# What Remains

SERIES ON
OHIO HISTORY AND CULTURE

# Series on Ohio History and Culture
Kevin Kern, Editor

Robert J. Roman, *Ohio State Football: The Forgotten Dawn*
Timothy H. H. Thoresen, *River, Reaper, Rail: Agriculture and Identity in Ohio's Mad River Valley, 1795–1885*
Mark Auburn, *In the President's Home: Memories of the Akron Auburns*
Brian G. Redmond, Bret J. Ruby, and Jarrod Burks, eds., *Encountering Hopewell in the Twenty-first Century, Ohio and Beyond. Volume 1: Monuments and Ceremony*
Brian G. Redmond, Bret J. Ruby, and Jarrod Burks, eds., *Encountering Hopewell in the Twenty-first Century, Ohio and Beyond. Volume 2: Settlements, Foodways, and Interaction*
Jen Hirt, *Hear Me Ohio*
S. Victor Fleischer, *The Goodyear Tire & Rubber Company: A Photographic History, 1898–1951*
Ray Greene, *Coach of a Different Color: One Man's Story of Breaking Barriers in Football*
John Tully, *Labor in Akron, 1825–1945*
Deb Van Tassel Warner and Stuart Warner, eds., *Akron's Daily Miracle: Reporting the News in the Rubber City*
Mary O'Connor, *Free Rose Light*
Joyce Dyer, *Pursuing John Brown: On the Trail of a Radical Abolitionist*
Walter K. Delbridge and Kate Tucker, editor, *Comeback Evolution: Selected Works of Walter K. Delbridge*
Gary S. Williams, *"No Man Knows This Country Better": The Frontier Life of John Gibson*
Jeffrey A. John, *Progressives and Prison Labor: Rebuilding Ohio's National Road During World War I*
John W. Kropf, *Color Capital of the World: Growing Up with the Legacy of a Crayon Company*
Steve McClain, *The Music of My Life: Finding My Way After My Mother's MS Diagnosis*
Jade Dellinger and David Giffels, *The Beginning Was the End: Devo in Ohio*
Peg Bobel and Linda G. Whitman, eds., *Native Americans of the Cuyahoga Valley: From Early Peoples to Contemporary Issues*
Carolyn Behrman and Timothy Matney, eds., *What Remains: Infirmary Burials, Memory, and Community in the Rubber City*

For a complete listing of titles published in the series,
go to www.uakron.edu/uapress.

# What Remains
## Infirmary Burials, Memory, and Community in the Rubber City

Carolyn Behrman & Timothy Matney, editors

*with contributions by*
Patricia Arnett
Patricia Connelly
Maeve Marino
Eric Olson
Morgan Revels
Robert L. Tucker

The University of Akron Press
Akron, Ohio

All material copyright © 2025 by the University of Akron Press
All rights reserved • First Edition 2025 • Manufactured in the United States of America.
All inquiries and permission requests should be addressed to the Publisher,
the University of Akron Press, Akron, Ohio 44325-1703.

ISBN: 978-1-62922-294-3 (paper)
ISBN: 978-1-62922-295-0 (ePDF)
ISBN: 978-1-62922-296-7 (ePub)

A catalog record for this title is available from the Library of Congress.

∞ The paper used in this publication meets the minimum requirements of ANSI/NISO z39.48–1992 (Permanence of Paper).

Cover photo: Lizzi Aronhalt, *Schneider Park*. www.lizziaronhalt.com. Cover design by Amy Freels.

*What Remains* was designed and typeset in Minion with Freight Sans titles by Amy Freels.

Produced in conjunction with the University of Akron Affordable Learning Initiative. More information is available at www.uakron.edu/affordablelearning/

*To the living community and those who came before us*

# Contents

| | |
|---|---|
| Acknowledgments | ix |
| 1  That Park on Mull Avenue<br>*Carolyn Behrman and Timothy Matney* | 1 |
| 2  How Did They Come to Be Here? A History of Schneider Park<br>*Eric Olson* | 22 |
| 3  Forgotten Graveyards and Rediscovered Bodies: Ethical and Legal Issues<br>*Robert L. Tucker* | 52 |
| 4  Science in the Public Eye: Archaeology at Schneider Park<br>*Timothy Matney, Maeve Marino, and Morgan Revels* | 92 |
| 5  Who Were They? A Demographic Analysis<br>*Patricia Connelly and Patricia Arnett* | 133 |
| 6  Reframing Akron History<br>*Carolyn Behrman* | 166 |
| 7  Closing and Openings<br>*Carolyn Behrman* | 204 |
| Appendix A. Death Certificates from the Summit County Infirmary | 222 |
| Appendix B. CADA Script | 242 |
| Works Cited | 295 |

# Acknowledgments

*from the volume editors*

Being professor-nerds, we have to start even our gratitude section by defining our terms. *To acknowledge* is to understand or come to recognize someone or something. To acknowledge a thing requires being able to name it.

The list of names at the start of this volume (the chapters' authors) and the list of names at the end (from the death certificates) bookend this entire exercise in acknowledgment. But we do not know the names of all those buried, and so we have tried to acknowledge them here obliquely by sharing what we learned of their history, hardship, marginalization, but also the community, care, and support that the County Infirmary could offer. We accept that there is more work to be done to properly acknowledge the people buried in what has become Schneider Park.

Regarding that first list of names, the authors, much of their hard work may appear effortless once the book is complete. Putting a book like this together is a sort of engineering feat in words. Each author needed time and space to gather their own data and thoughts. The chapters they constructed through multiple drafts highlight their particular talents and areas of expertise. Then they had to gather their patience as first we, and then the UA Press editorial board, asked for adjustments and changes. These scholars persevered. To the extent that the book stands well as a single story rather than poorly assembled parts, the authors deserve much of the credit. Any place where a reader experiences bumps is entirely on us.

We thank the UA Press editorial board and Director Jon Miller for insightful feedback at various stages and for guidance and support of this project. Thanks also to Thea Ledendecker for her clear and meticulous copyediting. We are beyond grateful to our production editor, the incomparable Amy Freels. Her recommendations were always well-reasoned, strong, and delivered with kindness even when she met with our reticence in the face of change. At this writing, we are just beginning our work with UA Press's Brittany LaPointe as she prepares to help us get this book from press to audience. We thank her in advance.

Collectively, the authors and volume editors acknowledge the residents and community partners who contributed to or assisted our work. It is a long list which includes but is not limited to The Akron Summit County Public Library and especially Special Collections librarian Michael Elliot, the Summit County Historical Society, University of Akron Archives' Vic Fleischer, Veronica Bagley, Mira Mohsini and her unclass students, and Josh Gippin and his unclass students. Wendy Duke and the cast members from CADA, the City of Akron, University of Akron Deans Linda Subich and Mitchell McKinney, and *Akron Beacon Journal* reporter and local historian Mark J. Price.

Numerous students, colleagues, and content experts made suggestions and offered critique for drafts or presentations of *What Remains: Infirmary Burials, Memory, and Community in the Rubber City*. Among those, we wish to especially thank Kevin Kern, Anoo Vyas, Linda Whitman, Karen Hackenberry, Felicia Konrad, Jane Greenland, Dani Jauk-Ajamie, Jennifer Bazar, and the students of Human Diversity.

Finally, we want to acknowledge that this work has unfolded over many years. Across that time family and friends have sustained us. Sometimes that sustenance has been in the form of long conversations testing ideas and tone-checking difficult topics. Sometimes it has literally been food. It has included the loan of a quiet house for a writing week, entertaining an author-parent who dropped in from out-of-town seeking headspace, and drone piloting at daybreak on a chilly morning. It also has meant indulging the nonlinear paths that research leads us down, like being asked to abruptly swerve onto a rutted, rural side road just because its sign read Poor Farm Road. Thank you, Rowan, Aidan, Natalie, Amy, Hillary, Sarah and Carrick, Dee, and Rinda.

## Chapter 1
# That Park on Mull Avenue
*Carolyn Behrman and Timothy Matney*

On the surface this is a story about a grassy park in West Akron, Ohio. A public, suburban space; a big brick church sits on one side, well-kept homes surround the other three. At the northern edge of the park is a brick-paved street, Mull Avenue, running between two main thoroughfares, Hawkins Avenue and Exchange Street, the latter of which leads into Akron's city center. But Mull Avenue is quiet. Many drivers choose alternate routes to avoid the knobby surface of century-old bricks. On any summer day you will find dog walkers, children dressed in soccer gear, or folks out for a stroll. In the autumn a game of flag football may appear. But there is discord between what transpires above and what lies below the surface of Schneider Park. There is a whispering history of people and institutions that, though scarcely visible, contributes to who we are, where we live, and what we value today. For seven decades, starting in 1849, the park area was a swampy corner of the land housing a poor farm, a working farm that housed and fed the poor and indigent in exchange for their labor. The poor farm later became Summit County Infirmary (the Infirmary, for brevity's sake going forward). This particular parcel of the Infirmary's land served as a burial ground for some of Akron's least influential residents. Our story of Schneider Park invites you to join in a process of discovery. We seek to engage your curiosity about Akron's past and the people—the Infirmary's dead—who remain among us, though not quite visibly.

This is not a book about ghosts, or at least not about the paranormal. Rather, this book is about memories and stories—how at times people collectively remember, forget, or even invent new pasts by tracing and uncovering their own histories. It is about what is worth remembering, what is better left forgotten, and who gets to decide. If successful, the story this book tells should lead you to feel that "ordinary life has gained a dimension" (Taylor, 2003:179). No two readers are likely to take the same message away. The authors of the chapters present many facts—legal, historical, archaeological, medical, and anthropological—and those facts appear solid, a framework upon which a proper, clear timeline can be built and populated with characters drawn from historical sources. But as we examine Schneider Park, the Infirmary, and its residents from these different angles, it becomes clear that no simple chronology tells the whole story.

## *What's in This Book?*

Each chapter in this book approaches Schneider Park and its burials through the lens of the author(s)' unique perspectives. Different ways of seeing bring different insights and observations, forging intertwining links between past and present.

In chapter 2, Eric Olson employs the tools of the historian: old maps, photographs, newspaper reports, journals, and letters to provide specific histories of the Infirmary and its cemetery. He traces from the land purchase and founding of the Infirmary in 1849, to the 1918 relocation of Infirmary residents (called inmates), to a similar state-supported institution in Munroe Falls. This time period overlaps what economists call *first globalization* (1870–1914), the rise of industrialization and urbanization of the US, heightened immigration, and the Progressive Era. In this last phase, the fracturing of old political party loyalties led to special interest groups that pushed for the breakup of industrial monopolies and the formation of labor unions, trade associations, and other special interest groups. The Progressive Era was particularly important for the implementation of political policies concerned with the promotion of social welfare and economic and moral reforms (Rodgers 1982). The importance of this larger social and historical context is covered in more detail, and with specific reference to the treatment of people at the margins of society, in chapter 6.

Fig. 1-1. Schneider Park in West Akron (Photo: Carolyn Behrman)

In chapter 3, Robert L. Tucker addresses the questions: who owns a human corpse, and what value does the body have once an individual has died? Tucker, a lawyer with extensive training and experience in archaeology, uses legal statutes and case law to address the broad issue raised by the discovery of bodies buried within an active city park. Who is legally responsible for them? What legal standing, if any, do the bodies have on their own? Distinct from the legal issues, Tucker also addresses the ethical considerations at play when authorities determine whether or not the dead can be disturbed in the thousands of public cemeteries spread across the country. Throughout this chapter, the reader will be reminded that politics, money, and the desire for "progress"—however that term is defined—are entangled with ideas of land ownership, individual rights, heritage, and respect for ancestors.

Having examined the legal, ethical, and historical context within which the Summit County Infirmary was run, in chapter 4 archaeologists Timothy Matney, Maeve Marino, and Morgan Revels share data collected and analyzed focusing on the burials. They present the results of an archaeological field-based class conducted by the University of Akron in summer 2017 at Schneider Park. Alerted to the presence of the burials at Schneider Park, and to how little was known about the physical remains of the cemetery there, the University of Akron's Department of Anthropology decided to conduct a minimally invasive survey class with undergraduate students. The goal was to teach students to use various geophysical survey instruments for detecting shallow subsurface features, such as human burials, without the need for excavation. But this sort of course is also about community engagement and the ways that academic, in this case archaeological, knowledge relates to contemporary communities. The students documented the location of over three hundred abandoned burials using drone photography and geophysical survey equipment. Residents and other visitors came to the survey area in the northwestern corner of Schneider Park to inquire what the students were doing, helping students to attend to and reflect on communicating their academic work. Chapter 4 discusses the ethical obligations of archaeologists, and other scientists, to present and discuss the results of their work to a curious public. The final exam took the form of a presentation at a local library branch, where over one hundred interested Akronites packed the small auditorium. While the scientific achievements of the students were lauded by all, the Q & A returned to two questions: are you sure there are dead bodies there, and what should we do about them?

In chapter 5, biological anthropologists Patricia Connelly and Patricia Arnett examine the people buried at Schneider Park from a forensic-demographic perspective. The authors introduce us to their field of study and offer ample background information to help us understand the physical conditions of life during their focal time period from 1908–1916, a brief period in which death certificates of those buried at the Infirmary's cemetery have been recovered. Connelly and Arnett then define three populations of people buried in Akron cemeteries during that time. Because there has been no modern excavation—only remote-sensing work—in Schneider Park to date, they rely on secondary source material documenting their three populations: cemetery ledger books and death certificates. The chapter carefully teases out what we can learn about the dead buried in the Infirmary's cemetery in comparison with two samples of other burials in Akron: one a population of destitute individuals from

Glendale Cemetery's potter's field and the other a population of wealthier people buried in Glendale Cemetery's elegant, primary grounds. Focusing on demographic trends within each buried population, chapter 5 considers, among other things, age at death, causes of death, and variables that indicate quality of life before death.

In chapter 6, one of us (Behrman), an anthropologist and specialist in community-engaged research, addresses the broader context of American ideals of social welfare, expanding on Olson's chapter 2 by adding information on the intellectual and political currents that drove the development of the county infirmary systems across Ohio and the United States, including a focus on the dynamics of marginalization. She describes the intellectual and social trends of the Progressive and Eugenics Movements and their role in shaping the Infirmary's practices. As D. T. Rodgers, author of "In Search of Progressivism," notes, a "language of social efficiency" took hold and created a broad US Eugenics Movement. Rodgers suggests it was "the merger of the prestige of science with the prestige of the well-organized business firm and factory that gave the metaphor of system its tremendous twentieth-century potency" (Rodgers 1982:123). Behrman explores in detail the impact of eugenical thinking and considers how this approach to social welfare and charity related to other marginalized populations. She discusses the Great Migrations and the economic and social challenges and successes specific to the Black community in Akron. She also draws attention to key aspects of the struggle for disability, women's, and racial rights across the time of the Infirmary and beyond.

In chapter 7, Behrman moves this volume fully into the present. She uses examples of contemporary, creative activity to illustrate ways we, as a community, have continued to write our story in light of what remains of this buried past. Behrman expands the conversation by describing how a spirit of engagement with this partially obscured history led to the production of new, local knowledge. Three groups responded to the 2017 archaeology project and to renewed public interest in Schneider Park and its history by asking what this old-new knowledge means for us today. These three groups represent diverse but overlapping perspectives. An anthropologist, two educator/dramatists, and an independent filmmaker, along with their students and actors, found the question of how we as a community are implicated in and impacted by the Infirmary's story compelling because it offers the Akron community the chance to reflect and grow. This chapter also includes a short epilogue illustrating one way the immediate neighbors are living in community with these currently unmarked burials.

Finally, this book has two appendices. Appendix A contains a summary of the information in the 308 death certificates analyzed in this volume. Included are the peoples' names, when available, and some details about their lives and deaths. Appendix B is a version of the script for the award-winning play *Along the Graveyard Path*, written and produced by Theatre on the Spectrum, a program of the Center for Applied Drama and Autism (CADA), which is reproduced here with permission from CADA.

Throughout the production of this book, the authors and their students encountered professionals, residents, and other community members who were interested in the burials. They kept pieces of the Infirmary story alive, tending to archives, transcribing and digitizing documents, writing newspaper articles and blog entries, asking their grandparents about Schneider Park in the "old days," and then passing those stories along to their children and grandchildren.

Since 1849, there has never been a time that this open space was abandoned by human activity, and in that sense, the people of Akron never lost the knowledge that people were buried there. The late nineteenth and early twentieth century was a period of significant economic growth in Akron. The rubber industry transformed the city, and with this productivity came ancillary business, an explosion in building, and a greater need for housing, development of schools, the arts, and public works. The bustling growth brought domestic migrants and foreign immigrants seeking labor and a foothold toward the middle class, but it also brought the dispossessed and others whose labor came cheap and therefore whose living conditions were rough. The stories of the leading industrialists of the time are often told, and now memorialized in public and private monuments and buildings, like the Stan Hywet mansion not far from Schneider Park, home of Goodyear Tire and Rubber Company founding family the Seiberlings. As a community, however, Akron seems to "fall asleep" on the knowledge, to let slip from mind even as citizens drive by or stroll over the ground, that the stories of some marginalized residents of Akron, persists under the grass.

The rest of this chapter contains sections offering terms and orienting concepts the reader may find useful for understanding the book as a whole.

## Useful Terms

There are a few general terms used in this volume. *Anthropology* is the study of humankind, where we come from, how we vary, and how we build and maintain societies. One of anthropology's subfields, *archaeology*, is especially exemplified in the chapters that follow.

There was a time when the terms *graveyard* and *cemetery* were not completely synonymous, although they are used interchangeably in casual conversation today. While human bodies were buried in both, the term *graveyard* originally referred to a comparatively small area that was part of a churchyard where burials were made, while *cemetery* referred to larger burial grounds that may or may not have been associated with a church. Many English dictionaries have abandoned that distinction (e.g., Funk & Wagnalls 1975 *Standard Encyclopedic Dictionary*). Legally speaking, at least in Ohio, there is no meaningful difference between a graveyard and a cemetery because the term *cemetery* has been defined in R.C. 1721.21 to include any place with one or a combination of more than one of the following: a burial ground for earth interments; a mausoleum for crypt entombments; a *columbarium* for the deposit of cremated remains; and/or a scattering ground for spreading human remains. In chapter 3, Tucker explains the legal statutes and their ramifications for how burial grounds are treated in greater detail. Here it is sufficient to note that we will use the terms *graveyard* and *cemetery* as synonyms.

In the US, state-run institutions for the care and housing of people deemed incompetent or lacking resources to care for themselves have evolved over time. During the era of state institutional development that is the focus of this book (the mid-1880s to 1920), those institutions, shaped by eugenic thinking (as discussed in chapter 6), lumped people together under broad and blurred categories that blended physical, neurological, and social disadvantages with assumptions that such hardship was also associated with moral "degeneracy" and even criminality. With the exception of otherwise competent, able-bodied adults disabled by accident, disease, or old age, people assigned to these institutions were referred to as "feeble-minded." *Feeble-mindedness* was often further defined with descriptors like insane, promiscuous or sexually immoral, alcoholic, or delinquent. It also had three subcategories: "idiot," "imbecile," and "moron," which were clinically specific and referred to mental capacities based on crude understanding of intelligence quotients. Chapter 6 explores the relationship between institutions and the evolving pseudoscience behind these terms and their use in detail.

## *Organizing Concepts*

Identifying several dominant themes may help the reader organize their thinking as they work through the detailed material presented in the specialists' chapters. The glue holding the chapters of this book together, apart from a focus on interred bodies, is that all the chapters have at least one trained anthropologist as an author. The authors came together because of a shared interest in how social memory of the Infirmary and the burial ground transformed through time as generations of residents moved in and out of the houses surrounding Schneider Park. They asked how *re*learning the story of the Infirmary's dead affects us today. Discussing this at a dinner together, the authors identified a few themes that weave among the chapters.

The first of these themes is *remembering and forgetting*. The authors explore how remembering and forgetting collectively impact individual and collective identities. This broad topic is considered in three parts: past, present, and future. Remembering and forgetting relate people and events together in a particular place and time. They are recorded in some way, and those records survive in some form. Then we encounter them in our own time and make sense of them relative to our lived experiences. We save, add, reinvent, or delete them, and in doing so, influence the ways those people and events are carried forward or forgotten for a future time. In the case of Schneider Park, the past context is the time when the Summit County Infirmary was active, from the mid-nineteenth through the early twentieth century in Akron. When thinking about the past, the authors highlighted two subthemes: *marginalization* and *worth*. In relation to the present context, a hundred years after the active Infirmary, here in the twenty-first century, the authors discuss *ownership* and *ethics*, and why we feel compelled to retell the story of the park. Finally, regarding the future, the authors asked what the accumulating knowledge about the past of the park should lead us to do. As you read, what stories are you developing to make sense of the information that is new to you? How will we as individuals, communities, and as a city, move forward in greater knowledge and understanding?

*Remembering and forgetting*

Perhaps the most immediate question that Schneider Park elicits is: how did the burials and cemetery fade from memory? Often, people just shrug off such forgettings—"it was such a long time ago, who can remember?" and there is some truth to this. In the complex social world, there is simply too much information, and it is too difficult to hold in mind everything that ever happened. So, some things are inevitably forgotten. Forgetting is only a choice or an act in that it is a letting go of the effort required to keep something in mind, to hold it in importance and consider how it relates to or connects to other things of consequence. This has been true for every generation. We fall into the routines of our lives and the minutia of work, children, home, kin and friends, travel, and it is easy to let some events, some people slide to the side and fade in our memories. But we also create markers, mementos to bring things of slippery significance back to mind. That photograph album from the trip you took with your parents when you were a child is a good example of a tangible marker that conjures up memories, details of a trip long past. It helps us remember and creates opportunity to pass on those stories to our children. When we die, our individual memories are gone, but there are still remnants in social memory of events that were, in part, shaped by us. These things continue on in some fashion, as stories, legends, and even myths.

Societies also forget and it is societal forgetting we focus on in this book. We are not so much concerned with how individuals forget, but rather how communities, whole societies can forget a series of events, such as the existence of a state-supported infirmary housing society's most marginalized people. The lives of the people who worked there, were inmates there, and some who died and were buried there have slid to the side and faded in our social memory despite occupying the same geographical space we occupy now. Great fires and dire storms, the collapse of a beloved bridge, the homecoming of a hero, the building of a college campus or a church or a park are all sufficiently important in the life of the community to be worth remembering, and so we make monuments, declare days of remembrance, and write history books. The societal function of such markers is to allow future generations to remember what we saw as important in our own time.

There is a great deal of scholarly writings about the concept of *social memory* from anthropology, history, literature, philosophy, psychology, sociology, and other academic fields (e.g., Brockmeier 2002; Jelin 1994; Van Dyke 2019). Reviewing that literature would be a lengthy undertaking, so instead here are a few terms and concepts drawn from those scholars. Van Dyke describes *social memory* as "the relational, contested ways that groups construct identities" with a variety of memory practices and perspectives (Van Dyke 2019:210). The important element of her definition is that it is an active process. Using storytelling, playwriting, filmmaking, erecting monuments, putting together photo albums, and the like, we call up and pass on information cast as shared memories. Second, social memory is a purposeful undertaking; remembering is a way of constructing identities. Across cultures, the stories we tell most frequently are those involving our own families, and it is those stories that help shape who we are and how we want others to perceive us as individuals. As a society, the same process is still at work, but rather than stories from our own past focused on our closest people, we expand outward to build an identity among many people as a neighborhood, or city, or culture. Choices to focus our national monuments on war heroes instead of immigrant workers, on captains of industry rather than mothers or operators of small businesses are purposeful decisions that contribute to the construction of our cultural identity; they mark what we outwardly value most. Third, Van Dyke notes the importance of memory practices, by which she means the particular, culturally defined methods or techniques we use to help us remember specific places, people, events, and histories. In discussing these definitions, Van Dyke reminds us that these processes of remembering are both relational and contested, that social memory does not develop in isolation, nor does it develop by consensus.

When considering remembering and forgetting together, it is useful to step away from the commonplace idea that remembering and forgetting are binary processes standing in stark opposition to one another. Social scientists such as Brockmeier conceive of remembering and forgetting as "two sides of one process, a process in which we give shape to our experience, thought and imagination in terms of past, present and future" and they see "memory as a movement within a cultural discourse that continuously combines and fuses the now and then, and the here and there" (Brockmeier 2002:21). As Brockmeier describes the concept of a social memory, he recognizes the need to lose some memories while retaining others, and in the process of continuously reinterpreting and reformulating social memory, distortions and contradictions are introduced, gaps created and gaps closed, as we reorganize social memories into a format—a "meaningful schemata"—that is relevant to us. Rather than a simple act of remembering or forgetting, the process of social memory is complex, combining, overlapping, privileging, and sidelining elements of the past to weave a new, modern narrative that is coherent to us. This process can be seen in the way that folk tales, fables, and mythologies are reformulated into novels, graphic novels, plays, musicals, video games, and films in which characters, settings, and storylines change, but the message, the moral lesson, remains fairly constant. It can be less easy to see this two-sided process at work when it is not part of a massive commercial enterprise, literally selling icons like superheroes drawn from Norse mythology. In the case of something that is just part of our landscape, like a quiet park not actively calling our attention, this way of thinking about forgetting is useful. It reminds us that we see and make sense of the world through an interplay of individual, cultural, and temporal lenses.

The creation of particular social memory, and the processes of remembering and forgetting, do not just happen. Individuals, communities and cultures have to somehow reach agreement that a thing is memorable or forgettable. People sharing a social memory in Akron allowed what happened across six decades on the land at the corner of Exchange and

Mull Streets to be socially unimportant, not relevant to the identity that the city's inhabitants wanted to project, or simply unrelatable to present day and, thus, removable from the telling. That is in fact what happened in the decades after the Infirmary was closed. Thus far, there is no evidence of a cover-up in the sense of someone deliberately hiding information about the bodies left behind as a housing development grew. But times change, ethical and moral frameworks shift, and with the aid of historians, archaeologists, archivists, and others, what was forgotten can be relearned, reexamined, reflected on, and ultimately reformatted into Brockmeier's meaningful schemata that tells a narrative that is useful to us, to who we are now and who we want to be as a community, city, and nation.

Summing up, the authors feel it is important to bear in mind that the social memory of a place like Schneider Park both relies on individuals remembering what happened at that place, and on a community's understanding that the stories of the Summit County Infirmary and Schneider Park are important enough for us to keep returning to and retelling. Additionally, time matters in the process of remembering and forgetting, so the next section is organized using past, present, and future.

*The past: marginalization and perceived worth*

Most Americans know only the vaguest stories of their ancestors from four generations ago. We might know the names, birthdates, marriage dates, children, or occupations of our great-great grandparents. Apart from such basic biographical details, however, their stories are largely lost to us. Yet, in the US we still commemorate a war of independence that happened nearly two and a half centuries ago, long before those great-great grandparents were born. Cultural markers of the events of that struggle engulf us: parades on the 4th of July, commemorative statues, place names, iconic images, songs, symbols of thirteen-starred flags, and so forth. The stories of most of the individual soldiers, excepting those few whose contributions to the revolution have become legendary, are lost to us. Their stories are limited to a few words carved in stone. We know no more about the average soldier in 1776 than most of us do about our own great-great grandparents.

In the case of Schneider Park, an important question is: Who exactly were the individuals buried in the unmarked graves of the Infirmary cemetery? Analyses of historical documents and death certificates presented in chapters 2, 5, and 6 offer insight into what happened as late nineteenth-century capitalism and immigration practices played out across a large segment of Akron's population. The burials included workers who lived and died serving the needs of industrializing Akron. Two themes dominated our characterization of the people buried at Schneider Park: marginalization and perceived worth.

Official attention of the time was trained on immigration. Country of origin was a space on every official document. There was a need for labor but also a generalized xenophobia. Often voiced was a concern that foreign governments were dumping their less desirable citizens on American shores. Local domestic Americans, often themselves second- or third-generation immigrants, highlighted distinctions between themselves and immigrants from backgrounds other than their own, setting boundaries and therefore margins of society in a wide variety of ways, including simply what they called people. In newsprint, journals, letters, and literature, newer immigrants are sometimes identified accurately by nation of origin but often with the dismissive or derogatory terms we all can still call to mind more than a century later. The newcomers were conceptually not part of mainstream nineteenth-century and early twentieth-century society, having come from elsewhere, often alone, and also often without fluency in English. Spatially they occupied the marginal zones of the city, first in the poorer and working-class areas of Akron and, if misfortune befell them and they became recognized as unproductive and therefore undesirable, they sometimes lost even that foothold and became inmates in places like the Summit County Infirmary, well outside the city limits at the time. Of course, not all the inmates at the Infirmary were foreign, working class, or poor. As chapter 2 discusses fully, other "undesirables" were also sent to the Infirmary: unwed mothers, unruly boys, the lame, the destitute without families, those suffering with alcohol and drug addictions, or seen as mentally incapable or insane. It is helpful to keep these two populations separate as we consider the history of the Summit County Infirmary.

For both the foreign-born and the "undesirable" inmates of the Infirmary, the concept of *worth* (worthiness, or value) in the judgment of mainstream Akron society of the mid-nineteenth to early twentieth century is important to the analyses in our chapters. Labor was value; muscles and physical energy drove the capitalist engine of the factories and built the canals and railroads that formed the economic foundation of the city. Immigrants also provided myriad services that supported industry, working for the merchants, shopkeepers, and craft persons who helped the city expand and grow wealthy. From the perspective of the twenty-first century, we can see that as much labor as possible was extracted from the bodies of workers. This lack of social support systems meant that laborers, once injured, exhausted, or too old to work, were deemed disposable and discarded (an arrangement that an anthropologist a century from now may also ascribe to our culture and time). There is no doubt that the conditions under which these laborers worked were harsh and, by contemporary standards, unacceptable. As discussed in chapter 2, some of the inmates of the Infirmary retained some worth after being discarded in a narrow and macabre capitalist sense; after death their bodies were turned into commodities and sold to medical schools—a practice that was banned as unethical in the early twentieth century.

Marginalization and worth are two conceptual axes for thinking about the human landscape in the US during this period. Those who have wealth or capital, and can use it to create more wealth, are seen as both at the center of the mainstream of society and as having great social worth, often called *social capital*, while those with little wealth and diminished ability to create more beyond the labor of their physical bodies are of lesser worth. When their capital and labor ran out, they became worthless in a financial sense. Following the logic of this model, people with few resources, undesirable attributes, or on whom society must spend resources populate the edges or margins far from that mainstream. This sort of organization puts the onus on the individual to prove themselves worthy of society, or to remove themselves if they are unable. Immigrants and others with less social capital were pressed by mainstream US society of the period to demonstrate their ability to create value or were forced to carry a stigma of reduced worth or even worthlessness.

By the time the Summit County Infirmary was finally shuttered in 1918, much had changed. The boundaries of the City of Akron had stretched with a burgeoning population and the area where the Infirmary sat was desirable real estate. Demands for new housing stock in the first three decades of the twentieth century were high. Standards and rules for what was acceptable practice at the county infirmaries in Ohio had also shifted, reducing the total number of inmates. When Philip Schneider finally deeded the land for the park to the city, the Infirmary buildings were quickly torn down, and a housing development owned by Schneider—Sunset View—was built. There are no known documents detailing Schneider's motive for donating the land for the park to the city. He was aware of how the park land had been used in the past; he knew there were bodies there. Did he seek to "disappear" the buried inmates by making no provision to memorialize them? Was his desire to create a new community with a history detached from the story of these poor souls? Perhaps he thought that the housing development was more likely to thrive without the reminder of such sadness underfoot? Did it simply not seem a matter of any importance? We cannot know. We do know that Schneider chose to live in the community with his family. It is interesting to note that one concern, expressed to the archaeology team by a resident of a house adjacent to the park in 2017, was that the acknowledged presence of burials in the park would "drive down house values" by association. Was the same true in 1921 when Schneider began selling houses?

*The present: ownership and ethics*

In chapter 3, Tucker discusses the legal statutes surrounding cemeteries and human burials and explains that when a body is interred there is no individual "ownership" exercised over the body. There is an inherent contradiction between the overt ownership of the land where bodies are buried—land being historically one of the original forms of private property in the US—and the property-less status of the individual physical human corpses. The issue of who has jurisdiction over an interred dead body is critical in assessing how those bodies are treated and ultimately cared for, across decades or in perpetuity. If the bodies belong to a recognized "imagined community" (Anderson 1983), then it is likely that care will be provided for them in the long term, like in many modern or active cemeteries. In the absence of this connection, however, the physical remains of the dead become unrelatable, untraceable, and perhaps even unknowable. A modern or recent body discovered by accident buried in a field or woods is typically turned over to a county forensic unit, a coroner, or the police for identification and, if possible, return to their kin for "proper" burial. This is the lawful process when dealing with dead bodies.

There is a stark difference between ownership, as Tucker discusses it, and responsibility or ethical behavior. A city, town, county, village, or even an individual can own the land on which a cemetery is situated, but what does this status of ownership demand in terms of its ethical management? In the case of active or maintained cemeteries, there is an expected stewardship, management, responsibility, and caretaking. Cemeteries found on private land are often maintained by descendants or long-time community members and can form a source of community identity. Neglected, abandoned, and destroyed cemeteries, on the other hand, often evoke passionate outcries from nearby residents who find such a situation distressing or disrespectful, even if the people buried there are not their ancestors. In the temporal context of the present, this idea of ownership is tied in part to *ethics*, defined here as the culturally specific moral principles governing our behavior and activities.

In the case of Schneider Park, legal ownership is clear. The park belongs to the City of Akron, whose elected officials make decisions as to how the park is to be used. Activity by the city in 2022–24 described in the epilogue of this book demonstrates that decisions about activities related to the park are being made in the context of caring for property held in common for the residents of Akron, presumably using knowledge of the history and former use of the land. The question of whether such action is ethical, however, is separate from that of whether it is legal.

Many people, when asked how to define the term *ethical*, will invoke concepts such as virtue, guilt, shame, and "doing what is right." These concepts came up again and again during the research and writing of this book. For clarity here, the definition of ethics above will be used, emphasizing these four aspects of an ethical code. First, an ethical code is culturally specific. Second, an ethical code is based on commonly accepted moral, not legal, principles. Third, an ethical code governs behavior and action, and fourth, an ethical code observed within any cultural group changes through time. An important outcome of this definition, then, is that there can be no universal ethical code. Likewise, there is no such thing as an individual ethical code. An ethical code only exists as a social contract among a group of people at a particular place and time.

These distinctions are important because this book time-travels in a sense. The chapters move from the context of the Infirmary as it was occupied and experienced in the past to the park with its hundred-year-old housing development and subterranean human bodies in the present. While we can decry how inmates were treated in the past as unethical, doing so comes from the culturally and temporally specific ethical code negotiated in the present. In other words, the unethical behavior we see in past practices may well have met, or even exceeded, ethical expectations of the 1850s, 1880s, or early 1900s. This relativistic perspective lies at the heart of all anthropological work. Most people who worked at the Summit County Infirmary were probably ethical people who thought they were "doing the right thing" by the inmates whose lives could well have been even more wretched, hard, or short without the support provided by that institution.

When we feel righteous, guilty, or ashamed about the past, or when we think about the "right thing to do" about Schneider Park in the present, we are deploying contemporary ethics. With this caveat in mind, what do our moral compasses tell us is the right thing to do? Why do some of us feel sadness, discomfort, or even anger at the way these individuals were treated in the past? For those people the desire to "do something" about Schneider Park is not really about the past, nor even for the people whose dead bodies lie under the turf. Our own sense of ethics may be demanding that we care now because the story of those inmates and what happened to them over a century ago resonates today. This historical moment is filled with revelations and rediscoveries of historically perpetuated social, economic, and racial injustices, and by the acknowledgement today of the long-term impacts of dehumanizing ideas, structures, and policies of the past. For many, perhaps for most people, there is a pull, demanding inclusiveness across kinds of human diversity once marginalized to the point of being forgotten. The work of this book, and the fact you are reading it, show that in some way, we all want to remember them, to reflect on what their lives can teach us, and to consider who we as a community are and want to be.

*The future: public-facing and engaged-academic challenges*

Each chapter below reveals some of the ways academic research is entwined with the non-university-based public. The researchers in this book share the ways they explain their work and/or engage residents and others in the fieldwork process. Fieldwork involves gathering data about people, with people, and from people. The goal is to produce knowledge for the benefit of the public. Now in the early twenty-first century, ivory-tower walls and paywalls that have kept knowledge development in the hands of elites are counterbalanced by open-access publishing and community-engaged research, which increasingly draw academic professionals into dialogue with community partners and the public. While this is generally positive, it brings with it a variety of ethical and pragmatic concerns. The case of Schneider Park illustrates the challenges and rewards of doing community-engaged research.

How should research goals, designs, data collection processes, and results be shared? Community-engaged scholars vary in their answers to these concerns. The example in chapter 4 involves academically driven goals, design, and data collection, but community engagement is emphasized when it came to sharing results. Reporting results for an academic audience or peer-reviewed publication involves writing to and for colleagues who share a narrow focus and specialized terms and concepts. For the archaeologist and archaeology student researchers in chapter 4, the pivot to community-engaged presentation of results meant reframing to an audience they knew less about, who might have some or no knowledge of the relevant technical and theoretical material, who might have a range of social, political, or economic concerns about the findings, and come with a variety of backgrounds and interests. Every case of public engagement encounters critics and supporters. One of the great benefits of public engagement is that, with the greater variety of backgrounds found in public forums, researchers can open up new lines of inquiry, new approaches, and new dialogues. A researcher is never done after reporting results; in fact, public response is arguably a second wave of data collection. How will people understand and react to the results?

Even this inclusive statement is not representative of all approaches to community-engaged research. Engaged or public anthropology has evolved beyond just informing the public of findings and listening to their perspective. The field has—for many years at this point—launched the research process in university-community partnerships. In these projects, goals are established, questions framed, data gathered, and results interpreted in a collaboration where both university and community partners play active roles at each step. Students learn research methods and relevant content, but they also learn to bring their own developing expertise to the table to collaborate respectfully with other kinds of expertise in the process of generating or expanding locally situated knowledge. In chapters 6 and 7, this idea is revisited in relation to concepts of marginalization, worth, ownership, and ethics through the media of contemporary oral tradition, filmmaking, and drama.

*Storytelling and memory*

This volume reweaves a story that remained only in threads of information, scattered documents, and forgotten bodies under an indifferent surface. In doing so, it sparks new consideration of the forgotten dead and of the ways reviving history can influence community.

It seems fitting to use a story to illustrate this. Carolyn Behrman relates how she came to know of the burials in Schneider Park.

> I am a fireside ghost-storyteller and mystery reader. I am also an anthropologist with experience sorting and identifying bones in the storeroom of a museum as the curators sought to comply with federal rules regarding the permanent archiving of human remains from ancient sites. This knowledge about unmarked graves should have grabbed my attention, but it was a hot day. I was single-parenting for the summer, worrying about groceries, laundry, and a demanding job at the university. The first time my daughter's team practiced soccer there, the coach didn't have a name for the place. It is called Schneider Park, but the directions he'd given us only specified cross-streets. None of the parents seemed to know the name of the park, even though most of us lived within a mile or two. "That open space along Mull." "You know, the big green space with the church on the rise at one end." "The field near St. Sebastian's School that isn't Forest Lodge Park." On the sideline, a parent told me it used to be an "unofficial graveyard." I am sure I looked concerned, and he quickly added that the graves probably were not where we were in the northwest corner but farther over to the south or east perhaps. (Spoiler alert: he was wrong.) The ground was hard, clay-filled dirt with sparse grass; it felt firm and dry. I turned my attention to my daughter on the field and my small son who, when I finally spotted him, had managed to climb way too high in a nearby tree. My concern about the dead was pushed aside by my more immediate concern for the living, both on the field and up the tree.

Several years later, I came across an article in the *Akron Beacon Journal* by Mark J. Price containing some details about the Summit County Infirmary and its use of the land that is now Schneider Park for burials. At the time, I was developing a unit for a course I teach on human diversity. I wanted to focus on the Progressive Era and the Eugenics Movement in the US, and I wanted some local material. I had learned about Apple Creek's Infirmary near Wooster, Ohio, as well as the two Summit County Infirmaries (Akron and Munroe Falls). Price's article said that the Infirmary building in Akron had been located just a few short blocks from Schneider Park and that the Infirmary grounds included the land of the contemporary park in its footprint. Locally, faculty in history and psychology departments at the University of Akron were also writing about the Eugenics Movement. Coincidentally, the American Anthropological Association—the principal professional organization for my academic discipline—was also drawing attention to this topic as a part of its Race Matters traveling exhibition. Some anthropology colleagues in Florida were beginning what would become a sensational and troubling anthropological and archaeological study of the Dozier School in Florida. I think it fair to say that interest in how our society has marginalized and undervalued some individuals over the past two centuries was coming under increased academic scrutiny and rising to the attention of the broader public.

Serendipitously, Eric Olson and I both raised the history of the Summit County Infirmary and the possible bodies buried at Schneider Park with archaeologist Tim Matney, who was planning a summer geophysical archaeology field course for his undergraduate students. He chose to focus the geophysical survey work on the graves in Schneider Park in the summer of 2017. From that point the work of this volume springs. It is a strange phenomenon. We always knew that the burials were there underfoot but, somehow, they are difficult to hold firmly in mind. Who lived and died at the Summit County Infirmary? Who is buried in Schneider Park? What does the fact that we do not know tell us about ourselves as human beings, as members of a community, as the most recent occupants of a landscape layered with the physical, social, and cultural histories that push some types of lives forward into our consciousness as ancestors—some with their names on plaques, streets, schools, and civic buildings—while others slide sideways away from our conscious focus, to the edges, and then out of mind?

Ghost stories and mysteries share a common element: the unknown. My brief concern on that summer day decades ago, and this volume's team of authors' subsequent musings, research, and conversations about the lives of the people whose bodies were buried in the park, have given us something to share with you—a narrative, a plot, characters, as well as an appreciation for the broader social stage on which this very real story unfolded.

## Chapter 2
# How Did They Come to Be Here?
## A History of Schneider Park
*Eric Olson*

At nearly fifteen acres, Schneider Park is one of the largest parks in the City of Akron. On the surface, it is a large grass lawn, with a dip in elevation to the south where water pools in early spring and fall. Water and soil play an important role in the history of this park. The seasonally wet area to the south is part of the reason this land was not developed when residential building spread through West Akron in the early 1900s. In the early twentieth century, as rubber manufacturing soared, Akron experienced its largest population boom, and housing construction exploded across the city. The area around Schneider Park, then plowed farmland, was highly desirable for would-be developers, including Philip Schneider. Much of the arable land was also buildable, but what would become Schneider Park overlays some of the most poorly drained soil in Summit County. The soil at the park's southern end is literally "muck" (Ritchie and Steiger 1974). *Muck* is not a colloquial term; it is a soil science classification referring to soils saturated with water for more than thirty days out of the year and of low agricultural production potential. One could argue that Schneider Park was established as parkland because it was not good for anything else.

As the reader now knows, there were other reasons why the ground in what would become Schneider Park was less than ideal for building houses. Just north of the muck, on a gentle rise in elevation in the park, is the abandoned cemetery that once served the Summit County Infirmary. This volume focuses attention on the Infirmary, which was established in 1849 and was in continuous operation until 1918. It housed some of Akron's poorest and most troubled citizens. The agriculturally useless land noted above was used as a cemetery for both the inmates who died at the Infirmary and for others who lacked the resources or the family connections for a more proper burial. To fully understand the history of Schneider Park and its burials requires a deeper dive into the history of some of Akron's other cemeteries (Middlebury, Spicer Hill, Dublin, and Glendale), the Ohio county infirmaries system (also see chapter 6), and the waves of immigration that took place in this Progressive Era of rapid industrialization and economic growth (also see chapters 5 and 6). The histories of cemeteries, infirmaries, and immigration explored in this chapter are at times uncomfortable for those of us who now inhabit these spaces as beneficiaries of the developments that enriched and empowered the builders while disappearing the lives and then the bodies of those who could not benefit fully from the progress of the era.

## *Burying Workers: Industry, Immigration, and the Story of Akron's Dublin*

Our journey to what will become Schneider Park does not begin in the park but farther east, near present-day downtown Akron. To understand how an unmarked cemetery could be in a public park, we must first look at the history of other cemeteries. The earliest cemetery in what would become the City of Akron was the Middlebury Cemetery, between Newton Street and Laffer Avenue, which was dedicated around 1808 (Lane 1892:232). A few years later, circa 1813, another small cemetery was dedicated north of Middlebury, known as Spicer Hill Cemetery. Spicer Hill Cemetery was dedicated by Miner Spicer and Paul Williams, two of the founding members of the City of Akron (Lane 1892:232; Knepper 1990:26). At that time, Akron was not Akron; it was the "Furnace Run" town. At least, that is according to James Geddes, lead engineer for both the Erie Canal in New York and the future Ohio and Erie Canal (Geddes 1823). Geddes had been hired by the Ohio Canal Commission to survey the state for the best possible routes for the newly planned Ohio and Erie

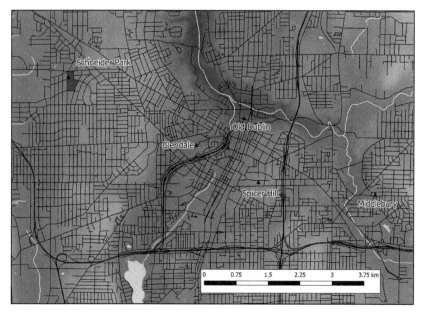

Fig. 2-1. Map of Akron showing location of places mentioned in the text (Map: Eric Olson)

Canal. Furnace Run town was small (less than two hundred people), with most people living along the Little Cuyahoga in what is today known as Middlebury. Geddes decided to route the canal west of this small town. Shortly after Geddes' recommendations, work began on the canal.

The City of Akron was established around the newly planned canal and was named Akron from the Greek word "acropolis" because it was located at the highest point along the canal (Grismer 1952). Akron was surveyed in 1825 (Hinshaw 1825), and construction of the first leg (from Akron to Cleveland) began the same year (Doyle 1908:65; Lane 1892:39). Based on Hinshaw's 1825 map, the city extended roughly from Cedar Street to State Street. Spicer Hill and Middlebury cemeteries were, respectively, a half mile and two miles east of Akron City limits in 1825. This was likely because the canal was placed to avoid destruction of property in the already extant town of Middlebury (Geddes 1823).

The opportunity for unskilled employment as part of canal construction drew manual laborers and was especially attractive to immigrants. Irish immigrants at this time were predominantly Catholic and spoke

## How Did They Come to Be Here?

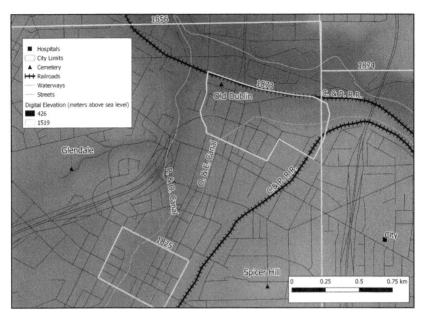

Fig. 2-2. Map showing the location of Dublin (Map: Eric Olson)

primarily Irish (or Gaeilge) rather than English. As is well known, Irish immigrants to the US at this time were not considered racially white. Facing broad discrimination and a number of stigmatizing stereotypes by mainstream Akron society, Irish immigrants were geographically marginalized, forced to establish their homes and neighborhood north of the city limits in the area just south of the Little Cuyahoga River that came to be known for a time as Dublin (see fig. 2-2). Samuel Lane (1892:39) described Dublin as the "lower lands of what is now called North Akron, being thickly dotted over with log and slab shanties." Lane (1892:233) placed Dublin "north of Tallmadge Street, and east of Main Street." However, Doyle (1908:65) places Dublin closer to the city limits of Akron at the time, "north of Federal Street and west of Summit." In 1908, Tallmadge Street (not to be confused with Tallmadge Avenue) was known as Federal Street. Whatever the exact boundaries were, it was certain that Dublin lay just north of Akron's city limits.

On the northern edge of Dublin was a cemetery used to bury, among others, those immigrants—overwhelmingly Irish—who died building the canal. The Dublin cemetery was north of Furnace Street, west of North

High, and operated from 1832 until Glendale Cemetery was established in 1838 (Lane 1892:233). An unknown number of Irish immigrants were buried in this cemetery. However, Lane (1892:39) estimates the population of Dublin at two hundred in the mid- to late 1820s. This likely puts the total number of interments at less than two hundred. Some of the individuals buried in the Dublin Cemetery were later moved in 1838 to Glendale Cemetery when it opened (Lane 1892:234). Dublin Cemetery was abandoned by the late 1830s because the canal had been in operation for many years, and the city had grown exponentially with industry and canal traffic. The larger population necessitated new space to bury the dead.

Around the same time Dublin Cemetery was in use, construction of another canal began. Ground was broken for the Pennsylvania and Ohio Canal in 1835, with operation beginning in 1840 (Lane 1892:71). This new canal cut up the eastern portion of Dublin and closed off that neighborhood from the rest of the city. The Ohio and Erie and the Pennsylvania and Ohio Canals formed physical barriers to the west, south, and east of this small neighborhood while the steep, almost cliff-like drop-off toward the Little Cuyahoga formed a northern barrier. While this small area was being physically isolated, greater Akron was becoming a hub of transportation and commerce. A new county was formed around this hub in 1840 when Summit County was created from portions of Medina, Portage, and Stark Counties (Perrin 1881:227).

This new canal water transport system quickly gained a rival when the Akron branch of the Cleveland and Pittsburgh Railroad (C&P) opened in 1851 (Ohio Commissioner of Railroads and Telegraphs 1906:79), connecting Akron and Cuyahoga Falls to the C&P in Hudson. The Akron branch still runs today through downtown Akron, east of Grace Park and Quaker Square. For the residents of Dublin, this railroad added train noise that echoed and coal smoke that lingered and settled in the Little Cuyahoga Valley.

The opening of the Akron branch of the C&P created opportunities for continued industrial expansion in Akron. One industrialist among the growing population of Akronites was Ferdinand Schumacher, the "Cereal King" (Doyle 1908:422; Lane 1892:155). Schumacher was born in Germany in 1822 and emigrated to Akron in 1851 (Doyle 1908:151). By 1859, he opened his first oatmeal mill and named it "The German

Mill" (Doyle 1908:151; Perrin 1881:771). Schumacher's business expanded and was renamed the Empire Barley Mills. In time it became the largest supplier of oatmeal in the United States, expanding rapidly across the 1870s (Perrin 1881:771). The American Cereal Company was founded by Schumacher and others in 1891 with capital from the sale of the Empire Barley Mills. This was transformed into the Quaker Oats Company in 1907 (Doyle 1908:152). The German Mill, also known as Quaker Oats Mills, still stands at the corner of Mill Street and Broadway. Akron's nickname was "oatmeal town" long before it became synonymous with rubber (Doyle 1908), and Ferdinand Schumacher was at the center of the industry. Residents of Dublin likely worked in the mill, which stood a stone's throw south of the neighborhood.

In the 1870s, as Schumacher's oatmeal empire was expanding, Dublin was surrounded by industrial factories and railroads. Any remnants of the Irish immigrant town were gone; new immigrants had come in to replace them, and the neighborhood was cut up by development (Doyle 1908; Lane 1898). An oil refinery was constructed just down the slopes from Dublin in the early 1870s. Not long after, this refinery was bought by John D. Rockefeller's Standard Oil Company (Tackbury et al. 1874). A new railway line between Cleveland and Akron, the "The Valley Railway," was constructed adjacent to this refinery so that the factories and oil refineries could transport their goods more easily. The Valley Railway also tied into the Cleveland and Pittsburgh railroad, and this important connection to wider rail networks ran right through the heart of Dublin (G. W. & C. B. Colton & Co. 1871; Gray 1873). In 1878 a train depot was constructed on the plateau near Furnace Street, cutting through Dublin and the Dublin Cemetery. Some individuals in the cemetery who had not been removed to Glendale Cemetery earlier were rediscovered (*Stark County Democrat* 1878). At the time, there was speculation that the unearthed bones might be from an "Indian burial ground," and someone suggested that at least one of the skulls was from the infamous murder of William Beatson, who had been decapitated (Lane 1892:233). While there were many tales about the bones, local newspaper reporters concluded that the remains were from the old Irish cemetery that was formally abandoned in 1838. The soil, and those burials still on the plateau, were "thrown into the ravine that is being filled up" (*Stark County Democrat* 1878). In recent years, the

Cuyahoga Valley Scenic Railway has revived this station, now called the Northside Station, one block north of current Furnace Street. The train is in daily use as one of the Cuyahoga Valley National Park's attractions. Based on historic descriptions from Lane (1892) and the *Stark County Democrat* (1878), the Dublin Cemetery site sits beneath the station.

Another Akron cemetery also experienced the trauma of removal in the name of development in the 1870s. In the case of the Spicer Hill Cemetery, the motivation was toward higher education rather than industrialization. Given the well-structured and free primary and secondary educational system that had been created in Akron, local Akron members of the Universalist General Convention (later the Universalist Church of America), with the financial backing of John R. Buchtel and other industrialists, founded a liberal arts college in the vein of Swarthmore or Middlebury Colleges. Spicer Hill, on the east side, and high above the main commercial activity by the river, was selected as the location for Buchtel College (Knepper 1990:13). Spicer Hill was also the site of Spicer Hill Cemetery. At the time of the college's founding, in contrast to the treatment of remaining graves from Dublin Cemetery mentioned above, there is good evidence that Spicer Hill Cemetery graves were known, respected, and transferred with the consent of living relatives in most cases. Approximately sixty-four bodies were removed and reburied in Glendale Cemetery (Knepper 1990:26). The grassy field on the north side of contemporary Buchtel Hall held many of these graves, including that of Miner Spicer, who was buried there in 1855 (Lane 1892:233). Avery Spicer, Miner's son, served on the committee that selected Spicer Hill for the College (Knepper 1990:13), and the family plot in Glendale Cemetery now holds both their graves. This relatively ideal outcome was not uniform, however, since, according to some student accounts in the 1880s, leftover bones from imperfectly removed burials could still be seen poking out of the grounds on particularly rainy days (Knepper 1990:27).

As Buchtel College grew and flourished, oil refineries were constructed in the Dublin neighborhood. In the 1890s, other parts of the city saw the construction of new rubber factories and a soap company (Burge 2014). Local topography suggests that the air quality of Dublin was likely some of the worst in Akron. The Little Cuyahoga River Valley is deepest in Dublin; the deep river valley and the steep hills to the east and west trapped smoke from factories, dust from wagons, and held moisture caused by runoff from the uplands. The soap company managed to be an especially egregious contributor to the fetid environment with its strident combination of odors from rendered animal fat, lye, and ash. Complaints about the smell eventually forced the factory to move outside the city limits (Burge 2014).

At the turn of the century, almost everyone living in the boarding houses on Bluff Street, Furnace Run, and North Street was an immigrant. These streets represent the remainder of what was Dublin. The immigrants at the turn of the century were mostly Austrians, Hungarians, Irish, Italians, and Polish (*Cleveland Plain Dealer* 1902; Doyle 1908:65). Immigrants, especially the Irish, did not have good reputations in Akron. Perrin (1881:500), describing an era when Irish immigration was more dominant, went into detail about a gang of Irish canal diggers who, wielding clubs, killed a German immigrant and buried him in a canal lock. To be fair, Perrin (1881) did not always corroborate or cite the sources of his information, and the example above does not appear in other Summit County histories (Bierce 1854; Doyle 1908; Lane 1898; Grismer 1952). Perrin's willingness to vilify the Irish is part of a general pattern of discrimination against Irish immigrants in the US and, in Akron, we find this echoed by Doyle almost thirty years later. Doyle (1908:65) had called the Irish "Paddy," which was as derogatory at the time as later terms like "Dago" for the Italians and "Hunkie" for Hungarians. In general, Irish workers' individual names did not make it into Summit or Cuyahoga County histories, only appearing in print on death certificates or newspaper notices.

Both the Dublin and Spicer Cemeteries have been destroyed in the wake of Akron's urban expansion and development; the Middlebury and Glendale Cemeteries still exist and take new burials to this day. However, there was another burial ground in Akron across this time, which was associated with a poor farm and later the Summit County Infirmary. In turning attention there, it is first necessary to consider the social experience of poverty and foreignness as they related to ideas about cleanliness and disease in this period.

## *Pest Houses and "Infectious" Immigrants*

Immigrants to the US in the late nineteenth and early twentieth century, in addition to being associated with degeneracy and criminality, were often also described as disease-ridden or dirty. Perhaps the perception of dirt was partially attributable to the harsh labor conditions for canal diggers and factory workers in industrializing America. As the industrial economy unfolded, a powerful anti-immigrant collaboration formed between some medical professionals and the press, which promoted narratives of "dirty" or "diseased" immigrants. The public perceptions generated by these news stories functioned to maintain ethnic enclaves like Dublin at the fringes of white, US-born Akron society.

One of the most influential medical professionals in the state was Dr. Charles Probst. Probst was the first secretary of the Ohio State Board of Health in 1879 (Ohio State Board of Health 1886). An example of the anti-immigrant propaganda Probst stirred up comes from a newspaper article in the *Cleveland Plain Dealer* where Probst submitted the names of immigrants traveling to Ohio, recommending they be "plac[ed] in pest houses for a week or two after their arrival" (*Cleveland Plain Dealer* 1892). The names came from the passenger list of a ship carrying immigrants to New York (the vessel's name was not printed), with their respective destinations in Ohio. The article reads like a warning to residents of the towns to which the immigrants were bound, a kind of medical "most wanted" list.

In the article, Dr. Probst claimed this ship of immigrants may be carrying varioloid (literally meaning "smallpox-like"). Varioloid was a mild form of smallpox that could infect someone who had been vaccinated or who had previously survived the disease. It was not uncommon, and Abraham Lincoln contracted varioloid on the day of the Gettysburg Address (Goldman and Schmalstieg 2007). In Lincoln's case, the disease was publicized as mild, but whether this was due to concern for public perception of the president's strength or to the actual mildness of the illness is not known. However, as early as 1824, varioloid was considered harmless. Dr. Alex Burnett concluded that varioloid "is in part genuine smallpox, and in part a disease somewhat similar, which is mild and runs a safe course" (Burnett 1824:136). Burnett shared the prevailing view of the time that this mild illness could not be prevented with a second vaccination. In 1886, however, the notion of re-vaccination was revived as a preventative measure (Ohio State Board of Health 1886:23–24). Probst assumed these immigrants were infected, even though none were confirmed as sick. He assumed the disease they carried was a dangerous disease, although the medical community had not considered it life-threatening since at least the 1820s. By raising this alarm, Dr. Probst stoked unwarranted fear.

*Pest houses*, Probst's recommended destinations for so-called infected immigrants, were quarantine locations for those without money to pay hospital costs (Jones 2016). They were usually outside cities, with a cemetery nearby for burial of those who did not survive their illness. Pest houses were, in some instances, created during or in response to epidemics, such as the Cleveland cholera epidemic of 1832 (Dubelko 2014) and the Ohio cholera epidemic of 1849 (Hall 2018). These crude quarantine facilities sometimes developed into larger public institutions, known as county homes, infirmaries, and poor farms (Dubelko 2014; Jones 2016).

County homes took in and cared for indigent sick people. These same facilities also removed the sick from public view since, without this aid, many would be left to struggle without shelter or care in the streets. This institutional system was used to house not only sick people who lacked social and financial resources but also disabled people, orphans, and the elderly without family to care for them, people in poverty, and those deemed by the standards of the time to be mentally insane. County homes and infirmaries *admitted* patients and residents; in other words, they retained the discretion to select whom to admit. Those admitted were called *inmates*. Inmates in poor farms and later infirmaries stepped into an enterprise that sought to use resident labor to be, in part, self-sustaining. To the extent they were able, inmates were expected to work to earn bed and board (Special Collections Division 2006:1).

While the term *inmate* may appear odd to contemporary readers, the etymology and origin of the term is rooted in the simple combination of *inn* and *mate*. The advent of institutions such as prisons, infirmaries, and asylums may be the cause for the shifted meaning from this historical root. Noah Webster's *Compendious Dictionary of the English Language* (1806) defines an inmate as a "lodger." This meaning continues from 1828 in Webster's *American Dictionary of the English Language* to the 1864 Merriam-Webster's *American Dictionary of the English Language* and appears in 1873 in Joseph Worcester's *Comprehensive Dictionary*. However, by 1890 the Meriam-Webster's *International Dictionary* definition shifts from "lodger" to "one of the occupants of an asylum, hospital or prison." By 1947, *Winston Dictionary, College Edition* defines an inmate

Fig. 2-3. The Summit County Infirmary in 1898. (Courtesy of Akron-Summit County Public Library: Summit Memory Collection, County Building, 1898. Public domain image)

as a "stranger lodger," but also "one who is confined to a prison, lunatic asylum, or the like." Thus, the use of the term *inmate* evolved away from the relatively neutral lodger, acquiring the tinge of suspicion or social undesirability across this period.

As noted above, many pest houses were established in the wake of epidemics and disease outbreaks. When a cholera epidemic struck Ohio in the summer of 1849 (Hall 2018), Summit County needed housing for the sick, infirm, and those people made homeless by loss of income, family, or both. Adding to the challenge in Akron, fires in June and September of 1848 and December of 1849 burned down a vast number of buildings, creating an influx of temporarily homeless people (Bierce 1854:28). The Summit County Infirmary was established in Akron at the end of the summer when the county purchased farmland from Joseph McCune (Perrin 1881:243; Lane 1892:1087). Summit County commissioners used McCune's existing farmhouse buildings on Market Street to begin housing inmates (*Akron Beacon Journal* 1849; Lane 1892:1087). Avery Spicer, the first director of the Summit County Infirmary, supervised the construction of new buildings that same year (Perrin 1881:244).

*How Did They Come to Be Here?*

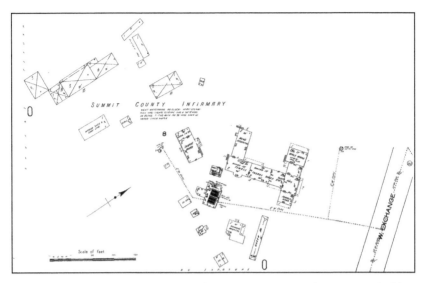

Fig. 2-4. A Sanborn Fire Insurance Map of the Summit County Infirmary, 1916. (Public domain image)

The housing originally constructed at the Infirmary in 1849 was soon deemed inadequate, likely due to the growing population of low-wage laborers and immigrants moving to Akron. By 1864 a new brick Infirmary was built, using inmate labor, with bricks made from the clay on the property (Perrin 1881:244; Special Collections Division 2006:3). The muck (Ritchie and Steiger 1974) in the south of what later became Schneider Park may have been a source for the clay.

The new Infirmary building stood on the corner of Exchange St. and Mull Ave. (Lane 1892:1089), where the present-day Westminster Presbyterian Church stands. The 1892 Sanborn Fire Insurance map of the Summit County Infirmary shows the layout of the main residence and its associated outbuildings, which postdate the major additions to the 1864 building (Lane 1892:1089–1090). Many of the buildings at the Infirmary were designed to sustain the functioning farm to limit the need for county funding. These included a cattle barn, hog pen, horse barn, corn crib, hospital, laundry, icehouse, and pond to harvest ice in the winter. The Summit County Infirmary had over 225 acres of arable land in addition to these facilities (Doyle 1908:124).

The major improvements in 1864 occurred at the start of a dramatic population increase in Akron. The United States Federal Census listed

Akron's population at 3,477 in 1860. By 1864, Akron's population surpassed 5,000 (Olin 1917:67). By 1870, Akron's census recorded population was over 10,000. At the turn of the century, Akron had over 40,000 residents. This population growth was the result of mass immigration of families from Europe. Roughly eleven thousand people from Poland, Hungary, Italy, Slovenia, Germany, Austria, Bohemia (present day Czech Republic), and Ireland emigrated to neighboring Cleveland in 1901 and 1902 alone (Cleveland Plain Dealer 1902).

In the decade from 1910 to 1920, Akron's population tripled to over 200,000 (Grismer 1952:376). The population explosion was felt at the Infirmary. In 1903, the Infirmary's superintendent demanded more rooms be built since he had inmates sleeping on the floor. The *Akron Beacon Journal* reported forty-five residents (*Akron Beacon Journal* 1903), while a very similar report in the *Cleveland Plain Dealer* reported fifty residents (*Cleveland Plain Dealer* 1903). In both news reports, the County Board of Visitors is cited as condemning the "close quarters at the infirmary." By 1908, an estimated 178 inmates were at the Summit County Infirmary (Doyle 1908:449). Thus, the population quadrupled in the five-year period from 1903 to 1908.

Perrin's (1881:244) description of the Summit County Infirmary in the late 1870s lists only six "heavily grated" cells for those considered "insane." Meanwhile, the attic had been converted into an apartment for "tramps." The influx of inmates at the Infirmary and the influx of immigrants into Akron is no coincidence. As Dr. Probst recommended, new immigrants were often sent to the pest houses (*Cleveland Plain Dealer* 1892), located on the Infirmary grounds.

Immigrants were not the only people who used the services of the infirmary system. Any person willing to swear an oath that they lacked worldly goods and needed assistance could be admitted (Blakemore 2018). Often, the social stigma of admitting poverty was used as a method of weeding out "undeserving" poor (Cottrell 1989). Immigrants were more likely to admit they needed assistance than others (Blakemore 2018). They had left their families behind, their primary social support network, in their home countries. Admission decisions were made by the board of directors and the Infirmary superintendent. In infirmaries across the US, these officers included physicians or were advised by medical professionals (Department of Charities and Corrections 1913; Wagner 2005).

The infirmary superintendent usually had the final say-so on admissions (Garman and Russo 1999).

Medical expertise was often instrumental in determining whether to send an individual to a county infirmary over a hospital or other more refined health care services. Professionals like Dr. Probst, collaborating with the popular press, promoted anti-immigrant rhetoric that played into these decisions. In the neighboring State of Pennsylvania, Dr. Benjamin Lee of the Pennsylvania Board of Health, who espoused similar anti-immigrant practices, stated:

> This institution [the county infirmary and quarantine station at Lewis, Pennsylvania] will be one of the utmost importance to Pennsylvania on account of the many ships which enter the port of Philadelphia and land immigrants for the entire country (*New York Times* 1889).

Dr. Probst had claimed a doctor in Latrobe, Pennsylvania, had failed to record, or had falsified, the cause of death on the death certificate of a deceased boy who had infected thirteen people with scarlet fever. Responding positively to Probst's claim, Dr. Lee argued the tragic events could have been avoided if immigrants had been immediately quarantined in county infirmaries.

Although wrong in his attitudes toward immigrants, Probst was a vocal and visible advocate for public health broadly speaking. He fought for ingredient labels on medicines, for vaccination and revaccination, and for water quality improvements (Ohio State Board of Health 1886). Among his primary concerns were combatting scarlet fever, cholera, typhoid, and smallpox. This more positive side of the influential Ohio physician had little overt impact on infirmary sanitation and medical practices, since oversight of the county home system was the responsibility of the Ohio Board of State Charities, which was often composed of nonmedical professionals (Ohio Board of State Charities 1887).

The Ohio Board of State Charities began overseeing and tracking data from institutions such as infirmaries, children's homes, and "insane asylums" in the 1860s. Urban county infirmaries, such as those in Summit, Cuyahoga, and Franklin counties had a tougher time with resources and facilities management than rural counties like Wood County. As late as the 1930s, the disparities between urban and rural social services were apparent (Anderson and Davidson 1937). However, the disparities were largely the result of disproportionate numbers of immigrants compared to US-born citizens in urban and rural counties (Garman and Russo 1999). Today you can visit the Wood County Infirmary, managed by the Wood County Historical Society. If the Summit County Infirmary was an example of how *not* to operate, then Wood County was the antithesis. Summit County represents the experiences of only one county within Ohio's eighty-eight counties. Most Ohio county infirmaries operated in rural areas.

## *Abuse at the Infirmary*

While inmates of the Wood County Infirmary are known to have had steak dinners and played board games thanks to records kept by a conscientious director (Wood County Infirmary Director's Journals, 1869–1900), we do not have the same level of historical documentation at the Summit County Infirmary. Those records which have survived focus mainly on the abuses that occurred in the Infirmary.

In 1887, the Ohio Board of State Charities opened a full investigation of the Summit County Infirmary to address accusations that Dr. Alvin Fouser, the physician caring for the Infirmary's inmates, was earning illicit cash selling corpses to medical schools. Compounding the scandal, the Infirmary's superintendent's son, Ralph Hamlin, was, for a time, the primary suspect in a rape case at the Infirmary. The rape came to light when an inmate's pregnancy was discovered which, based on her pregnancy stage and length of residency, occurred during her time in the Infirmary (*Akron City Times* 1887; Hagelberg 2010). The trial consumed the local papers for several days in February as witnesses testified against Dr. Fouser and superintendent Millard Hamlin.

Dr. Fouser was born in Stark County in 1854. He graduated from Akron High School in 1873 in a class of eleven students (Ohio Board of Education 1884:34). Fouser left for Cincinnati to study at the Medical College of Ohio, where he was mentored by former Union Army surgeons B. Chase and W. Underwood. Fouser graduated medical school in 1876, only three years after finishing high school (Perrin 1881:316). Historical records for Millard Hamlin were more difficult to find. Lane (1892), Bowen and Company (1898), and Doyle (1908) make no mention of Millard Hamlin beyond the years he served as Superintendent from 1882–1887.

The investigation and reporting of these events at the Summit County Infirmary lasted several months. The Ohio Board of State Charities in their annual report, mentioned the abuses:

> "The administration of the Summit County Infirmary was involved during the past year in a scandal, resulting from an insane woman giving birth to a child. A thorough investigation was ordered by the county commissioners, and subsequently changes were made in the immediate management, and additional facilities for the care of the inmates were provided." (Ohio Board of State Charities 1887:79)

The man eventually charged with rape was caretaker George Keck (Hagelberg 2010). Alvin Fouser, Millard Hamlin, and Ralph Hamlin were not convicted of crimes, though public opinion expressed in the local papers was that Ralph had raped the woman, and George Keck was a scapegoat. Dr. Fouser and superintendent Millard Hamlin tendered their resignations from their positions at the Infirmary on April 1, 1887 (Lane 1892:304). Dr. Fouser continued practicing medicine in Akron decades after the scandal (R. L. Polk and Company 1914:1281), serving as Summit County Coroner in the late 1890s, and is identified among those who worked to protect besieged prison-keeper, John Washer, during the violent riot sparked by a radical accusation of rape in the City of Akron in August 1900 (Doyle 1908:83–94).

Clearly, both Fouser and Hamlin were able to "save face" in the wake of these accusations. The trial for the illegal sale of corpses was one of the first in the state to charge medical professionals with both falsifying death certificates and illegally selling corpses. Falsifying death certificates allowed doctors to ship corpses like commodities out of their facilities and into the hands of medical schools and ensured that relatives who came looking for the deceased could not claim them or locate records that might cause suspicion of malfeasance. In 1881, the State of Ohio declared that unclaimed dead could be "donated" to medical schools for dissection (Frank 1976; Krauskopf 1958). Donated, to the modern reader, might imply a tax-deductible incentive; however, the intent was to legalize the transfer of corpses to medical schools for anatomical dissection. This simultaneously removed the financial motivation for rogue grave-robbing and gave physicians the power to designate particular human bodies as objects of study. As unclaimed dead, these corpses had specific attributes that allowed physicians, morticians, police, and the public at large to view them as different from other dead persons. Falsification of records to make someone unclaimable prevented descendants and relatives from claiming them. Likewise, making someone unclaimable removed any prestige or status that might otherwise protect them even if no kin could claim them. There were many medical schools in Ohio and Pennsylvania, and they competed for cadavers. Some medical schools incentivized physicians to acquire needed specimens by offering cash despite the legislation specifying that bodies be donated (Frank 1976).

The unclaimed dead law codified a two-tier division of human remains—the valued and the abandoned. It also enhanced an already close relationship between medical students and body snatchers (Frank 1976). A decade before the Ohio law, there was a well-known "spirited contest" between Cleveland medical students and two rival Akron physicians for the body of recently executed murderer John Henry Hunter (Lane 1892:976). Another especially infamous body-snatching scandal involved John Scott Harrison. Prior to his death in 1878, Harrison had been an Ohio senator, son of former president William Henry Harrison, and father of future president Benjamin Harrison. Benjamin Harrison discovered his father on the dissection table at the Ohio State Medical College, after body snatchers had disinterred him, among others, to provide cadavers for the school (Frank 1976:408). This widely publicized incident, among others, led to the 1881 legislation specifying that only state-owned or supported institutions could distribute unclaimed bodies to medical schools. With the advent of this law, selling corpses to medical schools should have decreased or disappeared. In practice, however, it became a conduit for these institutions to profit off the competitive medical schools through bribery and falsification of death certificates (Frank 1976).

There was growing public concern at the same time over the mistreatment of the dead. In 1886, an anonymous letter to the editor of the *Akron Beacon Journal*, signed "Humanity," decried the indecency of a late-night burial of a dead baby by an Akron health officer without a permit. Without such a permit, Humanity argued, there was no proof the baby was buried at all; even if a permit was issued, still the baby was buried "like a dog found upon the streets" (*Akron Beacon Journal* 1886a).

The public concern over bodysnatching impacted undertakers as well as health officers and medical schools. Less than a month after Humanity's editorial, disputes among undertakers led to formal charges being filed against prominent undertaker Captain George Billow for burial without a permit. Captain Billow, founder of Billow Undertaking Company (now called Billow Funeral Home), had a reasoned reply to his accusers that focused more on health data than social mores. "The main object... in keeping a record of the deaths was that in the future it might be referred to see what diseases have prevailed in the past, the number of deaths therefrom, and the means... to cure them" (*Akron Beacon Journal* 1886). Later, Captain Billow is identified by name as the agent burying at least eighty-three individuals at the Summit County Infirmary cemetery, while his funeral home, known then as Billow Sons Company, is associated with an additional forty-three individuals. His emphasis on the health data value of death certificates is the primary reason that the fraction of the known burials at Schneider Park have records, scant though the information on them may be, as discussed at length in chapter 5.

## *From Pest House to Public Park*

To say that conditions at the Summit County Infirmary of the 1880–1910s (*Akron Beacon Journal* 1903, *Cleveland Plain Dealer* 1906, Doyle 1908, Ohio State Board of Charities 1887, Ohio State Board of Health 1886) could have been better is a significant understatement. But the construction of new facilities was only likely if the county could sell the current property and move elsewhere. The Infirmary was quickly shifting from an institution on the fringe of Akron to one absorbed into an expanding city. Protests about the location of the Infirmary date to at least 1909 (*Cleveland Plain Dealer* 1909), though the residents of this protest argued the "past nine years" had seen unprecedented growth around the Infirmary. By 1910, housing developments had surrounded the Infirmary (Rectigraph Title and Abstract Company 1910). At least one buyer was interested in purchasing the Infirmary's land, with the stipulation that the Infirmary's cemetery be moved (Special Collections Division 2006:3). Though the buyer is not specified in the newspaper report of 1912, it was likely that the individual was Philip H. Schneider, who was the County Commissioner (Grismer 1952:587). Schneider was also a rising real estate developer and president of the Central Associated Realty Company headquartered in Akron.

It is worth our time to focus on Schneider here for two reasons. First, his actions led directly to the creation of Schneider Park. But he also stands as a societal contrast to the inmates of the Infirmary, a figure visibly enjoying success in his life. In 1916, Summit County sold the Infirmary to Schneider for just over $300,000 (*Akron Beacon Journal* 1916). Schneider gave the Infirmary three years to move the inmates (Special Collections Division 2006), after which time he had every intention of building a housing development with Central Associated Realty Company. With the money from the sale, the county began developing a new facility in what is today Munroe Falls Metro Park (Whitman et al. 2008).

There is scant information about Philip Schneider, a man of comfortable means involved in business and civic issues. The relatively limited information about a man whose name is now intertwined with one of the largest parks in Akron reflects the fickle nature of historical records. People with lower incomes and less stable supports might be nearly or even totally invisible in historical records of this period, by comparison.

Sometime after his birth in New York in 1865 or 1866 (the dates on his marriage and death certificate do not match), and before 1898, Philip Schneider lived in Lowell, Michigan, where he married his wife, Jenny (or Jennie) Winegar, in 1889 (Snivel 1935). Lowell is a small village in western Michigan, just east of Grand Rapids. Schneider appears in city directories, which have been indispensable in reconstructing his story. Prior to the phone book, residents of cities were listed in a large, indexed book by last name, with their home address and sometimes their business or occupation. Most city directories were published yearly and provide a useful timeline for tracking a person or family's residency. The first listing of Philip H. Schneider in Akron was in 1898, as manager for Taylor's Dry Goods Store, when Schneider was thirty-one years old (Burch Directory Co. 1898:577). Schneider lived with his wife in a house near Forge and Park Streets; that location is now the site of the Stark State College Akron Campus. By the following year's directory, Schneider had founded The P. H. Schneider Company, a dry goods, notions, cloaks, suits, and draperies store that replaced Taylor's (Burch Directory Co. 1899:591). By 1902 (Burch Directory Co. 1902:794), the Schneiders had moved a block east on Adolph Avenue, next to the City Hospital.

Fig. 2-5. The P. H. Schneider and Company on a rented trolley for a picnic, 1900. (Courtesy of The Summit County Historical Society of Akron, OH; housed at Akron-Summit County Public Library)

In 1906, there were no more listings of The P. H. Schneider Company. Instead, there was a listing for Philip H. and Jenny W. Schneider. A year later, at the age of forty, Schneider founded another new company, The Schneider Building Company (Burch Directory Co. 1907:833). Based solely on city directory data, it is not possible to say whether the shift in companies was an intentional sale, or a shuttering of a failed business venture. The 1910 US Census listed Schneider as a "novelty goods manufacturer." Schneider was County Commissioner from 1911–1913 (Burch Directory Co. 1911:946; Grismer 1952:587), and during this time, no company is listed in the directory (Burch Directory Co. 1913:1161, 1914:1222). The only other historical documents available referring to Schneider indicate that, in his mid-forties, he sought and won a 1914 patent for a five-seamed baseball (US Patent No. 1,109,183). Clearly, Schneider was an eclectic businessman.

In 1916, with the purchase of the land occupied by the Summit County Infirmary (*Akron Beacon Journal* 1916), Schneider became a developer directing the construction of the new Sunset View development. Today this housing development encompasses most of the homes east of Schneider Park and west of Exchange Street. A year later, fifty-year-old Schneider was listed as president of the newly created Central Associated Realty Company (Burch Directory Company 1917:1586).

The old Summit County Infirmary at Mull and Exchange Streets continued to operate through late spring 1919, when the new County Infirmary was finished in Munroe Falls (Special Collections Division 2006:3; Whitman et al. 2008). The Munroe Falls Infirmary included a cemetery space located southeast of today's Heather Knoll Nursing Home and north of the Summit County Fairgrounds, where an unknown number of burials from the old Infirmary's burial ground were reinterred at the same time living inmates were transitioned to the new facility (Whitman et al. 2008). Today, that cemetery is nestled in a small, wooded grove just off a trail in Munroe Falls Metro Park, with a fence and a few headstones. Most of the burials are unmarked.

The Summit County Infirmary at Mull and Exchange Streets was demolished in 1919, immediately after the opening of the Munro Falls location (Price 2009). By 1921, the Sunset View development had a handful of houses built, including Schneider's new home on Storer Avenue, with most parcels mapped but not yet built (G. M. Hopkins and Company 1921). The Infirmary's outbuildings were located on what is today Jefferson Avenue. The creation of that road and the new placement of other construction effectively obscured evidence of the Infirmary's existence.

Schneider built himself a second home on Rose Boulevard not long after, in 1925 (Adams 1978). Both Schneider's first and second homes still stand just a couple of blocks from his namesake Schneider Park, but his time at Sunset View development came to an early end. Schneider died October 9, 1935, of mediastinal cancer at the age of sixty-eight (*Akron Beacon Journal* 1935; Snivel 1935; Summit County, Ohio Death Certificate Vol. 1224, No. 63068).

Schneider had accumulated significant wealth across his lifetime. It is possible to glean information both about his financial standing and his and Jennie's values as citizens of the Progressive Era. The Schneiders had invested in rubber and real estate stocks (Snivel 1935), among his other business ventures of toy stores, baseball patents, and the Central Associated Realty Company. Schneider's will bequeathed the fifteen-acre park that became Schneider Park to the City of Akron (Price 2009; Akron Special Collections 2006). While the value of the acreage is difficult to calculate, another donation is revealing. As executor of the estate (*Akron Beacon Journal* 1935), Jenny W. Schneider donated $800,000 to the City of Lowell, Michigan, for new hospital facilities. Using the US Consumer

Price Index inflation calculator, this donation to the City of Lowell is equivalent to $18.8 million in 2025 dollars.

Jenny Schneider continued living in her home on Rose Boulevard (United States Federal Census 1940) and died at the age of ninety-six on October 30, 1964 (Summit County, Ohio Death Certificate Vol. 17848, No. 78724). Jenny and Philip Schneider are buried in Graceland Memorial Park and Mausoleum in Grand Rapids, Michigan.

Among the information lost in the history of Schneider Park is documentation regarding the removal of burials from what became Schneider Park to the new cemetery in Munroe Falls. Did the county move the burials in 1912, as suggested by the potential buyers, or were they exhumed by someone else? While many cemeteries in Ohio were mapped by the Works Progress Administration (WPA) during the 1930s, especially with the goal of locating the graves of US military veterans, no such map has been found for the Schneider Park burial ground. Informal oral histories from residents who passed by during the archaeological geophysical survey of 2017 (chapter 4) included stories of the WPA moving graves from Schneider Park to the new infirmary cemetery in Munroe Falls. Unfortunately, these are uncorroborated stories. No WPA records associated with the Infirmary burial ground in Schneider Park have been found to date.

## *Recovering the Stories of the Dead*

What we know of the inmates buried in the Infirmary's cemetery is very limited. The records from the newer Munroe Falls Infirmary are not much help. This section describes the principal sources of historical documents we have for identifying the individuals buried in the Infirmary cemetery. Later, in chapter 5, a thorough analysis of these records is made to understand the interred individuals as a population through mortality profiles, causes of death, infant mortality rates, recorded names, and nationalities. While that chapter discusses the dead as a group, the present section of this chapter examines what we can know about the individuals buried in the Infirmary cemetery. This discussion starts with a history of what was recorded and how many of the records were lost and then rediscovered.

### *Records of death*

From 1867 to 1908, Ohio required counties to record deaths within their jurisdiction. Beginning December 20, 1908, the Ohio State Board of

Health assumed responsibility for death certificates. Due to falsifications and unreported deaths by Fouser prior to 1887, death certificates for actual burials at the Summit County Infirmary form a patchy record. According to Whitman et al. (2008:29), the list of names and birth and death dates of individuals buried at the Munroe Falls Infirmary survived to the present because of the keen eye of a former Summit County employee, who spotted a copy of the burial records book in the trash in 1982. The originals were destroyed in a fire in 1981, according to local historian Marilyn Kovatch (Conn 2017). Whether intentional or not, many of the historical records of the people from the Infirmary buried have not survived to the present. In most cases, death certificates were the only historical records that remained of their life stories.

Michael Elliott, retired Akron-Summit County Public Libraries special collections librarian, took a particular interest in this subject and gathered relevant death certificates over decades (Price 2009). Elliott compiled a list of death records and certificates with burial locations of "Infirmary" or "County Home" (meaning the Munroe Falls Infirmary) for this research. The data he shared were gathered by combing through newspaper and public records microfilm for burials before 1919 and associated with the Infirmary. Due to the transition between the old and new Summit County Infirmary sites, deaths between 1916 and 1919 may have been buried at Schneider Park or Munroe Falls. Without the original record book, destroyed by fire, or the records of the purchase between Summit County and Philip Schneider, there are no additional data to help us distinguish between the two.

Elliott's data includes 308 death certificates associated with the Infirmary cemetery in Schneider Park. Aside from a handful of interviews with inmates in 1919 (Price 2009), these certificates are almost all that remain of their histories. Together, these certificates tell stories about ancestry, languages, health struggles, neighbors, and even roommates. Of these 308 records, only 138 represent inmates who died in the Infirmary. The rest are the unclaimed dead of Akron.

Death certificates provide basic historical information, including place of birth, place of death, former residence, occupation, parents' place of birth, and cause of death. Every death certificate has a section with the location of the burial. The number of years, weeks, and days at the Infirmary are also recorded on the death certificate. For individuals buried in the cemetery while it functioned as a potter's field, they did not have Infirmary residency information. These individuals usually had the location of death and place of former residence without any additional information as to the length of residency.

An overwhelming majority of death certificates in this dataset (287 out of 308) occurred after 1908. Most of the remaining certificates post-date 1889 (N =17), which may reflect the change in administrations after Fouser and Hamlin resigned. Most of the deaths recorded in this collection occurred between 1908 and 1916 (n=283), with a precipitous drop-off after 1916. This drop-off likely reflects the transition between the two institutions in Akron and Munroe Falls.

One of the more striking patterns in the data are the ages of the pre-1908 deaths. Eleven of the seventeen death records from this period are for people over fifty, with three records not listing ages. Where possible, other data were used to approximate ages of individuals. For example, Robert Thompson had a son who lived independently in another state, putting Thompson's age estimate over thirty (*Akron Daily Democrat* 1902). There is not much we can do with these early records in terms of a statistical analysis, but it is useful to note that the inmates buried in the Infirmary cemetery were old individuals. Chapter 5 examines the death certificates from 1908 to 1916, when a much fuller analysis can be undertaken.

*The city's dead*

In addition to those who died in the Infirmary's care, the Infirmary's cemetery also doubled as a potter's field, or a cemetery for the unclaimed dead, for the City of Akron's morgue (Special Collections Division 2006). When the Infirmary cemetery began burying non-inmates is unknown; the oldest records clearly indicating this practice come from 1908. In fact, many of the 308 known dead buried in the Infirmary Cemetery did not hail from Akron, or even Ohio. The unclaimed included immigrants without family to identify them, or whose families did not come forward, and unidentified bodies. Any single adult, immigrant or migrant, without kin in town to claim them could end up in the Infirmary cemetery while it served as a potter's field to the city morgue.

The death certificates are, unfortunately, often exceedingly terse in the details they provide. For example, the occupation is often described by a single word, and the most common occupations listed include laborer, domestic, and farmer. The general term laborer was the most common, with just over a quarter of all occupations being described in this way. The other fifty-three listed occupations included (in decreasing frequency): domestic, farmers, brick layers or masons, barbers, rubber workers, and carpenters. There were also unique occupations such as a match maker, a bookkeeper, an editor, and a professor.

The professor is one of a handful of cases where their death was reported in the newspapers. Professor David D. Evans gives us some insight into non-inmates interred in the Infirmary cemetery. His obituary in the *Akron Daily Democrat* (1901) reads:

> Without funeral services—not even a prayer; without flowers—not even a pansy, his favorite flower, the mortal clay of Prof. David D. Evans was buried in the potter's field at the Infirmary farm Saturday afternoon. A grave was dug, the cheap pine coffin, whose dull black paint could not conceal its look of poverty, was lowered and the excavation in the earth filled in. That was all. It took but a little time, and the men who do the work shouldered their shovels and trudged away. The watch which Supt. [superintendent] S. B. Stottler, of the Infirmary, had hoped to sell to give the unfortunate man's body decent burial, is said to be worth $40. Half of this sum would have been sufficient for the purpose, but a purchaser for the old-fashioned but still handsome time-piece could not be found.

The unclaimed dead of Akron were not memorialized, even when they were known in the community. As unclaimed, Professor Evans exemplifies the disposition of all who were consigned to the potter's field. However, his eulogy in the press is atypical of burials in the Infirmary cemetery. Duffin Russel (*Akron Beacon Journal* 1913) and Robert Thompson (*Akron Daily Democrat* 1902) are more typical cases in which only a brief notice is given to anyone who might claim their bodies. Robert Thompson's obituary (*Akron Daily Democrat* 1902) reads:

> The body of Robert Thompson still lies unclaimed in Parks' morgue. Mr. Parks telegraphed to the son of the deceased, who lives in Clearfield, Pa., but late Wednesday afternoon had received no reply. The remains

will be held a few days and then if no one makes a claim, they will be interred in the potter's field, or turned over to some medical college.

Newspaper accounts suggest a likely association between the cost of burial and failure to claim bodies. The Infirmary cemetery served as the final resting place for those who left no money to cover burial expenses.

*The Infirmary's own*

Many of the death certificates indicate length of residency at the Infirmary prior to death. Any amount of time in residency on the death certificate represents formal admission as an inmate in the Summit County Infirmary. In the absence of the Infirmary's admissions records, this is our only corroboration of inmate status for these individuals buried in the Infirmary cemetery. The person with the longest residency, according to the known death certificates, was William Scappin, who lived at the Summit County Infirmary for thirty-four years. Many of the deceased inmates were simply recorded as "5 + [years]." On the other end of the spectrum, some inmates spent only days or a few weeks at the Infirmary, likely as indigents requiring the free medical facilities and services of the staff. Looking at just the records dated after 1908, the number of dead who were not among the Infirmary inmate population (those unclaimed from the city morgue) represent 73 percent of known death certificates (n=210) while inmates with residency over a year account for 13 percent (n=36), and inmates with residency under a year at time of death make up the remaining 14 percent (n=41).

*Immigrants and their places of origin*

The inmate population receiving the benefit of social services at the Summit County Infirmary were largely of Western European and US origin, while most of the people who can be identified as Eastern European or from outside the Euro-American regions were among the unclaimed dead from the Akron city morgue subsequently buried in the Infirmary cemetery.

This distribution is partially the result of the overall proportions of the general immigrant population from these regions in the general Akron area at the time. However, the high proportion of unclaimed dead coming from Eastern Europe and from further abroad also illustrates that the most recent immigrant groups often experienced the greatest privations while having the least social capital. They also experienced anti-immigrant bias, which may be reflected in these data. The death certificates contain a few examples of reckless record-keeping that hints at such bias. For example, the Kleten triplets passed away due to birth complications, but they died on different days. Two of the children were recorded as "Romanian," while the third was "Hungarian." John and Eva Kleten were Romanian, and all three infants were recorded by the same physician. In another case, a man could not be identified because he had been struck by a train. No name was recorded, but his country of birth was identified as "Hungary." It is possible that the physician used the location of death, tracks near where immigrant encampments were known to be, as a context clue to the ethnicity, despite the immense level of speculation encoded into that context.

In chapter 5, we examine the death certificates from 1908–1916 in greater detail. We are able to examine indicators of health, working conditions, disease, and trauma in that chapter by expanding our sample size to include other contemporary cemeteries that provide us with a greater context for the records that survive from the Summit County Infirmary.

## *Conclusions*

To close this chapter, we return to the map. Downtown Akron and neighborhoods like Dublin were dominated early on by Irish canal diggers and later, in the late nineteenth and early twentieth century, by Italian and Eastern European immigrants (Doyle 1908:65). Our potter's field death certificates offer addresses, or at least streets of residence for eighty-two of the individuals in our dataset (26 percent) from within this area. Others cannot be more specifically geo-located because they simply indicate broad place names such as "Akron," "Barberton," or "Cuyahoga Falls."

The map in figure 2-6 shows the locations of known street addresses for people buried at Schneider Park who were not Infirmary residents. While most were in downtown Akron, along Broadway, High, and Main, many lived in Dublin or in the valley between Perkins Park and Spicer Hill. Downtown Akron sits in the historical stream-valleys formed by the Wolf Run and the Little Cuyahoga Rivers (Geddes 1823). These valleys offered reasonable sites for building but also served to trap smoke and reverberate industrial noises from factories as Akron businesses grew.

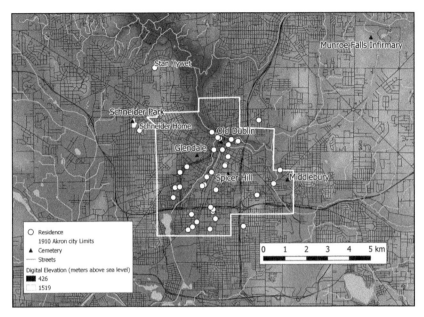

Fig. 2-6. Known locations of homes of the deceased buried in the Summit County Infirmary cemetery (Map: Eric Olson)

Open, stagnant water trapped atop the clayey soil of the area facilitated infections and supported disease-carrying mosquito populations (World Health Organization 2013). It is notable that these people did not live to the west of downtown Akron. Across the evolution of the rubber industry, it became clear that the stench, airborne particulates, and the attendant grime they generated blew west to east with prevailing winds and settled in valleys. The hills to the west of the city became prime real estate for people accruing wealth from rubber production and other Akron manufacturing booms. The Seiberlings completed their mansion, Stan Hywet, on the western hills of Akron in 1915, with many lower-level capitalists following in their footsteps. Another West Akronite of wealth was Philip Schneider. It is not a surprise that the Summit County Infirmary's large property became the object of desire for Schneider as a developer or that those in power in Akron supported the transition of this space into luxury housing, houses of worship, and a high-quality private school.

When we look at the physical legacy left behind by late nineteenth- and early twentieth-century poorer people in Akron, there is little to see.

Dublin and its cemetery have been paved over. The Infirmary is gone, replaced with a church and parking lot. Its former fields are now residential streets and houses. Many of the workplaces that drew them, canals and the iconic factories, have fallen into disuse or been demolished. Only a handful of the houses that immigrants and lower-income Akronites of the era lived in still exist. The pest houses used to quarantine newly arrived immigrants are gone. Dr. Alvin Fouser's home is now the Morley parking deck on Broadway. Captain Billow's original funeral home was demolished to make way for the Martin Luther King Jr. Beltway. However, Schneider Park still stands open, a reminder by his name of the development that flourished and by its openness of both a time when suburban development engineers could not tame wet and mushy land, and before that, a time when inmates of the Infirmary and the unclaimed dead of the City of Akron found a resting place in otherwise undesirable land. Philip Schneider's house on Rose Boulevard also still stands.

Akron's booming economy created a demand for a workforce to supply the growing industries that characterized the late nineteenth century. Immigrants made new homes in Akron with the prospect of a better life. They made new friends, celebrated old traditions, spoke different and common languages, built new communities, and buried their dead. As the city they helped build grew, the need for new spaces also grew.

The Infirmary was created to support the low income, immigrant, and indigent people of the county, many of whom worked and lived in Akron. All these inmates lived under the same roof. For people who had survived war, transatlantic voyages, hazardous working conditions, and poverty, the Summit County Infirmary was one of very few forms of aid available. It was hazardous, cramped, and dirty. The inmates were often not treated with dignity and could end up quarantined in the pest house. Still, for most, it was better than living in the streets and, in some cases, it provided a stable means of support. For better or worse, the Summit County Infirmary in Akron closed its doors in 1919, and the living inmates were moved to other places, including the new facility at Munroe Falls. Chapter 6 takes up the story of how society viewed and treated the poor, indigent, and sick, following national trends in social support past the end of the infirmary system, and it provides a larger context for considering how modern views and norms shape our treatment of these people today. Much about the individual's life stories of the inmates has been lost, but even the scraps of evidence we have left tell a compelling story and are worth remembering.

## Chapter 3
# Forgotten Graveyards and Rediscovered Bodies
## Ethical and Legal Issues
*Robert L. Tucker*

The town of New Haven, Connecticut—home of Yale University—is centered around a bucolic green space known as New Haven Green. Bordered on two sides by Yale, the Green consists of approximately sixteen acres of open area, plus three churches. Sidewalks used by thousands crisscross the Green, and during warm weather, crowds spread their blankets on the green to listen to jazz fests or other forms of entertainment (American Planning Assn. 1950).

But it wasn't always so. Between 1638 and 1796, the New Haven Green was used as a burial ground for local residents. After 150 years of use, the Green became too cluttered with gravestones, so a new graveyard (the Grove Street Cemetery) was established. When the Grove Street Cemetery opened in the early 1800s, most of the headstones from the Green (except for those directly situated under Center Church) were moved to the new cemetery. But the bodies were left *in situ*, and it is estimated that the remains of at least five thousand (and perhaps as many as ten thousand) early colonists still remain buried under New Haven Green (Blake 1898, 247–255; Henri 2017). Many of the graves are quite shallow, as evidenced in 2012 when Hurricane Sandy blew down a 103-year-old

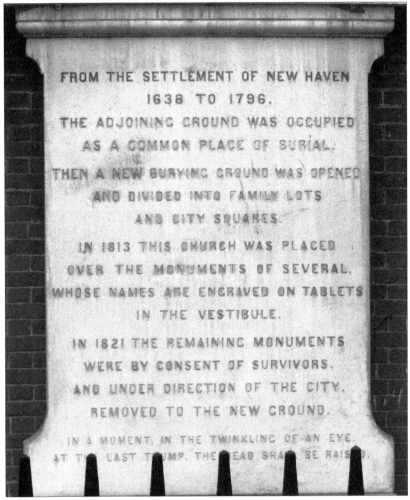

Fig. 3-1. Plaque commemorating those buried beneath the New Haven Green (Photo: Robert L. Tucker)

tree, exposing two of the skeletons (Winter 2012). A marble plaque affixed to the side of the Center Church on the Green memorializes the dead.

The New Haven Green is just one example of the conflict between the desires of the living to utilize the land and a decision made decades or centuries earlier to bury the dead at that location. There are many others. For example, in 1823, a municipal ordinance was passed that prohibited ground burials in certain parts of Manhattan. Twenty-eight years later, a second resolution was passed forbidding any new cemeteries in the borough. Many of the previously existing Manhattan burials were moved to Queens in the nineteenth century to permit the land to be developed and used by the living (Marsh 2012, 197). Similarly, in 1858, the sanitary superintendent for the City of Chicago sought the abandonment of the city's downtown cemetery. By 1866, all burials in Chicago had been disinterred and relocated to cemeteries on the edge of town (Marsh 2012, 197).

This repurposing of graveyards has continued into the twentieth and twenty-first centuries. In 1900, the San Francisco Board of Supervisors prohibited any future interments from taking place in the city. After the 1906 fire, most existing burials were removed and relocated elsewhere. In the mid-twentieth century, the Tennessee Valley Authority moved thousands of graves to assemble land for its many reservoirs (American Society of Planning Officials 1950, 202). In the mid-1940s, the City of Baltimore moved more than 170 bodies that were buried in several small cemeteries and family burying grounds, which required the city to obtain the consent of survivors, exhume the bodies, and purchase suitable graves elsewhere so that the bodies could be reinterred (The Baltimore Sun 1946:19). Similarly, in 1957, St. Louis moved its potter's field burial ground for the indigent to make way for a housing project (American Society of Planning Officials 1950, 202).

In 2005, the City of Chicago petitioned a court to allow it to move the historic St. Johannes cemetery, where 1,300 century-old graves occupied the ground where a new airport runway was planned. In reporting on this request, National Public Radio reported that "as cities and suburbs grow leaving precious little undeveloped land, cemetery relocations seem to be increasingly common" and that "few communities seem willing to make room for new cemeteries" (Schaper 2005).

Similarly, in 2009, human remains were discovered at the site of a new hospital being built in Eugene, Oregon. The bodies were the remnants of a family plot from the 1800s, and the family "missed a few" of the bodies of their relatives when they disinterred and reinterred them many years later (Joiner 2010). Again, in 2011, graves that dated from the early 1800s were found beneath softball fields in an Indiana city park, which was being examined as the proposed site for a new convention center. The cemetery closed in 1862, then became overgrown, and was later converted to a city park in the 1920s (Castleman 2011).

Even cemeteries owned by religious denominations are sometimes converted to other uses. In 2012, the Catholic Diocese of Toledo contemplated selling one of its cemeteries for use as a housing development. The gravestones had been removed from the burial grounds in the 1920s, and the land had been farmed for nearly a century thereafter. Controversy developed when the diocese planned to sell the burial grounds to a residential developer (Kelly 2012).

Cemeteries may be abandoned, or the use of a graveyard may need to be changed, for any number of reasons. Problems develop when cemeteries fall into disuse and neglect or when they become health hazards. Those hazards arise from either decomposition of the bodies or from the use of formaldehyde (a known human carcinogen found in almost all embalming fluid). The presence of a cemetery near a residential area may depress property values, and city administrators often find cemeteries to be expensive and tax-exempt headaches that drain municipal resources (Gardner 2015, 220).

Land use problems associated with burial grounds develop for several reasons. Frequently they occur because the living would now prefer to use the land for other purposes. But land use problems also arise when prehistoric burials are found in areas where they were not previously known to exist. To cite just a single example, a road in Vermont cuts through an area thought to have been populated by the Abenaki peoples for centuries before the arrival of European colonists. Most of the land along the road is privately owned, and the area has become popular for residential construction in recent decades. Since the early 1970s, the remains of more than one hundred bodies have been found at residential construction sites along the road, and it is estimated that perhaps as many as eighty thousand Abenaki were buried in this area over the past ten thousand years (Cusick 2003, 469). Land use problems associated with these burials first arose in 1973, when a landowner discovered human remains while digging a hole for a cellar. Construction halted, and skeletal remains of more than eighty bodies were exhumed and examined. The ensuing dispute over the use of this land took twenty-three years to resolve. The matter was concluded when the state purchased the parcel using funds provided by the Vermont legislature and an anonymous private donor, and the remains were reinterred in a closed Abenaki ceremony.

But that was not the end of the matter. By 1992, Vermont authorities believed that at least two other burial sites had been disturbed along the same road in the previous two decades. Recently, in May 2000, excavation for modular homes unearthed still more human remains. Again, the use of that property was resolved only when the state ultimately purchased the land for nearly twice the assessed market value (Cusick 2003, 468–470).

A patchwork of cemeteries (both ancient and modern) across the landscape is causing land use problems, especially given the growing population and the permanency (at least in the United States) of modern burials. If current notions of "perpetual care" of the dead in cemeteries consisting of single graves persist, then eventually all available land will be used for the interment of the dead, leaving no place for the living. The land use problems caused by the burgeoning number of graveyards were noted by an English judge in the 1821 decision in the case of *Gilbert v. Buzzard and Boyer*. In that case, Sir William Scott observed that as time goes on, the land near cities will increasingly be given over to graveyards, thereby depriving the living of the ability to use it:

> The comparatively small portion of the dead will shoulder out the living and their posterity. The whole environs of this metropolis must be surrounded by a circumvallation of churchyards, perpetually enlarging by becoming themselves surcharged with bodies; if indeed landowners can be found willing to divert their ground from the beneficial uses of the living to the barren preservation of the dead.

To illustrate, in 1935, the US Department of Commerce estimated that there were approximately fifteen thousand cemeteries in the United States, which then occupied an estimated 140,000 acres (mostly in or near areas of comparatively high population density). Since that time, at least two thousand more acres have been used for graveyards each year. Current full body inhumation burial practices with standard plot sizes allow 620 burials per acre. Using the Center for Disease Control's 2015 estimate of 2,712,630 deaths per year and taking into account the fact that 48.6 percent of deaths result in cremation rather than burial, approximately 2,126 acres will be devoted to full body inhumations per year (Centers for Disease Control 2018; American Society of Planning Officials 1950, 200).

Given crowded municipal conditions and (at least in older cities) the absence of any planned green spaces in urban areas, municipal graveyards have often been converted to public park space (just as the Summit County Infirmary graveyard has now been rededicated by the City of Akron as Schneider Park). In cities with high population densities, inner-city cemeteries may be the only open space left. A full century ago, an English commentator exhorted the idea of converting these inner-city burial grounds into park land that could be enjoyed by the living:

> In many cities—most strikingly in London—where land values have become so high as almost to discourage municipal purchases for the creation of open spaces, and where the crowding is so severe that there is excuse for fear that an arbitrary reduction of the habitable area in a given section may increase rather than diminish suffering and the pushing of the urban boundaries into a distance that the poor cannot traverse make pitiful appeal for public open areas, there has been a utilization of ancient graveyards. They are transformed, with excellent sanitary effect, to serve as breathing places, garden spots, and playgrounds. But their location as regards the street plan is obviously without system.
>
> ... Finally, the community use of the cemetery as a park is simply a pathetic confession of the public need of park reservations. Speaking artistically, the cemeteries have lately shown vast improvement. From a type originally comparable to stoneyards they tend to become more and more park-like.... But the great significance of a community's park-use of a cemetery is the proof of the need of park. It is a use to be encouraged and approved, until the park is provided, for all the reasons for which parks are approved. (Robinson 1918)

It is therefore not surprising that lands once used as burial grounds increasingly are put to other uses. But doing so can create endless legal and regulatory headaches. It has been observed that "the disposal of the dead is enmeshed in religious doctrine, custom, fear, superstition, complicated statutory law, and crusading burial reform." Even more to the point, when city planners propose removing bodies from cemeteries to use that land for other purposes, the public relations issues can be delicate (American Society of Planning Officials 1950, 200).

The burial grounds at Schneider Park in Akron—like the graveyard located at what is now known as New Haven Green—illustrate this recurring conflict. As the above examples show, the perceived highest and best use for a parcel of real property changes over time. This raises a pointed question that has still not been fully resolved: if one generation of humans has designated a parcel of real property to be used as a cemetery, is that decision perpetually binding upon all future generations? Or is it permissible (both legally and ethically) to repurpose the land? If the land use may be changed from the cemetery to some other purpose, what (if anything) must be done with the bodies that were buried in the tract while it was dedicated and used as a cemetery?

Legal and ethical questions necessarily arise when human remains are discovered in places where they were not known to be buried and when the living seek to disinter the dead from cemeteries so that the land can be put to other uses. Among others, these issues may include the following: Who (if anyone) "owns" (or has the right to possess) the body of a deceased human being? What uses of land should be permitted when bodies remain buried beneath the surface? When may (or must) the living disinter the dead and reinter the bodies elsewhere before using a burial ground for residential or commercial purposes?

## *The Ethical Issues*

Chapter 1 raises two important points that bear repeating. First, "there is no universal ethical code." Second, even within a specific cultural group, the "ethical code observed within [that] cultural group changes through time." The question of what conduct is right or wrong is one of value. Different religions, and different ethnic or cultural groups, have different views on whether, when, and to what extent human remains may be excavated or studied and to whom (if anyone) they should be returned.

Ethical issues are particularly keen when there are multiple and inconsistent interests and claimants. The decision as to what conduct is morally or ethically correct depends upon the relative weights assigned to the different and competing values and interests. Reasonable people of good will may not always agree on the priority or weight to be assigned to each of those values.

There is no absolute authoritative answer as to whether morals and ethics require, for example, the immediate reburial of human remains or whether they may fairly be curated and studied (at least for some period of time) before their ultimate disposition. The major religions hold different views on that issue. Some, such as orthodox Jews, consider the dead to have an absolute right to remain undisturbed and require that any human body accidentally excavated be reburied immediately. Interestingly, however, Israel's Antiquities Act requires only the reburial of human remains that are less than five thousand years old because remains older than this are considered by orthodox Jews to predate creation, and therefore are not "human" (Pearson 2008, 177, fn. 18).

But other ethnic and religious groups, including most Christians, have far less absolute views on the subject. The Church of England, for example, has no particular opposition to the disturbance of human remains, in part because removal and disturbance of graves were both regular and necessary aspects of churchyard burial. Thus, the members of some ethnic groups within modern British society are actively involved in excavating and researching their own ancestors from eighteenth and nineteenth-century London. But other ethnic groups (including some that feel marginalized or oppressed) consider disturbance of their dead to be unthinkably repugnant (Pearson 2008, 184).

It should therefore come as little surprise that the published ethical codes are short on absolute moral imperatives and long on recommendations for consultation and negotiation. Many organizations that are associated with anthropological research or the curation of artifacts have attempted to create codes of conduct or other statements that address the ethical and moral issues associated with investigation of the dead and of the land where they are buried. The absence of imperatives about the investigations that either are or are not permissible, combined with heavy reliance on strategies for seeking buy-in and consensus, illustrate that these issues are not generally decided on the grounds of moral absolutes but are instead resolved by attempting to achieve consensus based on a negotiated compromise.

For archaeologists in the western hemisphere, the most important of these ethical codes may be the one published by the Society of American Archaeologists, which is an organization dedicated to the research, interpretation, and protection of the archaeological heritage of the Americas. Founded in 1934, the SAA seeks to stimulate interest and research in American archaeology, advocate for the conservation of archaeological resources, encourage public access to and appreciation of archaeology, halt the excavation and sale of looted archaeological materials, and serve as a bond among those interested in American archaeology.

In May 1986, the SAA's board of directors adopted the "Statement Concerning the Treatment of Human Remains," which was reaffirmed in March 1999. The SAA Statement includes four noteworthy components. First, it recognizes that both the scientific and indigenous interests in human remains and funerary objects are legitimate. The Statement acknowledges that "[m]ortuary evidence is an integral part of the archaeological record of past culture and behavior in that it informs directly upon social structure and organization and, less directly, upon aspects of religion and ideology."

Second, the Statement notes that the scientific value of human remains and funerary objects varies depending on each object's ability to contribute significant information about the past. It reflects upon some of the many legitimate areas of scientific and cultural inquiry that are involved, saying that "[h]uman remains, as an integral part of the mortuary record, provide unique information about demography, diet, disease, and genetic relationships among human groups." It goes on to say that "[t]he scientific importance of particular human remains should be determined by their potential to aid in present and future research" in these and other areas.

Third, the Statement supports the notion that repatriation and reburial should not necessarily be an inflexible rule. It explicitly states that the SAA "opposes universal or indiscriminate reburial of human remains, either from ongoing excavations or from extant collections." Instead, the statement suggests that "the weight accorded any claim made by an individual or group concerning particular human remains should depend upon the strength of their demonstrated biological or cultural affinity with the remains in question."

Finally, the statement argues that this individualized determination should be made in the context of negotiations on a case-by-case basis. As the SAA Statement puts it, "controversies involving the treatment of human remains cannot properly be resolved nationwide in a uniform way."

Archaeologists in Europe face the same concerns of local stakeholder populations when they excavate sites where human remains are present.

In 1997, the organization known as Historic Scotland published a policy document titled *The Treatment of Human Remains in Archaeology*, which was amended in November 2006. That policy statement emphasizes the need to balance and accommodate the interests and desires of both the scientific community and the cultural descendants of the deceased. The document begins by requiring that measures be taken to avoid the "needless disturbance, damage or destruction of human remains, their graves or funerary monuments." It then encourages and recommends "discussion on any issues relating to the treatment of human remains" and expresses the expectation that archaeologists will "handle any controversy which may arise from these debates with sensitivity and the hope that, where differences of view persist, mutual respect between protagonists will remain."

The same emphasis on respect for mortal remains, the wishes of the decedent, and the interests of the local community is featured in international codes of ethics. For example, the *Vermillion Accord on Human Remains* was adopted by the World Archaeological Congress in 1989. It urges that "agreement on the disposition of fossil, skeletal, mummified and other remains... be reached by negotiation on the basis of mutual respect for the legitimate concerns of communities for the proper disposition of their ancestors, as well as the legitimate concerns of science and education." It also recognizes that "the concerns of various ethnic groups, as well as those of science are legitimate and to be respected," and anticipates that respectful negotiation "will permit acceptable agreements to be reached and honored."

In 1991, the World Archaeological Congress adopted the *First Code of Ethics*, which consists of eight "principles to abide by" plus seven "rules to adhere to." The "principles to abide by" emphasize the importance of Indigenous cultural heritage in general, and the "special importance of indigenous ancestral human remains." They recommend the establishment of "equitable partnerships and relationships between members and indigenous peoples whose cultural heritage is being investigated," and instruct that the views of the Indigenous population should be "considered as critically important in setting research standards, questions, priorities and goals."

The "rules to adhere to" also emphasize the need to "negotiate with and obtain the informed consent of representatives authorized by the indigenous peoples whose cultural heritage is the subject of investigation," and urge "deference and respect to the identified indigenous people" in presenting the results of any investigation.

In 2005, that same organization adopted the *Tamaki Mauka-rau Accord on the Display of Human Remains and Sacred Objects*. It consists of three unnumbered paragraphs, followed by six very brief principles that must be "taken into account" by any person or organization that considers displaying human remains and sacred objects. The unnumbered paragraphs begin by recognizing that "the display of human remains and sacred objects is recognized as a sensitive issue," while also acknowledging that "the display of human remains or sacred objects may serve to illuminate our common humanity." The Accord concludes with the now-familiar refrain that stresses the need for "consultation and collaboration with communities," seeking permission from those communities, making sure that any display is "culturally appropriate," and engaging in "regular consultation with the affected community."

All of these ethical statements agree that there are no generally accepted moral absolutes associated with the investigation and treatment of human remains and cultural artifacts. These statements generally acknowledge the legitimacy and importance of scientific study of our past and the world around us, while simultaneously urging researchers to learn, respect, and accommodate the beliefs and customs of Indigenous communities, even if those beliefs are not in accord with—or even if they are wildly at odds with—Western science.

## *The Legal Issues*

Given that professional organizations have been unwilling or unable to opine on the question of whether the needs and desires of the living (whether they be for the repurposing of land or for scientific investigation of bygone cultures) should take precedence over past or present local cultural values, it should come as no surprise that courts and legislatures throughout the western world have struggled with those same questions.

Even within the borders of the United Kingdom alone, the laws concerning excavation of graves vary widely. For example, in Scotland, all human remains are said to have a "right of sepulture," and the deliberate violation of a burial—for any reason—is a criminal act. This stands in stark contrast to the situation in England and Wales, where the Burial Act of 1857 has long permitted human remains to be disinterred from unconsecrated ground by obtaining a license from the Secretary of State after the bodies have been located. When excavation takes place in known cemeteries of more recent vintage, the Disused Burial Grounds (Amendment) Act of 1981 (which amended legislation that was originally enacted in 1884) allows disinterment where prior notice of the removal is given by developers both in the newspapers and on the land in question. Similarly, the same 1981 Act controls where church crypts can be emptied and removed because of land use development (Pearson 2008, 183).

In England, most cemetery excavations are not carried out by archaeologists, but rather by commercial enterprises that specialize in clearing cemeteries so that the land may be redeveloped and used for other purposes. This is done using low-cost exhumation methods, including heavy power machinery. The relative ease of obtaining these licenses can lead to loss of important historical data because the issuance of the license does not require consultation with English or Welsh advisory bodies on heritage matters. In one notable case, battle-scarred skeletons of combatants in the Battle of Towton in 1461 (one of the bloodiest battles during the Wars of the Roses) were found buried in a series of large pits. A license to excavate those remains was issued without any requirement that any archaeological investigation be conducted before removing the bodies. Fortunately, one of the contractors realized that important historical information was being lost, and archaeologists were called to the scene. A careful scientific examination of these remains yielded a great deal of information about medieval face-to-face combat. This information was derived from the concentration of injuries in the form of crushing (by mace, flail, or morning star), slashing (by use of a sword or dagger), or piercing (by use of pole axe or battle axe). Further, the rugged muscle attachments on their bones provided information about their physically strenuous lives, and their occupational injuries were documented by traumatic lesions likely caused during archery practice.

In the United States, there are comparatively few instances where legislatures (at either the federal or state level) have addressed burial, disinterment, and reinterment issues, and even fewer where they have done so in the specific context of archaeological and scientific investigation of bodies and funerary objects. The absence of legislative directive has resulted in a sketchy and inconsistent patchwork of judicial precedent, which leaves large gaps in the legal landscape insofar as property rights (both as to the graveyards and the bodies contained within them) are concerned.

There are several reasons why the law governing both graveyards and "found bodies" is so poorly developed in the United States. First, the notion that each individual is entitled to be the sole occupant of a burial plot in perpetuity is of recent vintage in the United States and does not exist in most of the rest of the world. Only in comparatively recent times has there been a widespread perception that an individual will be buried in a marked grave that will be cared for in a designated cemetery—which shall be used for no other purpose—in perpetuity. In the seventeenth and eighteenth centuries, the concept of a burial ground was that a limited public space would be used to store the remains of all deceased members of a community, regardless of how congested the space became. Documents from that time mention that bits of bone and teeth were often found in earth excavated for a new grave. But as time went on, toward the end of the eighteenth century, burials in small family plots began to occur in New England. Many tiny cemeteries from that era may be found throughout rural Massachusetts. It was only in the early nineteenth century that the concept of a modern cemetery was adopted, which incorporated well-defined burial plots limited to one body per plot (Deetz 2010, 89–90).

The American notion that graves are individual, permanent, and perpetual stands in stark contrast to expectations in most of Western Europe, where some form of "grave recycling" and/or multiple burials in a single plot is the prevailing model. For example, in Greece, remains are buried in a rental burial site, where they decompose for a period of twenty to fifty years. They are then disinterred, and the bones are reinterred in a communal ossuary. Similar "grave recycling" laws exist in Switzerland, Australia, and Norway, all of which lease graves for periods of twenty to twenty-five years. Singapore, Hong Kong, and Taiwan allow interment for a comparatively short time (usually fifteen years), followed by mandatory exhumation and cremation. Even in England, whose laws and customs form the basis of most American law, the government permits the reuse of graves that have been untended for more than seventy-five years (Horlick 2015, 211–215).

Second, court decisions in both the United Kingdom and the United States recognize that there comes a time when a body has decomposed to the point that it can no longer fairly be considered as anything other than a part of the earth. In part, this results from English common law, which considered the burial of a human body as only a temporary appropriation of space (an "accession to realty"), resulting in a pseudo-easement that was extinguished as the body decomposed (Jackson 1950, 124–134). Thus, as early as 1898, the court in *Carter v. City of Zanesville* held that a statute that prohibited the unlawful possession of a "body" or "corpse" could not be interpreted to "include the remains of persons long buried and decomposed."

Similarly, in *State v. Glass*, the defendant was a land developer who had purchased sixty acres of land. The tract included a small cemetery with four graves. Three of the graves had headstones, and the fourth was marked with a "big rock." The developer obtained a permit from the health department to remove the bodies, hired a licensed undertaker to move them to another cemetery, and paid the costs of moving the associated stones. However, despite these good faith efforts at complying with applicable laws, the developer was charged with the offense of grave robbing and was convicted at trial. But on appeal, the Court of Appeals reversed. The court held that a "grave" is an excavation in the earth containing a dead body. Since the remains in question had been buried for at least 125 years and were thoroughly decomposed, the defendant did not "open a grave to obtain interred valuables or to remove the body," which is the definition of grave robbing:

> A cadaver is not an everlasting thing. After undergoing an underfined [sic] degree of composition, it ceases to be a dead body in the eyes of the law. Disinterment of anything not remotely identifiable as a human corpse, though carried out with no good intent, could not amount to "grave robbing." (*State v. Glass*, 898).

A third reason for the lack of clarity in the law is the fact that rules that apply to other types of property do not readily translate to dealing with human remains. In 1905, in the case of *Louisville & N. R. Co. v. Wilson*, the Georgia Supreme Court was called upon to address the nature and extent of a widow's interest in the unburied body of her deceased husband, whose coffin, body, and shroud had been damaged by the negligence of a railway company in transporting it for burial. Before discussing historical English common law concerning the rights of the decedent's survivors, the court explained why the law concerning human remains must necessarily be different from the rules pertaining to other types of property:

> Death is unique. It is unlike aught else in its certainty and its incidents. A corpse in some respects is the strangest thing on earth. A man who but yesterday breathed and thought and walked among us has passed away. Something has gone. The body is left still and cold, and is all that is visible to mortal eye of the man we knew. Around it cling love and memory. Beyond it may reach hope. It must be laid away. And the law—that rule of action which touches all human things—must touch also this thing of death. It is not surprising that the law relating to this mystery of what death leaves behind cannot be precisely brought within the letter of all the rules regarding corn, lumber and pig iron. And yet the body must be buried or disposed of. If buried, it must be carried to the place of burial. And the law, in its all-sufficiency, must furnish some rule, by legislative enactment or analogy, or based on some sound legal principle, by which to determine between the living questions of the disposition of the dead and rights surrounding their bodies. (*Louisville & N. R. Co. v. Wilson*, 25)

Finally, the recurring conflict between the needs and desires of the living and respect for burial grounds of the dead is of comparatively recent vintage. The earliest decisions involving efforts to repurpose land previously used as cemeteries appeared in the early to mid-nineteenth century. For example, in the 1850 Pennsylvania Supreme Court decision of *Brocket v. Ohio & Pa. R. R. Co.,* the court held that a cemetery had to be relocated so that a railroad could run through the land previously occupied by the cemetery. The court concluded that it could not demand that the railroads instead use a different and more hazardous route that would subject train passengers to considerable danger.

Similarly, in 1837, a New York court in *Brick Presbyterian Church v. Mayor of New York* refused to prevent the sale of a church in Manhattan (including its graveyard) for use as a public street. The court held that it was not right that "a comparatively small portion of the dead will shoulder out the living and their posterity." The court quoted with approval Sir

Walter Scott's opinion in *Gilbert v. Buzzard*, which implied that the right to an undisturbed burial "may be subject to a limitation for the period during which the bodies are intact."

Again, in *Schoonmaker v. Reformed Protestant Dutch Church of Kingston*, the New York court ruled in 1850 that

> the common cemetery is not... the exclusive property of one generation now departed, but it is the common property of the living, and of generations yet unborn, and subject only to the temporary appropriation. (*Schoonmaker v. Reformed Protestant Dutch Church of Kingston*, 271)

As indicated in the introductory portion of this chapter, as cities and populations have grown in size, the needs of the living to repurpose land formerly used as cemeteries has become even more pressing, and this trend is likely to continue. As one commentator put it, "as development of land throughout the United States increases, and society struggles with the need to both bury its dead and make room for the increasing population, courts will probably see more cases of this type" (Karinshak 1997).

In almost every state, English common law forms the basis of state jurisprudence, and property rights are almost exclusively matters of state (rather than federal) law. An understanding of those English common law precedents is therefore essential to an understanding of current state law and the theoretical underpinnings for modern court decisions concerning the dead and the places where the dead are buried.

## English Common Law

The relevant English common law began with the *Haynes' Case* decision in 1614. In that case, an action was brought against an individual named William Haynes, alleging that he "had digged up the several graves of three men and one woman, in the night, and had taken their winding sheets from their bodies" (*Haynes' Case*, 112). The court determined that the sheets were not owned by the decedents but were instead still owned by "him who had property therein, when the dead body was wrapped therewith; for the dead body is not capable of it... a dead body being but a lump of earth hath no capacity."

The rule that a dead person cannot own property means, of course, that a decedent does not "own" the plot they are buried in. At common law, English courts viewed human burials as a *temporary* appropriation of space, sometimes referred to as an "accession to realty," rather than as the ownership interest in the land. Most modern-day American courts agree that title to a burial plot remains with the grantor or his successors and that title to the plot may be transferred to others, subject to an easement granting the decedent the right to occupy the burial space and the corollary right of family members to visit that grave (Shaffer 2003:486–487).

The *Haynes* decision originally stood for the proposition that dead people can't own property, but the court's holding was misreported in two important English legal textbooks that inverted the nouns and omitted the qualifying verb. Consequently, rather than saying that "a corpse cannot own property," the textbooks instead stated that "there can be no property in a corpse." Over time, through repetition of this maxim in numerous court decisions, it became settled law that dead bodies and parts thereof were not "property" that could be owned by the living (Campbell-Tiech 2002, 809). These English court decisions were, however, consistent with earlier Roman law, which also generally held that human remains are not property (Marsh 2015, 183).

The common law principle that the body of a deceased person belongs to no one is known as "*corpus nullius in bonis.*" The common law rule was adopted in the United States and has been a linchpin of subsequent development of American law relating to human bodies. Since the law generally does not recognize any property interest in the body, the constitutional protections that apply to government interference with property interests are inapplicable. And since there is no owner, a great deal of litigation takes place simply to determine who has the right to decide whether, how, and where a body will be buried (Madoff 2010, 17).

One exception to the rule that no one can own the dead body of another developed in the twentieth century when the High Court of Australia rendered its decision in *Doodeward v. Spence*. In that case, Doodeward obtained the mummified corpse of a two-headed child that he sought to exhibit on tour. The police seized it as indecent or obscene, and Doodeward sued for its return. It was argued that since there was no property in the corpse, Doodeward could not possibly have a right to possession and that his action must therefore be dismissed. The court held that Doodeward was entitled to the return of this corpse because it had been subjected to "the lawful exercise of work or skill so...that it has acquired some attributes differentiating it from a mere corpse awaiting burial." Put differently, because skilled work had been applied to the corpse, it became something for which Doodeward could claim at least a right of possession.

The *Doodeward* precedent has been cited and applied by English courts. In *Dobson v. North Tyneside Health Authority*, a woman died of a brain tumor. Her brain was removed and preserved in paraffin during a postmortem examination and was stored at the hospital. The rest of her body was returned to the family for burial. Two years later, as the first step in a contemplated action for alleged negligence in failing to properly diagnose and treat the tumor, the family's attorney requested samples of the tumor. But by that time, the brain and other stored samples of the tumor had been destroyed. The family brought an action against the Health Authority for failure to preserve the brain. The court applied the original common law rule that there was "no property in a corpse," and indicated that the *Doodeward* exception did not apply since the act of preserving the brain was not an application of human skill sufficient to render it "property."

The *Doodeward* exception was explicitly adopted and was outcome determinative in the case of *Regina v. Kelly & Lindsay*. In that case, an artist had been granted permission to sketch anatomical specimens that were kept on display and were used to train surgeons. The artist organized the removal of a number of body parts that were then used as casts for models, some of which were exhibited at a gallery in London. A complaint was registered by a passerby, who incorrectly identified one of the casts as being that of her grandmother. This led the police to investigate the provenance of the works of art, and the artist was arrested.

When the artist was tried for theft, the defense argued that because there was no property in a corpse, the Royal College of Surgeons had no superior right to possession of the body parts, and the indictment should therefore fail. But the Court of Appeals applied the *Doodeward* exception and held that because these body parts had been subjected to the skill of a previous generation of service in both their preparation and preservation, they had therefore become "property" that was capable of being stolen.

One English commentator has noted that the law is not always consistent in the treatment of bodies and body parts. For example, amputated or removed body parts are rarely returned to their owner and are almost never accorded any sort of burial or other dignified form of handling. That commentator felt that the law might be more consistently applied if it protected the rights of an owner of a dead body, rather than protecting some presumed expectation on the part of the decedent:

> The overriding reason why this area of the law has developed in such an extraordinary way lies in the lay (nonmedical) attitude to the body after death. Legislators and courts have assumed for at least two centuries that no matter how little regard the populace pays to the welfare of its members whilst alive, in death the body of the citizen must be accorded a dignity which its erstwhile occupant might well have preferred to enjoy somewhat earlier.
>
> I wonder to what extent this assumption holds true today, if ever it did. Few patients ask their dentist for the return of the extracted tooth. A request by an amputee for custody of his leg might well prompt an investigation of a psychiatric nature. There is no constituency for the belief, echoing St. Augustine, that within the body or in the sum of its parts, lies the human soul or spirit, or more prosaically, the individual self.

◇◇◇◇◇◇◇

It may be that a future Court of Appeal will accept the invitation of Rose L. J. and revisit the whole question of ownership and right of possession when a suitable case comes along. This is of little assistance to those who have to act within the law as it stands, still less to those charged with advising them what the law really means. (Campbell-Tiech 2002:811)

## *The Development of American Law*

Given that everyone dies, one would expect that the law concerning bodies and burials would be well-established and fully developed. But that is not the case. As one leading treatise on American cemetery law puts it, "the common law of cemeteries has not changed significantly in the past six and a half decades—or, for that matter, in the past two centuries." Indeed, one of the most central pronouncements of American cemetery law is not found in a statute or a court decision but is instead the text of an address given by US Supreme Court Justice Joseph Story at the dedication of a cemetery in Boston in 1831 (Marsh 2015, 2–4).

Two important principles underlie modern American burial law. The first of these is the concept of dedication, which refers to setting aside a portion of real property for the burial of the dead, regardless of whether it has been used as such. Further, once a parcel of land has been characterized as a cemetery, either by dedication alone or by use as such, it may not be used for other purposed except to the extent permitted by law. A cemetery may be either a "public" cemetery (meaning one that is used by the general community, occupants of a neighborhood, or members of a church) or a "private" cemetery (used only by one family or a small segment of the community).

The second key principle is the common law right of sepulture. In *National Archives & Records Admin. v. Favish*, the United States Supreme Court has recognized this right as a "well-established cultural tradition acknowledging a family's control over the body and death images of the deceased...." In general, sepulture has been defined as "the right of the next of kin to control and direct the burial of a corpse and arrange for its preservation..." (*Whitney v. Cervantes*, 2014). Before interment, the right of sepulture attaches to the actual bodily remains. After the body has been interred, the right attaches to the grave or tomb, and allows the holder to take steps to protect it, but the remains themselves are not property. Instead, after interment, human remains are considered part of the real estate in which they have been interred.

Interestingly, at common law, the right of sepulture cannot be transferred by gift or will but passes solely via intestate succession (Marsh 2015, 12–13). But at least in Ohio, this rule has largely been abrogated by the passage of Ohio Rev. Code §2108.70(B) in 2006, which grants any adult of sound mind the right to make a written declaration assigning to a representative the right to direct the disposition of the declarant's body after death. In the 2022 decision in *In re Disinterment of Glass*, the court held that the right of "disposition" relates solely to events that occur immediately after death and not to later disinterment (which is governed by two other statutes).

But there is another aspect of the right of sepulture, which is known as the right of access. This right is a perpetual easement that arises by operation of law, and it permits the descendants of the deceased to cross private property to access their ancestor's grave or tomb.

The right of sepulture is also associated with the strong common law presumption that, once interred, human remains should not be disinterred except with the consent of the holder of the right of sepulture and a court order. That being said, it is also important to note that this presumption is far from conclusive, as will be shown below, and as an Ohio appellate court recently noted in the case of *In re Estate of Eisaman*, this presumption—and R.C. 517.24 which is one of the two statutes that govern the disinterment and reinterment of human remains—require only a showing of good cause before a probate court may order disinterment.

Throughout much of English history, human bodies were buried in nothing more than a sheet or some other type of shroud. During the reigns of Edward II (1307–1327) and Edward III (1327–1377), even citizens of distinction were customarily buried in bare earth. Given the lack of any mention of coffins in the burial service of the Church of England, it is believed that when the service was compiled (circa 1546), unconfined interments were common because only the body or corpse alone was mentioned. Likewise, during the reign of Queen Elizabeth I (1558–1603), the common custom was to bury the dead only in winding sheets. Burial in coffins, as a near-universal custom, first began in the 18th century (Wickes 1884, 113).

Other than the speech by Justice Story, a second important exposition of widely recognized common law principles is a document written in the middle of the nineteenth century. The so-called Ruggles Report was written by a referee (a type of inferior magistrate in some state court systems) named Samuel B. Ruggles. A lawsuit had been filed in New York state courts relating to the city's appropriation of a portion of the Brick Presbyterian Church cemetery so that Beekman Street in lower Manhattan could be widened. The portion of the cemetery proposed to be taken included twelve vaults that the church had sold (or in some cases, leased for a 999-year term) to the plaintiffs. The dispute concerned 1) whether it was the church or the purchasers of the vaults that were entitled to the $28,000 paid by the city for the appropriation of the property and 2) whether the church was obligated to pay, at its own expense, the cost of reinterring the human remains of one individual who had been removed from his vault and temporarily placed under the church.

The Ruggles Report laid out a comprehensive exposition of the law that ranged from the history of burials in churchyards to the legal principles associated with repurposing land previously used as a graveyard. More than thirty years after it was written, in the case of *Renihan v. Wright*, the Indiana Supreme Court praised the Ruggles Report, stating that it is a "learned investigation of the law of burial, and it is believed to be the most accurate and elaborate collection and statement of the law, upon that subject, yet published." (*Renihan v. Wright*, 824).

## US Federal Law

In the United States, most laws governing the disposition of bodily remains or the ability to convert a graveyard to some other use preferred by the living exist at the state level. Similarly, virtually all of the laws relevant to the disposition, possession, and trade of human remains, and the disturbance of graves, exist solely at the state level (Marsh 2015, 192). In many cases, state-level statutory controls are sparse. It is possible (and in all but three states, perfectly legal) to buy and sell human remains other than those that are governed by the Native American Graves Protection and Repatriation Act ("NAGPRA"), 25 U.S.C. §§3001-3013 (2006).

NAGPRA serves three primary purposes. First, it extends protections for Native American graves located on federal and tribal lands. Second, it prohibits commercial trafficking in Native American cultural items. Finally, it provides a structure for the repatriation of Native American remains and cultural objects that were in the position or control of either federal agencies or museums as of the effective date of the statute. In order to comply with this mandate, federal agencies and museums were required to inventory their Native American remains and funerary objects, notify all federally recognized tribes about the status of their collections, and engage in consultation with the tribes to establish cultural affiliation (Tsosie 2012, 816–817).

NAGPRA protects the rights of Native Americans to four specific categories of cultural items: human remains, associated and unassociated funerary objects, objects of cultural patrimony, and sacred objects. However, the statute does not require repatriation of items that lack sufficient evidence to establish cultural affiliation with a modern tribe (and are thus "culturally unidentifiable") and items that were affiliated but not claimed by the relevant groups (known as "unclaimed" items) (Tsosie 2012).

NAGPRA was, of course, not relevant to the investigation conducted at Schneider Park, since there was (and still is) no reason to believe that the site harbors any graves of Native Americans. For that reason, a detailed discussion of this difficult and often confusing aspect of federal funerary law is unnecessary. For a reasonably comprehensive treatment of the law on this subject, the interested reader may wish to consult one of the leading treatises that addresses laws pertinent to archaeology and the excavation and curation of relics of every stripe, including human remains (Cunningham 2005, 692–836).

## State Law

As noted above, property and funerary law in America—including the ownership, treatment, and disposition of human remains—is primarily a matter of state law. Federal law, other than the NAGPRA requirements that relate to Native American remains, is largely irrelevant to issues of disinterment. Consequently, disinterment questions are governed exclusively by state law.

Only about seventeen states have laws that forbid the "abuse of a corpse," which makes it a crime to "treat a corpse in a way that [the actor] knows would outrage ordinary family sensibilities." At least one commentator has observed that the failure of the law at both the federal and state level to protect the commercialization of human remains is not surprising, given the neglect of the "law of the dead" by legislatures and other policymakers, legal scholars, and the public (Marsh 2015, 193).

In each state, some court (usually the probate court) has the equitable power and the obligation to exercise jurisdiction over disinterment of the dead. This was recognized by no less an authority than the United States Supreme Court in its 1829 decision in *Beatty, et al. v. Kurtz*, in which it held that:

> [I]n the event of an interference with the sepulchres of the dead], [t]he remedy must be sought, if at all, in the protecting power of a court of chancery; operating by its injunction to preserve the repose of the ashes of the dead, and the religious sensibilities of the living. (*Beatty, et al. v. Kurtz*, 585)

Like most states, Ohio derives its foundational legal principles from the common law of England. As the Ohio Supreme Court once put it in its 1861 decision in *Drake v. Rogers*, "in the absence of legislative enactments and as auxiliary to, and for the enforcement of such enactments...the common law of England has always been received and accepted as the common law of the state." This echoes the statement made in its 1854 decision in *The Cleveland, Columbus and Cincinnati Railroad. Co. v. Keary*, wherein the Ohio Supreme Court said that:

> We profess to administer the common law of England, in so far as its principles are not inconsistent with the genius and spirit of our own institutions, or opposed to the settled habits, customs, and policy of the people of this state... (*The Cleveland, Columbus and Cincinnati Railroad. Co. v. Keary*, 205).

Given Ohio's historical adherence to English common law, it comes as little surprise that in 1893, the court in *Hadsell v. Hadsell* held that "a dead body is not property." (*Hadsell v. Hadsell*, \*\*3). In 1926, in *Hayhurst v. Hayhurst*, the court held that "there can be no property in a dead body and therefore a man cannot by will, dispose of same..." (*Hayhurst v. Hayhurst*, 375).

In fact, Ohio courts have gone so far as to hold that there is not even a quasi-property interest in the body of another. In its 1986 decision in *Carney v. Knollwood Cemetery Assn.*, an Ohio court refused to characterize a surviving relative's rights with respect to the treatment of the corpse of the decedent as a quasi-property right. Three years later, in *Everman v. Davis*, another Ohio appellate court agreed that no quasi-property right in the body of a deceased relative is recognized under Ohio law.

This principle was recently reaffirmed by the Ohio Supreme Court. In *Albrecht v. Treon*, the plaintiffs' son died, and the county coroner performed an autopsy. After the autopsy was completed, the body of the plaintiffs' son was returned to them for burial, except for the brain, which had been retained for further examination. The son's brain was then disposed of by the coroner's office, which prompted the plaintiffs to file a suit for damages for failure to return all of their son's remains to them for burial.

The Ohio Supreme Court was called upon to decide whether the next of kin of a decedent have a protected property right under Ohio law in the decedent's tissues, including those that have been removed and retained for further examination. The Ohio Supreme Court—citing the cases discussed above—held that no such property right exists. The court based its decision on several principles. First, it observed that Ohio courts had traditionally held that there can be no property right in the body of another. Second, the court looked to the statutory definition of an "autopsy" adopted in 2006, which specifies that any "retained tissues… or any other specimens from an autopsy are medical waste…"

In view of these authorities, the Ohio Supreme Court held that the plaintiffs did not have a property right in the body of their son that would support an action for damages against a coroner who failed to return all of their deceased son's tissues to them. Instead, the high court declared that "the interest that Ohio statutes… give next of kin in an autopsied decedent's body is to inter or cremate the body after the autopsy has been performed." (*Albrecht v. Treon*, 358).

This holding was generally consistent with earlier Ohio cases that had recognized a "right of disposition" in the surviving spouse or other next of kin. For example, in *Federman v. Christ Hospital,* the court recognized a "right of disposition" in the surviving next of kin (usually the surviving spouse), which confers upon them the right to "direct the disposition of a deceased person's body, to make and purchase funeral arrangements, and to make arrangements for burial, cremation, or other manner of final disposition of the body." And in *Spanich v. Reichelderfer,* the court recognized that there is a well-established public and legal policy holding that once a person has been buried, the body should not be exhumed except for the most compelling reasons.

However, the next of kin's right to dispose of the body as they see fit—and the decedent's presumptive right to remain undisturbed—are not absolute. In the case of *In re Disinterment of Frobose*, the decedent's wife and son agreed on the place of burial of their decedent. But after the burial, the decedent's wife (who was not the biological mother of the decedent's son) felt that she was not welcome to be buried in the cemetery where other family were buried and sought to have her deceased husband's body disinterred and buried elsewhere. The court noted that applications for disinterment—both by surviving spouses and by others—are governed by Ohio Rev. Code §§517.23 and 517.24. While surviving spouses generally have the right to disinter their decedent and reinter them elsewhere, the same statutes permit any other person to oppose that disinterment decision and litigate the issue in probate court. The court found that when ruling upon a request for an order of disinterment, equitable standards demand that the court consider a variety of factors including 1) the degree of relationship that the party seeking reinterment bears to the decedent; 2) the degree of relationship that the party seeking to prevent reinterment bears to the decedent; 3) the desires of the decedent; 4) the conduct of the person seeking reinterment; 5) the conduct of the person seeking to prevent reinterment; 6) the length of time that has elapsed since the original interment; and 7) the strength of the reasons offered both for and against the proposed reinterment.

The *Frobose* court found that the factors in favor of preventing disinterment outweighed those in favor or permitting it. These included the decedent's continued ties to the local community, the fact that 274 of his family members were buried in that cemetery (including the decedent's parents and grandparents), the close proximity of the cemetery to living relatives, and his wife's initial agreement to burial at the cemetery.

The same factors were employed in the case of *In re Disinterment of Swing*. In that case, the decedent was survived both by the decedent's mother and by the decedent's son. Sometime after his father's death, the decedent's son attended an event at the home of his grandparents, where he saw a box containing his father's remains. When he requested that the remains be given to him, Jean Swing (the decedent's mother) told him that "your dad's going to stay with me, because he's my baby."

Sometime thereafter, Jean Swing died. But rather than giving the ashes of the deceased to his surviving son, Swing's husband, who was also the father of the decedent, asked a funeral worker to place the ashes inside of Jean Swing's casket. This was done, and the casket containing Jean Swing's body and the ashes of her son was buried, albeit in contravention of a cemetery rule that required a permit to bury two people in a single grave.

The decedent's son later learned via a Facebook post that his father's ashes had been buried with his grandmother. The son then brought an action seeking permission to disinter his father's remains and rebury them elsewhere. The probate granted the application. On appeal, the Court of Appeals affirmed. In doing so, it considered the same factors used by the *Frobose* court. In this case, the court held that the equities weighed in favor of disinterment, even though technically the decedent's parents (the grandparents of the plaintiff) had the "right of disposition" under Ohio law. The court held that the right of disposition could be overcome where—as in this case—the equities weighed in favor of allowing the decedent to be disinterred and reinterred elsewhere.

Naturally, this raises the question of what can and should be done where a cemetery has fallen into disuse, especially in those cases where the living want to put that land to some other use. The land use problems that can develop with the passage of time were summarized in the 1893 decision in *Methodist Prot. Church of Cincinnati v. Laws*. In that case, a cemetery had once been far beyond the city's borders, but over time the city expanded to bring the cemetery within its limits. Years earlier, the City of Cincinnati had passed an ordinance prohibiting any further interments in the cemetery, which allowed the land surrounding it to be fully developed. In time, some of the city's wealthiest residents lived immediately adjacent to the cemetery. While the question before the court dealt with whether building a gate at the cemetery entrance would interfere with an easement that allowed visitors to pass through the cemetery, the court elegantly described the effect of changing circumstances on once-remote cemeteries:

This land was purchased for cemetery purposes. It is undoubtedly true that at the time there was no other intention but that it would be used for a cemetery for all time. The parties at that time could not have contemplated that within sixty years it would be in the center of a thickly populated city, surrounded by streets and magnificent residences. It was to be a place of residence for the dead, and not for the living.

The most recent and most comprehensive Ohio decision addressing when human remains that have been laid to rest may be disinterred is the 2021 decision in the case of *In re Disinterment of Glass*. This suit involved an application brought by a son to disinter the remains of his parents and reinter them elsewhere. One of his sisters supported the application, but a second sister opposed it. The *Glass* court thoroughly reviewed the history of disinterment proceedings extending from their origins in England's ecclesiastical courts, through the courts of equity that handled such matters in early American times, up to the present where the power to disinter has been vested in probate courts using the procedures specified in Revised Code sections 517.23 and 517.24. The court recognized that it has long been the "policy of the law to protect the dead from disturbance and maintain the sanctity of the grave." (*In re Disinterment of Glass* (2021), 26). The court added that this policy comes "down to us from ancient times, having its more immediate origin in the ecclesiastical law." (*Id.*).

But in a subsequent decision in the same lawsuit rendered just two months later, the same appellate court explained that under the current statutes, "the probate court may issue a disinterment order if good cause is shown." (*In re Disinterment of Glass* (2022) at ¶37). The court also agreed that where a petition for disinterment is contested, the probate court must apply the "flexible, multifactor-equitable standard" that was used in the *Eisaman*, *Swing*, and *Frobose* decisions cited and discussed above (*Id.*)

As noted above, disinterment of bodies is required before land that has been used as a cemetery may be sold and repurposed. The Ohio legislature has addressed the sale, transfer, and repurposing of cemeteries, but the statutory scheme is something less than a model of clarity. Three different statutes in three unrelated sections of the Ohio Revised Code (Chapter 517, Chapter 1715, and Chapter 1721) all contain provisions relevant to the acquisition, use, and sale of land used for cemeteries. As we have seen, Revised Code Sections 517.23 and 517.24 address whether and when bodies may be disinterred. In general, those two statutes unartfully suggest that the rule in Ohio is that land used for cemeteries may not be repurposed unless the cemetery has been "abandoned" (the meaning of which is addressed below) or unless the continued use of the land for burial purposes will be detrimental to public welfare or health. The statutes also provide that cemeteries may not be sold without disinterring the human remains on the premises and reinterring them elsewhere. They do not, however, address what constitutes human remains, nor do they address the repurposing of land by the owner (such as a church or family) that no longer desires to use or recognize the land as a burial ground.

A related question is whether and when land used as a cemetery may be sold to others. As recently as 2003, the Ohio Attorney General opined that "if the human remains interred in a public cemetery have not been removed from the grounds…[Ohio law] does not authorize a board of township trustees to sell and convey the cemetery to a grantee." (OAG 2003-034, 2-286). But if there is no "sale," then it is possible that cemeteries can be converted to other uses without removal and reinterment of the bodies.

One of the earliest cases suggesting this possibility is *Pansing v. Village of Miamisburg*. In that case, an old cemetery belonging to a church had been used as a public burying ground prior to 1860. But for the next forty years, there were few if any new burials in the cemetery. In the early 1900s, the village council decided to appropriate the land through eminent domain proceedings in order to erect public buildings. The court held that the village had the power to appropriate the cemetery for public purposes since it had not been in "use" for forty years. Interestingly, the court held that the right of sepulture only existed until the remains had been buried for a sufficient length of time to permit thorough decomposition, after which use of the premises for other purposes would be permissible:

> In this case it appearing that interments were made on payment of a fee, no title to the ground being granted to individuals, the only rights acquired by the survivors were to have the bodies of their dead remain long enough for thorough decomposition, and removed to another burying ground, when the property should be used for secular purposes. (*Pansing v. Village of Miamisburg*, 135)

This is a matter of some consequence as the burial of a single person on private property can render the premises as a cemetery. In 2007, the Ohio Attorney General was called upon to decide whether the burial of a single deceased family member on privately owned family property qualifies the property as a "cemetery" (that was required to be registered) or a "family cemetery" (that is exempt from registration). The Attorney General determined that neither the township board of trustees nor a local board of health have the authority to prohibit private burials of family members on private property and ruled that the burial of a single individual on privately owned property constitutes a "family cemetery," albeit one that is exempt from registration requirements that apply to commercial or public burial grounds.

In determining whether a burial ground may be converted to some other use, the courts look to whether the cemetery has been "abandoned."

In *City of Newark v. Crane*, a parcel of land had been conveyed to the city for use as a cemetery. A three-cornered strip of land had been deeded to the town of Newark in 1848. It was still in use as a graveyard by as late as 1871, although it had never been deeded to any person or association for that specific purpose.

In 1868, the town of Newark passed an ordinance prohibiting any further burials in the graveyard. Seven years later, a second ordinance was passed that required notice to be given to survivors to remove the bodies from the premises by November 1 and allowed the cemetery trustees to remove any bodies or tombstones that remained after that date had passed. Nevertheless, four years later, a resolution was passed referring the matter of the removal of the remaining burials to a special committee, which necessarily implies that not all of the bodies had yet been removed.

In the late 1880s, most of the remaining gravestones were taken down and were laid into their respective graves and covered by soil. Ultimately, in 1905, city council passed an ordinance selecting this as the site for a proposed municipal hospital. That action resulted in a quiet title action being brought by the city to resolve the controversy over the ownership and use of the land.

While the case was pending, the city laid cement blocks diagonally across the premises, built a fountain in the center, laid pipes, and strung electric wires, all of which was done for the purpose of converting the land into the Sixth Street Park. The defendants in the quiet title action claimed that this meant that the city was no longer using the land as a burial ground. Since the 1848 deed stated that the conveyance of the land to the city was "for the sole purpose of a burying ground and for no other purpose whatsoever," the descendants of the transferors claimed that the city had abandoned the graveyard and that title to the land should revert to the descendants of the transferors.

The Court of Appeals agreed, holding that because the city had abandoned the land for the purpose of a graveyard (even though some burials remained), it should be required to remove its improvements and reconvey the property back to the descendants of the original owners.

But on further appeal, the Ohio Supreme Court reversed. In a one-paragraph decision, the Ohio Supreme Court held that the mere fact that there had not been active burials for many years and that many (but not all) of the earlier burials had been removed was not a complete abandonment. In holding that the City of Newark still had good title to the land, the Ohio Supreme Court determined that, despite the absence of recent burials and the other improvements that the city had made, there still had not been a complete abandonment of the land's use as a graveyard:

> The court finds that the Court of Appeals erred in its conclusion that the plaintiff had abandoned said premises as a graveyard...

◇◇◇◇◇◇◇

> The court finds that, notwithstanding interments have not been made in said graveyard for many years, and that many bodies previously buried there have been removed therefrom, it appearing that many bodies still remain, there has not been a complete abandonment of said premises to purposes inconsistent with its preservation as a graveyard. The court further finds that the improvements made by the plaintiff are not inconsistent with such use and preservation. Coming now to make the decree which should have been entered herein by the Court of Appeals, it is hereby ordered and decreed that the title of the plaintiff in and to said premises—which shall be preserved and improved as a graveyard, but not otherwise—be and hereby is quieted as against the defendants... (*City of Newark v. Crane*, 538).

In an opinion that was rendered about forty years after *City of Newark v. Crane* was decided, the Ohio Attorney General found the question of when a cemetery may fairly be said to be "abandoned" to be much more problematic. In OAG Opinion 1953-2978, the Perry Township trustees asked the Ohio Attorney General for his opinion on what constitutes "abandonment" of a cemetery. The issue arose because under Section 3465 of the Ohio General Code (now codified at Rev. Code 517.21), the township trustees may order that the abandoned cemetery be discontinued, and that all remains buried within it be removed and reinterred elsewhere, along with re-erection of the accompanying monuments.

The Ohio Attorney General began by noting that this form of "abandonment" was more in the nature of an abandonment of a duty (such as the obligation to support one's spouse or child) than it was of an "abandonment" of a property right. In the Attorney General's words, "there is no element of loss of a right; rather, there is implied an escape from something in the nature of an obligation." That being the case, the Attorney General ruled that "an abandoned cemetery is one in which those responsible for the burial of a deceased person or those standing in such relation that they might be expected to take care of the final resting place, either deliberately or by pure indifference or neglect or for some other reason fail to render any such service."

The Ohio Attorney General cited and discussed the Supreme Court's decision in *City of Newark v. Crane*, which found that "it appearing that many bodies still remain, there has not been a complete abandonment" of the premises as a graveyard. Still, the Attorney General ultimately found that abandonment could occur in either of two ways. First, a cemetery will be considered abandoned when most or all of the bodies had been removed. Second, a cemetery will be deemed to be abandoned where no burials have been made within it for a long period of time, where the cemetery has been so neglected as to lose its identity as such, and when it is no longer known or recognized or respected by the public as a cemetery. This raises the question of whether Schneider Park might be considered to be "abandoned" as that term is used in R.C. 517.21. There is, of course, no evidence or reason to believe that most or all of the bodies have been removed, so the first of the two possible bases for finding an "abandonment" has not been satisfied.

The second basis has three separate elements, all of which must be met before a court may find that an "abandonment" has occurred. As to the first element, it is certainly true that no burials have been made within the perimeter of Schneider Park for a long time.

But the second and third elements are doubtful. The second element requires that the cemetery "has been so neglected" as to lose its identity as a cemetery. Schneider Park has not been "neglected"; it is routinely and carefully maintained, albeit as a public park rather than a cemetery in the traditional sense. But as the City of Newark case cited and discussed above teaches, the Ohio Supreme Court has held that the improvements made by a municipality to allow the land to be used for park purposes by the public are not inconsistent with its use as a burial site as well.

The third element is also in doubt. It would require that the public no longer recognize or respect the land as a cemetery. But the public has been informed of the burials on many occasions in many ways in recent years. The rectangular bare patches on the earth that mark the locations of many of the burials are still plainly in evidence. As noted in the introduction, many neighborhood residents are aware of the character of prior uses of the land, and tell ghost stories about the place, or recall oral traditions about real or imagined efforts by the Civilian Conservation Corps to move some of the bodies. Articles informing the public about the park's history have appeared in the *Akron Beacon Journal* and in other news outlets on a number of occasions, discussed in chapter 2, and the results of the 2017 geophysical survey were disclosed to a packed house in a branch of the Akron-Summit County Public Library. Even the publication of this book is powerful evidence that Schneider Park still is recognized as the place of burial of many of the city's residents from more than a century ago. In a sense, we never lost the information that people were buried here.

Against this backdrop, there is one (and only one) Ohio decision that directly addresses whether and when a landowner (without having sold the property to another) may discontinue its use as a graveyard and instead use it for some other purpose. In *Schaeffer v. Unknown Heirs,* the First United Presbyterian Church of East Cleveland owned property that has been used as a cemetery. The church filed a suit seeking an order that would permit it to vacate a portion of the cemetery for the purpose of building a Sunday school building on the land, without removing the bodies interred in that area. The construction of the building was to be done without need for excavating the area, since no below-ground cellar or foundation would be erected.

The court began by recognizing that the Ohio legislature has determined that the sale of a cemetery without removal and reinterment of the bodies is against public policy. However, the Ohio statutes did not apply to the situation before the court because there had been no sale of the property and no commercial use of it was being proposed.

The court acknowledged that the issue was one of first impression not just in the State of Ohio, but even across the entire United States. In the eyes of the court, the issue was whether the construction of a Sunday school building over the graves "would constitute a desecration of the dead that are interred there." (*Schaeffer v. Unknown Heirs*, 777). In answering that question, the court carefully considered all of the evidence. It noted that the Sunday school building was to occupy an area of ground approximately 50 feet by 130 feet. Within that area were the remains of six graves, only two of which had legible inscriptions. While there were other grave plots in the area, they were not marked, and the names of the decedents were not known. The last burial had taken place in the year 1900, and most of the other burials had been made before 1850. The cemetery had not been visited by friends or relatives for many years, and the graves were not cared for by anyone except the church.

The church's intention had been widely publicized, and no objection had been raised within the church or in the community. The church planned to remove the headstones from the area and build a memorial to the dead on the northernmost portion of the church property. The proposed inscription was to read:

> There lie buried in this church-yard, early settlers of the city, friends of the church, veterans of our county's wars and many others named and unnamed. This memorial is erected that coming generations may hold the memory of their deeds in lasting honor. (*Schaeffer v. Unknown Heirs*, 778)

In view of all of these considerations, the court concluded that the proposed use of the property would not "constitute desecration of the dead." (778) The court therefore granted the church permission to build a Sunday school addition without disinterring and reinterring the bodies buried within that portion of the property.

No further guidance on these issues have come from the Ohio courts or legislature, although there have been some unsuccessful efforts to pass legislation that would have addressed these issues. In September 2013, for example, the Ohio General Assembly passed a resolution to create the Ohio Cemetery Law Task Force, which was authorized and directed to review all laws related to cemeteries, and to permit stakeholders to present their view on the current state of cemeteries in Ohio.

The term "stakeholder" is frequently used in discussions about cemeteries and funerary practices, but it is rarely if ever explicitly defined. For example, the 2021 SAA Statement Concerning the Treatment of Human Remains alludes to "descendant communities, affiliated groups, and other stakeholders whose interests have not been previously recognized or acknowledged." It furnishes no basis for identifying those unrecognized or unacknowledged stakeholders, or for discerning how much weight their views should carry.

Insofar as the Ohio Cemetery Law Task Force goes, the General Assembly directed that its eleven members include representatives of various state and local governmental authorities and individuals who could represent the interests of cemetery owners, genealogists, archaeologists, Native American groups, historians, and real estate professionals. Forty "stakeholders" were invited to submit input, although no indication is given as to how these forty were selected. Sixteen "stakeholders" presented oral and/or written submissions on behalf of themselves or groups that they purported to represent. Submissions were received from individuals and organizations who represent the interests of archaeologists, historians, veterans, religious groups, cemetery owners, townships, Native American groups, the Association of Gravestone Studies, and the Bureau of Workers Compensation.

Whenever previously unknown deposits of human remains are found or when relocation of burials is being contemplated, there are of course other groups who have interests as well. The medical and scientific communities may be interested in the diseases or genetics of long-dead individuals. Archaeologists and anthropologists have a legitimate interest in being permitted to photograph and study (at least for some period of time) grave goods and cultural artifacts that may accompany the burial. The owners of the land upon which the remains were discovered certainly have interests to be considered. Law enforcement may need to be consulted. Persons related by blood, marriage, cultural, or religious affiliation may need to be contacted and their voices heard. And government officials who have proposed repurposing the land, as well as individual members of the community of the living who might be expected to utilize the land for other purposes, should have their interests kept in mind.

The final report and recommendations of the Ohio Cemetery Law Task Force was issued on September 29, 2014. In the Executive Summary, the Task Force reports that "one tenet became clear and was a driving force in the meetings. All burial sites and human remains, regardless of historic period or culture, deserve the same level of protection and respect." (Task Force Report & Recommendation, 3).

That statement appears to be derived from a Florida statute that governs unmarked human burials. Under Fla. Stat. Ann. §872.05(1), the Florida legislature has decreed that: "all human burials and human skeletal remains be accorded equal treatment and respect based upon common human dignity without reference to ethnic origin, cultural background, or religious affiliation." Several other states have adopted similar "unmarked human burial statutes," including Delaware, Louisiana, Massachusetts, Missouri, Nebraska, and North Carolina (Olexa 2006:65–66).

However, despite its agreement in principle that human remains are worthy of protection and respect, the Task Force conceded that it was unable to arrive at specific recommendations because the issues were so broad, and opinions were so varied:

> The time constraints faced by the Task Force and the natural tension between private property rights and interests in preserving all burial sites prevented a more thorough analysis that might have resulted in more specific recommendations. (Task Force Report & Recommendation, 24)

The difficulty in achieving consensus on these issues is further illustrated by the inability of Ohio legislature, working in conjunction with stakeholder constituent groups, to enact legislation similar to the NAGPRA scheme that exists at the federal level. In 1989 and 1990, companion bills (styled as H.B. 720 and S.B. 244) were introduced into the Ohio House and Senate during the 118th General Assembly. Under that proposed legislation, if human remains were found during an excavation, the county coroner would be notified. If the decedent's closest living relative could be identified, then that individual would determine the disposition of the remains. But if the next of kin could not be determined, the remains would be turned over to a newly created State Administrator of Human Remains from Antiquity. If the State Administrator determined that the remains were those of a member of "recognized contemporary ethnic group," then consultation with a representative of that group would have been required before disposing of the remains. But if no ethnic affiliation could be determined with reasonable certainty, then the remains would be "curated" and made accessible for "legitimate scientific purposes."

These two bills met with opposition from several stakeholder groups, all of whom felt that their interests were not appropriately address or protected. Because of the controversy created by this contemplated statutory scheme, the proposed bills were scuttled (Evans 1993, 731–733) and the law was never adopted.

## *Conclusions*

This chapter opened by posing a series of ethical and legal questions. Some may find it disconcerting that neither the law nor recognized codifications of ethical standards provide bright line answers to those questions.

The law is reasonably clear that no one "owns" human bodies, although one or more surviving relatives of the decedent may have a right of sepulture or a right of disposition that would authorize them to direct how and where their decedent's remains will be laid to rest. But for individuals who died centuries or millennia ago, identifying all of their now-living descendants or collateral relatives is virtually impossible. Further, even if all of the surviving family members could be identified, the law furnishes no clear answer on how conflicting preferences among those survivors would be reconciled.

◇◇◇◇◇◇◇◇

Similar uncertainties abound with respect to converting land previously used as a place of burial to other purposes. Must the bodies be relocated before the land is repurposed? Under what circumstances should the bodies be disinterred and reinterred (or otherwise disposed of) before converting the land to other purposes, and when (if ever) is it appropriate to use the land while bodies remain buried beneath the surface? Again, there is no definitive answer to these questions, and they are typically resolved by the courts on a case-by-case basis. These are matters upon which reasonable minds can (and often do) disagree.

The absence of black-and-white answers to these recurring and important issues may be frustrating to some. But there is a growing sense in many quarters that issues such as these are often best resolved through a process of consultation and negotiation with all affected stakeholders rather than by creating, recognizing, or imposing legal, ethical, or moral absolutes. This so-called "multiculturalism without illusions" accepts the undeniable fact that value conflicts are inevitable when societies include groups with different mores, norms, and lifeways.

Once the law recognizes absolute "rights" in any complex and diverse society, it becomes impossible to satisfy multiple conflicting notions of what any group's "rights" are or should be. Multiculturalism without illusions recognizes that "rights talk" which posits that some groups have rights that are final, absolute, and undeniable under any and all present or future conditions and circumstances silences debate, negates the possibility of negotiated solutions, and leads to heated political discourse that undermines social peace (Brown 2003, 230–231).

Modern political philosophers like John Gray hold that the search for consensus values in pluralist democracies is unrealistic. Instead, they suggest that large, complex democracies with multiple groups holding value sets that are at odds with one another can sustain themselves only through compromise and a constant and never-ending quest for a *modus vivendi*. Under such a "value pluralism" society, apart from a small set of core values, negotiated solutions are preferred and are the norm because they are "usually perceived to be more legitimate than legal procedures which end in the promulgation of unconditional rights" (Gray 2000, 7, 117).

One of the principal advantages of political solutions is the fact that they are never final; the solution may change over time to reflect changing sentiments and shifting local realities. Negotiations—as distinguished from the creation of absolute "rights"—provide opportunity for the development of unique and culturally appropriate solutions that may vary from place to place and from time to time (Brown 2003, 233). After all, time marches on, and the law marches with it (Zander 2004, 204; Tucker 1999, 1). Those of us living in the twenty-first century may imagine that our generation's ethics and morals are the pinnacle of civilized society and right thinking and are vastly superior to those of our forefathers in the age of exploration. But our descendants several centuries hence may in turn consider our views to be singularly unenlightened. Negotiated solutions to problems of cultural control more readily allow for flexibility and change over the long run.

The conversion of Schneider Park from a cemetery to a public park is an example of a change in use that has been achieved by consensus rather than by the conferring or recognition of absolute rights. The modern-day use of the former Summit County Infirmary cemetery (which, so far as is known, still has bodies beneath the surface) as a public park is indistinguishable from the conversion of the New Haven Green from burial grounds to public park that opened this chapter. As the City of Akron grew, its borders expanded outward and eventually encompassed the Infirmary property, which had once been considered to be very remote from the city. In view of the age of the Infirmary and the changing character of the land that surrounded that property, Summit County residents voted in 1915 to sell the Infirmary property and build a new Summit County Home in Monroe Falls. Infirmary residents were moved to the new facility in May 1919 (Price 2009). In the meantime, Philip Schneider—in his capacity as the President and a director of Central Associated Realty Company—submitted a bid of $301,879 to acquire the property and to develop it into the "Sunset View Subdivision." Advertisements for these lots were featured in the May 15, 1918, edition of the *Akron Beacon Journal*.

The Summit County records show that Philip Schneider personally took title to all of Lot No. 11 in the A block of Sunset View Subdivision on December 17, 1919. The warranty deed that he received contained a number of deed restrictions that limited the types of structures that could be placed on the land. But that 1919 deed contained no significant limitations on the use of that part of the land that had been devoted to use as a burial ground.

When Schneider died in 1935, the land that is now known as Schneider Park was deeded (through the vehicle of the Central Associated Realty Company) to the City of Akron. The 1939 deed to the City of Akron contains a metes and bounds description of that part of former Lot No. 11 which is now the park, but contains a rather odd deed restriction that provided as follows:

> Said premises herein conveyed to the City of Akron, is made for and upon the following consideration, conditions and reservations:
>
> That the portion of said premises not necessary to be used for street purposes, as set out in the blue print made by the City of Akron March 1934, shall be used exclusively by the City of Akron for a public park, excluding the right to use the same for hard baseball games.
>
> The deed further explicitly required that "the name of said Park shall be the "PHILIP H. SCHNEIDER PARK."

There is no record of the reason for the prohibition against using the land for "hard baseball games," nor is there any contemporaneous explanation of why other types of games, activities, and sporting events were apparently to be permitted. Whether this restriction was intended to show respect for the dead that were buried on the premises, or whether it was intended only to protect passersby and vehicles from injury and damage inflicted by flying baseballs, is purely conjectural.

But as of this writing, no signs or markers have been placed on the park premises to memorialize the dead, or to recognize the role that these people and this land played in the formative years of Akron history. While the use of this property as a city park is well established by 80 years of precedent and is generally accepted in the community, one might fairly ask whether there is at the very least in ethical or moral obligation to publicly recognize Schneider Park for what it is—the final resting place of many of the least fortunate of Akron's earliest residents.

# Chapter 4
# Science in the Public Eye
## Archaeology at Schneider Park

*Timothy Matney, Maeve Marino, and Morgan Revels*

As any student enrolled in an introductory archaeology course soon discovers, archaeology is not really about swashbuckling adventurers seeking golden statues in the remote jungles of South America, despite the romantic portrayals long cherished by Hollywood and the popular media. In fact, most of archaeology does not involve being in the field at all. Long hours analyzing finds in the laboratory, tabulating results, writing catalogs, filing grant reports, and writing technical publications consume most of an archaeologist's time. When archaeologists do go into the field, it is often to decidedly mundane venues. Many surveys and excavations take place in urban centers and suburban parks, under parking lots, and in agricultural fields. In this chapter, we move from the historical context that created Schneider Park and Akron's economic boom at the start of the 1900s, and one outcome, a housing development—to the story of what remains, literally, under the park's grass.

We tell the story of an archaeological survey conducted in the mundane venue of a city park in 2017. Two things make this story interesting. First, our data demonstrate that Schneider Park is indeed a cemetery: we discovered over three hundred "missing" graves there. The second interesting part was the engagement between our university team (university students and their professor) and the community. We had not anticipated the level of excitement and interaction our project would draw from neighborhood homeowners, dog walkers, joggers, and others who came across our team at work. They asked questions that challenged the students to become good communicators regarding their research. We also learned from these community members. They became another source of data that our archaeological equipment would not have detected. So, in addition to being a study of the bodies in Schneider Park, this chapter illustrates how public archaeology—in the form of visibility in our mundane, grassy field, transparency in our information sharing, and engagement with community members—helps change the way we as humans remember or respond to the tendency to forget people who were marginalized in life.

The stream of visitors was fairly constant and in recognition of these intrusions into our workday, we have chosen to intersperse our observations and discussions about public archaeology and our thoughts on how archaeology should be conducted "in the public eye" into the normal narrative of a scientific report. These interjections break the flow in a way that some readers will find jarring, but this is deliberate and desirable. One of the obligations of archaeology is to let the public know why this work is important, even if it means breaking our concentration and workflow to answer questions.

When dealing with human graves and remains, archaeologists work under three important mandates. First, permission must be obtained to dig at cemeteries and to study the bodies; second, remains may not be commodified, as discussed in chapters 2 and 3; and finally, respectful treatment of the remains during and after study is required.

### *What is Public Archaeology?*

Public archaeology is a sub-discipline of archaeology dealing specifically with how archaeological information is interpreted and relayed to the nonacademic, nonprofessional public interested in archaeology. It is a type of archaeological outreach that has become increasingly popular in recent decades. Those scholars working in public archaeology study what happens once information is disseminated: how it is received and understood by the wider public. They also study social reactions to archaeological work, which influences how future work is handled, interpreted, and discussed.

In the United States, public archaeology is also often equated with cultural resource management (CRM). CRM emerged in the 1960s as federal and state governments enacted mandates to preserve prehistoric and historic sites and materials in response to the destruction of cultural resources, such as archaeological sites, through rapid expansion of the nation's infrastructure. Public archaeology also encompasses the idea of "educational archaeology" which involves shaping archaeological information in ways that are easily understood and making sure this information is located in highly relevant places so the public can encounter it. It also involves an attempt to "empower the public to participate in the critical evaluations of historical and archaeological interpretations that are presented to them and to better understand how and why the past is relevant to the present" (Jameson 2004:22). Public archaeology and CRM function within the sphere of public discourse and are often seen as distinct from purely "academic" archaeology which is focused more narrowly on research-based fieldwork and peer-reviewed publication. As shall be obvious from this chapter, we prefer to blur this somewhat artificial distinction between public and academic archaeologies.

The term "public archaeology" has been around since the early 1970s (McGimsey 1972; Smith and Ehrenhard 1991), and in recent decades it has become established as a formal sub-discipline within archaeology. This is seen, for example, in the creation in 2000 of an international, peer-reviewed quarterly journal, *Public Archaeology*, dedicated specifically to the field. Likewise, university programs specializing in some aspect of public archaeology (e.g., graduate programs at California State University in Northridge, the University of New Mexico, the University of Georgia, and the University of South Florida) are producing a generation of archaeologists for whom concern for engaging with the public, and especially under-represented groups and nontraditional communities, both past and present, is important. As Shackel noted: "One cause for the development of a new community-based archaeology program is that a growing number of professionals now accept the fact that archaeology is more than implementing scientific methods to collect and interpret data." (Shackel 2004:2) In 2008, the Society for Historical Archaeology dedicated their national conference to the theme "The Public Benefits of Historical Archaeology." In short, there now exists a rich and developed literature focused specifically on the complex interplay between archaeologists and other stakeholders who share an interest in understanding "what happened in history."

The University of Akron has a public archaeology program housed within the Department of Anthropology. Since the 1990s, this informal program has been called the Community Archaeology Program, and through it we have run scores of field schools and other hands-on field, laboratory, and public presentation projects. This program is one type of public archaeology; we use the term *community* in the title to reflect that our focus has been almost entirely on the City of Akron and the immediate vicinity of Summit County. From the inception, we have worked primarily with community partners, especially the Summit Metro Parks, the National Park Service, and a host of local landowners, to explore the archaeology and the history of the region while also providing our students with an opportunity to work actively with the community and strengthen ties between UA and the City of Akron. This is part of a trend within public archaeology referred to as "community-engaged archaeology."

There is also a growing movement to include marginalized communities in archaeological fieldwork and interpretation of buried ancestors, from enslaved Africans in the Caribbean to the child burials at Canadian Indian Residential Schools (e.g., Atalay 2012; Ferguson et al. 2015; Flewellen at al. 2022; Wadsworth et al. 2021). Community-engaged archaeology goes beyond educating the public about archaeology: practitioners seek to involve descendant communities and stakeholders at every step of an archaeological project and give them decision-making power over sites and knowledge production (Atalay 2012). In the case of Schneider Park's cemetery, there are no known descendants. The burials at the Infirmary occurred in large part precisely because there was nobody to care for the inmates and nobody to claim them after death. The information recorded on the burial records is perfunctory and partial. Our public archaeology project thus focused on making connections with the residents living in Akron today who, while not direct lineal ancestors of the inmates buried in the park, need to be informed of what remains and to understand and interpret in their own way the implication of these graves and their history, allowing them to make decisions on how the site should be handled once our archaeological investigations concluded.

## *A Summer Field School in Suburban Akron, Ohio*

In the summer of 2017, a dozen undergraduate and graduate students at the University of Akron enrolled in a five-week intensive summer course to learn archaeological geophysical survey techniques. This class, which Matney has taught for nearly two decades, typically involves lectures, laboratory demonstrations, exercises, and fieldwork at a venue within driving distance of the university. In the past, field sites for the class had varied from Native American encampments in the Cuyahoga River valley to the grounds of historic cemeteries and structures in the area. The goal of the class is to learn survey technology, which, as briefly explained below, is adaptable to many different types of prehistoric and historic archaeological sites. For the 2017 class, the selected field site was an open field that historical documents suggested had been a cemetery at Schneider Park in West Akron.

Typically, the fieldwork component of the course is done in a quiet, often isolated place where prior disturbance of anything lying below the surface is minimal. Unlike these usual venues for the class, Schneider Park is within Akron city limits, bounded by busy Mull Avenue on one side and residential streets of well-kept homes on the others. The park itself is ideal for teaching geophysical survey. The ground is flat, with few bushes and shrubs, and is mowed regularly. There is some street parking, and the wide, flat vistas of the park allowed the students ample room to work in teams without constantly running into one another. Importantly, Schneider Park also has a clear target of archaeological interest because of the unmarked graves from the Summit County Infirmary.

Although the course was designed to address the issue of communicating about archaeological work with the public, we were surprised by the level of interest we encountered. For the neighbors, our presence amid survey tapes, ropes, odd equipment, and pairs of students walking slowly in straight lines for hours on end was a curiosity, to say the least. Over the course of the five weeks, approximately eighty visitors came to the Schneider Park survey site, including those curious neighbors, newspaper and television journalists, and even a young filmmaker who asked permission to record our work and interview us for a documentary film he planned to submit to a local arts festival. We even became, so we are told, the subject of a Sunday sermon at one of the local churches.

The university students signed up to learn the science and skills involved in geophysical measurement of various properties of the earth's shallow subsurface. Learning and using these were key to achieving success in the class. However, they found they also needed to master the skill of explaining basic principles of geophysics and their specific activities clearly to the people who visited our work. While not a common part of most university coursework, it is an anticipated and important part of public archaeology or community archaeology classes. Although built into the syllabus for this field class, the students still found the intensity of the engagement challenging but doing science in public quickly became routine for them, and some found they both liked and excelled at it.

The goal of this chapter is twofold. First, we present the straightforward scientific results of our survey work at Schneider Park. The archaeological project turned out to be quite productive, and the class was able to locate and map several hundred possible graves in the northwestern part of Schneider Park. To be clear, no excavation took place, we do not know if there are still bodies present in the graves, although there is no record of more than a few bodies being moved to the Munroe Falls infirmary cemetery, so most of the graves will still have skeletal remains in them. Before turning further to the results, we will briefly discuss the technology used to collect and process the geophysical data, describe the resulting maps, and provide an interpretation of what our evidence suggests is immediately below the park's surface. The second part of the chapter's goal is to interrupt this scientific narrative, much as our own fieldwork was interrupted by an understandably inquisitive public, by examining three ways in which our interactions with the community demonstrated to us how complex, political, and messy science can be when queried and confronted with different perspectives and concerns. First, we examine the range of preconceptions, biases, and differing perspectives brought to the project by members of the public. Second, we discuss what it means to be an "authority" or "expert" in the eyes of different parties. Third, we explore the role of media in describing and interpreting our work as they share it with the public. One of the more valuable lessons this class provided was that knowledge is not a concrete thing that scientists produce and simply place in the public sphere. Knowledge production happens in contexts—in this case, a very local setting with a great deal of interaction, consideration, and reconsideration. This archaeological project demonstrated that local knowledge is the negotiated product of scientific data collection and analysis interacting with social, political, and ethical issues in a public forum.

## Inception of the Schneider Park Survey

In 2009, Behrman showed Matney an *Akron Beacon Journal* article entitled "Local History: Poor Lost Souls of Akron" by Mark Price (2009) that she planned to use in a unit on eugenics as part of her *Human Diversity* class. For Matney it was an interesting piece of local lore, but it didn't connect with his research at the time and was quickly filed away. He was reminded again of the cemetery in the spring of 2016, by Eric Olson, a former UA undergraduate and, at the time, an archaeology graduate student at Ball State University. In consultation with Behrman, Olson, Shanon Donnelly (UA Department of Geosciences), and Jerrad Lancaster (UA Department of Anthropology), Matney decided to explore the idea of using the cemetery at Schneider Park as a location for the summer geophysical field class. A quick reconnaissance was made using a drone to create aerial images of the site, followed by two days of testing using an electrical resistance meter in the summer of 2016. The resistance survey, although confounded by very dry soil conditions at the time, still suggested that this would make an excellent location for a field class, and Olson requested— and received—permission from the City of Akron Planning Department to use the park for the 2017 UA summer field class. Schneider Park is a fifteen-acre grass-covered public park. The criteria that made it a good site for geophysical survey included: a small number of large trees, sparsely scattered, mostly on the edges, with only a few mature trees on the park's interior. In the northwest portion of the park is a disturbed area of grass, with clear rectangular patches of thick vegetation and soil depressions.

Figure 4-1 is a drone photograph of the northwestern portion of Schneider Park in the fall of 2016. The linear arrangement of rectangular features is clearly visible and represent the location of graves, most of which were also visible on the ground during the 2017 field class. The rectangular patches are roughly 2.00m (6' 6") by 0.70m (2' 4"). One of the most striking features of these rectangular features is their long, evenly spaced, linear arrangement. Initially, Matney and Olson interpreted these visible depressions as the locations of graves for inmates from the Summit

*Science in the Public Eye*

Fig. 4-1. Drone photograph showing the NW portion of Schneider Park (Photo: Jerrad Lancaster)

County Infirmary, given the size of the features (about what one would expect of a human grave) and their spacing. Previous investigations (Price 2009; Whitman et al. 2008) referenced a cemetery of the Summit County Infirmary in Schneider Park without mentioning any specific grave count or cemetery boundaries, so this seemed to be a logical initial interpretation or hypothesis. For the history of the Infirmary and a detailed historical discussion of the property starting in the mid-1800s, see chapter 3.

## Field Methods and Techniques

The aerial maps from our drone work showed the location of numerous possible graves. These images mirrored other remote sensing images, including Google Earth satellite images and historic aerial photographs, all of which show slightly irregular rows of rectangular surface features near the northwestern edge of the park. Figure 4-2 is a Google Earth image showing the northwestern portion of Schneider Park. This satellite image shows the locations of the graves similar to those in the drone image, although the resolution is not as good as that of the drone.

Fig. 4-2. Satellite image showing the northwestern portion of Schneider Park (Photo: GoogleEarth)

The fieldwork conducted by the students began with a visual surface survey of the northern area of Schneider Park to determine the visible edge of the grave distribution. Possible graves at the time of the surface survey in late June 2017 were clearly visible as there was differential growth of grass and other plants immediately above the rectangular features. Archaeologists frequently interpret differential plant growth in terms of shallow subsurface features. Old pits such as graves, even centuries after they are filled in and depending on the local context, can hold moisture better than the surrounding earth and will support more verdant plant growth. Plant growth is facilitated by breaking up the soil, allowing air and nutrients to reach deeper into the soil. On the other hand, stone wall foundations or concrete features buried immediately below shallow soils retard plant growth and can, likewise, create differential growth patterns visible on the surface. At Schneider Park, the greener grass plots likely signify a place where the soil had been disturbed by past activities such as digging a grave. From the aerial photograph, we can also observe very large circular features, probably tree stumps that have rotted in place, as well as long linear features caused by the ditch of a buried sewer line. As a working hypothesis, we chose to call these rectangular features "graves" during the fieldwork because of the strong circumstantial evidence presented earlier in this volume. Had we been working in an unknown context, we would have adopted a more neutral term, such as "feature."

We were able to trace a total of 114 separate graves based solely on visible surface features. The northern side of the site has what appears to be a group of six rows of graves; each row contains between five and eighteen graves evenly spaced about 1.10m (3' 7") apart. To the southwest of these, there is a group of at least four, and possibly five, rows of graves numbering between three and thirteen graves per row. A final grouping of graves lies in the southeastern part of the survey area. There appeared to be at least five graves somewhat spread out in a long row. All the rows of graves at Schneider Park are oriented a few degrees west of magnetic north. Not all the graves were equally distinct from the surface, especially those at the ends of the rows. Once all of the visible grave edges were determined, the class set about creating a map in preparation for the geophysical survey to find graves that were not visible from the surface. The geophysical survey involved setting out an overall site grid extending at least 10m beyond the limit of the last of visible graves. We hoped this additional buffer around the features that could be seen on the surface would allow the team to define the edges of the cemetery more accurately.

First, a few very basic definitions are required. An electronic total station is a type of modern surveying equipment employing a laser and reflecting prism system to measure and record the location of finds, features, and other items of archaeological interest quickly and accurately. Advanced students learn to use the electronic total station during the UA field school. Magnetic field gradiometry is a geophysical survey technique that measures fluctuations in the Earth's magnetic field caused by magnetic materials and features at or below the ground surface. A second geophysical technique, electrical resistance survey, introduces a subsurface electrical field between two probes and measures the differential resistance of the soil to the passage of an electrical current due to buried materials and features. Finally, a transect is a line along which a field survey is conducted. Typically, in archaeology, a survey area of interest is, in effect, divided into long, parallel strips with space in between each transect, and data are gathered at points along the transects. This represents an effective sampling over large areas.

◇◇◇◇◇◇◇◇

The overall extent of the survey area demarcated for the class project was 140m running north to south and 80m running east to west with the alignment following magnetic north. The total area we hoped to survey was, thus, 11200m² (1.12 hectares, or 2.77 acres). Using an electronic total station, the students surveyed and plotted the location of the corners of each of the visible graves relative to the site grid which established a base map of features onto which additional datasets would be overlain. The edges of the streets, trees within the survey area, and a few fixed points such as benches and fire hydrants were also mapped for reference. Likewise, topographical data were collected so that the overall site plan of Schneider Park includes the contours of the park.

Finally, the entire survey area was subdivided into 20m x 20m meter grids for magnetic field gradiometry survey and 10m x 10m grids for electrical resistance survey. Thus, the survey area comprised 28 magnetic gradiometry grids and 112 overlapping electrical resistance grids. A grid system is used in archaeology to keep data in order according to its three-dimensional location. Each grid square is numbered by reference to the southwestern corner of the overall site grid; this reference point is called the site datum. In our case, we designated the site datum as N100E100. The "N" and "E" refer to a northing and easting, while the following number is a measurement in meters. So, N120E160 is the point 20m north and 60m east of the site datum. This system allowed the team to place the data in their correct spatial locations and to overlay different data sets easily.

One of the difficulties we encountered with our spatial data was that while the surface mapping and the two geophysical techniques all used the same base grid for measuring, the aerial images were made prior to the imposition of our site grid. Furthermore, the drone could only image a portion of the survey area at one time; subsequently, we needed to tile together many separate images to produce an overall site view. Because the drone did not remain exactly level with respect to the ground surface as it was flown across the large park, the images themselves were somewhat skewed, an effect that was intensified when they were subsequently stitched together into a single view of the park. This distortion required us to break the aerial image into three sections (roughly the northern, southwestern, and southeastern areas) during the analysis phase when we aligned the aerial imagery with the maps generated from on-the-ground measurements. Despite some minor spatial errors, the correlation between the drone images and the surface survey of visible features was quite strong.

## *Differing Perspectives*

The world is full of preconceptions and viewpoints that make up an individual's sense of how things work and how stories come together to form a roughly integrated meaning or history. The project that took place at Schneider Park generated its own set of stories and opinions. As the undergraduate and graduate students learned geophysical techniques in archaeology, they also became engaged with public relations and shared meaning-making.

Just as the professor held the position of authority or expert for the students, the team found that, in general, they were placed that position by the people who came to ask questions at the site. Some people knew a little about the history or shared stories about their experiences in the park. Nobody came forward claiming to be a descendant of someone who had been an inmate at the Infirmary. This is not surprising; it will likely be difficult to find living relatives of the inmates, especially those who were buried at the facility because they did not have kin caring for them. For the most part, there was excitement and curiosity about the work and the history that inspired it. However, that was not always the case, which became especially clear during the public presentation of our findings at the close of the class.

The final project for our class was to present the methods and results of our survey to the public. Matney stressed during the class that archaeologists have an obligation to keep people informed and to consider their responses to what we do. This open event was one way to put that dictum into practice. Fourteen students stood in front of an audience of over a hundred people at the Highland Square branch of Akron-Summit County Public Library with a PowerPoint presentation illustrating our methods, results, and interpretations. During our presentation and especially during the question-and-answer period, we were met with fascination, additional volunteered information, and speculation from the audience. We also encountered some criticism of the whole project.

Actual opponents to the work were few, but they were vocal. One resident commented that we "were depreciating the value of our [the] homes" surrounding Schneider Park. Several others challenged us, asking, "How do you know bodies are really buried there?" Although most of the people who attended the presentation were interested in the techniques we used, the history of the Infirmary, and wanted to know what other technology or methods could be used to explore Schneider Park, others pointed out how our work was hurting the community (*Akron Beacon Journal* 2017b). To have a member of the community stand up and tell us the work we were doing was harmful to their community is something no archaeologist wants to hear.

As archaeologists, we try to bring light to past events, no matter how painful those events may have been. It is not our job to hide, downplay, or negate the facts of the past, nor is it to exaggerate, pretty up, or sensationalize them. Rather, we see our job as documenting past events and presenting them as objectively as possible while considering alternate interpretations of our findings. The idea of an objective detached scientific archaeology has been significantly criticized for decades (e.g., Shanks and Tilley 1992). In the context of public archaeology, for example, Pyburn has said that:

> Archaeology began in the U.S. with the investigation of ancient indigenous cultures; although historical archaeology has grown, most U.S. archaeologists still focus on people whose history they do not share and whose descendants continue to be an economically and politically oppressed minority. Consequently archaeology's home has been in anthropology, traditionally the study of 'other cultures' outside the context of western history. Americanist archaeologists have emphasized expertise over engagement, since their claim on the past is academic rather than personal (Pyburn 2017:30).

As a remedy to this shortcoming, Pyburn argues that for public archaeology to work well, it needs to engage community members in solving problems that matter and make sense to them. The approach we have taken here represents something of a philosophical middle ground. We agree with Pyburn that contextualizing our project at Schneider Park for the public is vital for an open dialogue; but we also accept there are hard facts that can be presented and expertise in methods such as the geophysical survey techniques described here which lead to an interpretation that is grounded in an imperfectly objective science.

We tried to provide our interpretation through a range of public activities to raise public awareness and understanding of Schneider Park as a cemetery, both on- and off-site. During our public presentation, we explained that we used many separate modes of data collection and that our conclusions about the graves at Schneider Park were strengthened by the observation that each of the data types pointed toward the same conclusion. It was frustrating to hear that some individuals in the audience, no matter how thoroughly we explained the methods and results, refused to acknowledge the facts that were before them. One older man made it clear that no matter how many forms of data we had, they would always be insufficient to change his opinion that there were no bodies under the ground at Schneider Park.

We explained at several points during the presentation that no remote sensing method can deliver "total certainty" about what lies below ground; this same problem extends to almost all of science. Without excavation, we can only say with some degree of likelihood that there are still bodies buried at Schneider Park. There is overwhelming historical and archaeological evidence that it is a cemetery and that bodies were buried there and stayed in the ground for some time. We know that some bodies were disinterred and reburied approximately a hundred years ago, as noted in chapter 3. Our public presentation offered this historical evidence and the results of multiple scientific techniques in support of our hypothesis that evidence of the bodies buried there still remains. Because good science builds arguments in this fashion, we did not assert that the bodies are there but that the historical and scientific evidence we had assembled strongly supports our hypothesis. The older man in the audience loudly concluded that there was "no proof" that there ever were graves: "How can you say that kids are playing on a cemetery when you can't even say for certain there are bodies?"

To the students, as archaeological scientists in training, the multiple sources of evidence point to the existence of graves and support our understanding in a convincing manner. To this resident, our circumspect language sounds uncertain. We have no particular stake in the historical or current reputation of the park, but this resident's home is located there, and he is struggling to reconcile conflicting images of a space with which he has a relationship. When engaging with individuals like this, the appropriate path for public archaeologists is to present the data, share in the dialogue, and support each person as they assemble their own new understanding.

Informally at our project site, and again at the presentation, people from the community asked what should happen at the park as a consequence of our work. Some members of our team suggested that the city could erect a memorial or plaque to commemorate the history of the site and the people buried there. There were concerns that the park would be fenced in or that activities that had taken place at the park for decades would suddenly be banned. To be clear, physical access to the park has not been affected by our work. In our presentation, we did discuss the historic deeding of the land to the city and the restrictions that Schneider made for its use in his deed (see chapter 2), but only as an observation of historical fact. We made it clear to all our contacts in the community that we, as a class, were not advocating for any particular action or indeed any outcome at all. Schneider Park is an important green space and is easily accessible to the community for a variety of activities. In this vein, the physical accessibility of the site also gives value to Schneider Park as a public archeological site where people can learn and experience the history of their own neighborhood (e.g., Grima 2017).

## *The Science of Finding Graves*

A magnetic gradiometer is a machine used for measuring minute fluctuations in the Earth's magnetic field caused by features buried immediately below the surface (a number of excellent introductory texts to this technique and others in archaeology are widely available; see Clarke 1990; Gaffney and Gater 2003; Johnson 2006; Witten 2006). Typically, in archaeology, magnetic gradiometry can easily detect ferrous metal (iron), burnt features such as hearths, and features in which there are significant contrasts between the magnetic properties of juxtaposed materials immediately surrounding the feature. This latter case includes the detection of graves, in which the soil surrounding the pit cut for an inhumation has slightly different magnetic properties than the material replaced in the pit after the burial. When a pit is dug for a grave, the depth typically cuts

Fig. 4-3. Photograph showing the FM-256 fluxgate gradiometer in use by Maeve Marino at Schneider Park in the summer of 2017 (Photo: Timothy Matney)

through the topsoil and into various subsoil layers; the removed topsoil and deeper soils are mixed together in the process of refilling the grave (now containing a human body). The gradiometer is able to measure and map the differences in the magnetic properties of the soil inside the pit and the undisturbed soil immediately outside of the pit.

Kvamme (2006) provides a good basic overview of the sources of magnetic properties of soil, including thermoremnant magnetism, which comes from the firing of clays, soils with varying amounts of iron oxide, fermentation of hematites, and bacterial concentration of magnetic compounds in the soil. He identifies six human causes of magnetic variation: deliberate fires, features made with fired materials, magnetic enrichment of the surface soils by human occupation, the removal or accumulation of topsoil, use of stone and other materials for construction with varying magnetic properties, and the presence of iron tools and other artifacts.

The basic principle behind magnetic field gradiometry is that the Earth's magnetic field, caused by the rotation of its semi-molten iron core, is immense and extends far out into space. It has both a direction and a strength. At any one point on the Earth's surface, there are minute fluctuations in the Earth's magnetic field caused by highly localized conditions, some of which are the result of human activities. Depending on the nature of the localized magnetic disturbance (e.g., its size, strength, orientation), it can either add to or subtract from the overall Earth's magnetic field. This is best visualized as a simple bar magnet. Depending on the size of the magnet, its strength, how deeply it is buried below ground, and the relative orientation of the positive and negative poles, the bar magnet might add to or subtract from the strength and direction of the Earth's magnetic field. Of course, a bar magnet is infinitesimally weak compared to the Earth's magnetic field, but our equipment is able to measure these differences and map them.

In our survey, a GeoScan FM-256 fluxgate gradiometer was used to survey twenty-seven out of the twenty-eight grid squares (each 20m x 20m) in our overall site grid. The gradiometer is a handheld device that incorporates a pair of extremely sensitive sensors, one at each end of a short (0.5m) long tube. The top sensor, more remote relative to the Earth's surface, measures the Earth's magnetic field, while the bottom sensor, being closer to the ground and the shallow subsurface, has an added component of measuring both the Earth's magnetic field and localized disturbance. By subtracting one reading (measured in nanoteslas, nT) from the other, the difference or gradient represents the effect of buried features and artifacts down to a depth of about 1m. Due to its sensitivity, such contrasts can include the differences between soil conditions caused by pitting, digging graves, or other anthropogenic activities. Unlike a metal detector, a magnetic field gradiometer requires no energy input from the machine itself; rather, the FM-256 employs a passive measurement of the earth's magnetic field. The gradiometer records measurements of the Earth's magnetic field while the operator walks along a straight transect following the site grid. At the same time, the distances between measurements were timed and converted into spatial coordinates, as discussed in a later section.

One of the difficulties in using a magnetic field gradiometer in an urban setting is that the machine is sensitive to numerous different types of interference. For example, the one unsurveyed grid square at Schneider Park had too much modern metal (most notably a modern park bench) and too many large trees for a good survey to be conducted. The strength of the localized magnetic field caused by the iron in the park bench was immense relative to the differences in magnetic soil properties in a century-old grave, and any information that could have been learned from that grid square would have been obscured by the highly magnetic park bench.

In addition to magnetic field gradiometry, we also employed electrical resistance survey, a technique used in archaeology to measure the resistance of the soil in the shallow subsurface to the passage of a subsurface electrical current generated between two probes. Like magnetic field gradiometry, the goal is to identify patterns in which human activities, such as building constructions or pits excavated into the ground and then refilled, interfere with the flow of electricity below ground. Differences in water content, salt content, and soil that has been packed down, disturbed by digging or replaced with a different soil will have differential levels of resistance and can be detected by electrical resistance survey. Electrical resistivity is an active technique, requiring energy to be put into the ground (in this case electricity) creating a circuit between probes. In archaeology, typically we use two pairs of probes connected by a long, insulated wire. One set of probes (the remote probes) remains fixed in the ground throughout the survey and, in effect, provides a stable background reading. A second set of probes (the mobile probes) is mounted on a frame and moved systematically through the survey grid. Each set of probes includes one probe between which a current is passed and a second probe at which voltage readings are made. The resistance meter records the resistance of the soil to the passage of electricity in ohms ($\Omega$). The spacing between the probes determines the depth of current flow. In our survey, the probes were spaced such that the bulk of the current flow was within the top 50cm of the soil. For this survey, a GeoScan RM15-D resistance meter was used.

One of the drawbacks of using an electrical resistance survey is that it is very slow in the field. The speed of the survey is dictated, in part, by the need to reset the location of the probes after each reading. Thus, a smaller area of Schneider Park was surveyed first using electrical resistivity, then a larger area was surveyed using magnetic gradiometry. In

Fig. 4-4. Photograph showing the RM-15D electrical resistance meter in use by Robert L. Tucker during the 2017 field season at Schneider Park (Photo: Timothy Matney)

the survey area, 40 out of 112 grids, each 10m x 10m, were completed. Using the RM15-D is a far slower process than using the gradiometer, meaning fewer data points were collected during the short survey time. Another problem we encountered with the electrical resistance survey was the dryness and compaction of the soil. In general, the park is hard-packed through use, especially athletics, making it difficult to push the probes very deep in the ground. When this factor was combined with the dry conditions we encountered in our mid-summer survey, we had significant difficulty in overcoming surface resistance to the introduction of an electrical field. Short of using a power driver of some kind, pounding these probes into the hard soil is not practical, in part because the probes would bend or break. We were often unable to get the probes deep enough into the ground to reach a layer with sufficient moisture to create a stable electrical current. The effects of this can be seen in the electrical resistance map below.

## *Archaeology and Authority*

"Do you have a permit to work here?" "Who gave you permission to do that?" Hidden behind the science, the public, and the excitement of making new discoveries in the field is a forest of forms and an entanglement of official relationships. Anyone who has ever led an archaeological expedition is familiar with permits, insurance and liability forms, copyright and intellectual property issues, the ethics of survey and excavation and of disturbing the dead, and even the idea of who owns the past and has the right to present it to the public. On overseas projects, we seek approval from multiple ministerial departments and regional museums before digging or even before surface survey. This might mean coordinating with the local imam when modern graves were exhumed by accident (modern Islamic graves do not have grave goods and are, therefore, sometimes difficult to date, especially when first discovered) and spending countless hours negotiating with landowners over the rental of their land to conduct surveys and excavations. There is one universal constant in this field: bureaucracy. By comparison, the project at Schneider Park was easy. Of course, we did not want to dig at Schneider Park, we still needed clear permission to conduct any fieldwork, including our minimally invasive geophysical survey. A series of emails between Eric Olson, Jason Segedy (Director of Planning and Urban Development for the Akron Mayor's Office), John Nutter (Superintendent of the Akron Parks Maintenance Division), and John Moore (Director of Public Service for the Akron Mayor's Office) was all it took to obtain permission to undertake the geophysical survey at Schneider Park. City officials were happy to cooperate with our plans; it didn't hurt that this was an official class offered by the University of Akron and run by one of the tenured faculty in the Department of Anthropology. This is one form of authority that comes from holding a PhD and working at a university. Whether applying for an excavation permit from a foreign government or asking a city government for permission to conduct archaeological survey, the doctoral degree and professorial rank are generally accepted bona fides.

In an informal way, the same is true when working in the public eye. Being considered an authority or as having expertise is part of the social dynamic that public archaeology needs to consider. "The Professor" is treated as the expert, and her or his interpretation is often seen as the final word on the work being undertaken. Several of our students experienced this to some degree when interviewed formally by the media or informally by community members. In those cases, they served as educators and authorities, especially our team leaders, who were both graduates of the program at UA and experienced field hands. Doing good archaeological fieldwork requires a combination of formal training ranging from theory to a detailed knowledge of case studies; it also requires experience and the ability to troubleshoot in the field. Because of this, we *are* the real experts in many ways. That said, many of our local visitors knew far more about the history of Schneider Park than we did, having lived near the park or grown up in the area. There is a folklore surrounding the park (see chapter 6). Visitors to the site listened carefully to our explanation of the magnetometer and resistance meter and the methods we employed, but then were disappointed when we did not have a definitive answer to the seemingly simple questions of "how many people are buried here?" and "where are all the graves?" There is sometimes the mistaken assumption that scientific expertise means we already have all the answers.

Archaeological Field School is the official name of this University of Akron class, and the instructor is an employee. Thus, the team on this project can be seen as representatives of the university. Normally this is not particularly important when a class meets in a university lecture hall and students are engaged with library research, writing papers, or attending lectures and discussion groups. Much of the teaching work at the university does not extend beyond the campus walls and is conducted out of public view. Increasingly, students are engaging in community-based research and service-learning courses or other experiential learning classes that happen in part or entirely outside of the university classroom. In Akron, this brings the faculty and students into deep and important interactions with the larger community. To some degree, then, the class and especially the professor become university spokespersons to the community.

At Schneider Park, this was important for two reasons. First, not all the residents were happy or supportive of our fieldwork in their neighborhood. While the overwhelming number of local visitors felt that this was a good project for the students and that our work was respectful of the memory of the people buried in the cemetery, some felt quite the opposite. In the few (very minor) conflicts that arose during our weeks in the field, tensions were diffused by listening and providing a clear explanation of what we hoped to achieve at Schneider Park. This is part and parcel of all archaeological fieldwork. Finding ways to communicate with upset landowners, farmers, residents, or government officials is a skill we all learn.

Our work raised the question from the community but also from our team members of what should be done as a result of the accumulating knowledge regarding the park. Once it was understood that the data indicate that Schneider Park was a cemetery, a dissonance was created between the way the space is used now as an active city park and the treatment afforded other cemeteries in American culture which are typically fenced off and less actively used. The team discussed various options with both the residents and among themselves. These included putting a fence around the cemetery, marking the individual graves, erecting a commemorative marker, banning the playing of soccer, football, and other sports, and even exhuming the bodies for reburial elsewhere. Here the potential for serious conflict was real, and the limits of our authority would easily have been overreached. This minefield needed to be carefully navigated as it became clear that there were potentially four constituencies in this issue. First, there were the Akron city officials. We have no official guidance on what the city might want to do, if anything, at the cemetery. Clearly ongoing park maintenance was important; it is well maintained with regular mowing, tree trimming, and other minor repairs. A few large-scale projects involving excavation had been necessary, e.g., storm sewers and sanitary sewers had been installed in the park after its use as a cemetery ended. At the same time, one of the few clearly posted rules—golfing is not allowed—is not enforced, and soccer leagues were allowed to practice on the park grounds.

The neighbors, who form a second constituency, use the park for their own activities: jogging, dog walking, playing, and having picnics. They also clearly kept an open eye and informally policed what was happening in their park. Several residents were concerned that our work would lead the city to restrict their access to the park if it became an "official" cemetery. Fences, grave markers, or an outright ban on use of the park would seriously impact their enjoyment of the green space that has been open to them for generations. At the same time, many also felt that it was appropriate to acknowledge the suffering of some of Akron's most unfortunate citizens. The third constituency was the University of Akron officials. Although it was not our intention to generate publicity with our class project, within a few days of starting work, we were dealing with media representatives, and it was clear that there was widespread interest in our Schneider Park project. Whether or not the professor and students enrolled in the class had the authority to speak "for" the university is a gray zone. Naturally, the University of Akron administration does not have a specifically formulated position on what should happen at Schneider Park. It was important not to misrepresent our own opinions as representatives of the university, especially given possible disagreements among city officials, residents, and local or even outside groups concerned with how this cemetery and history fit into the larger pattern of treatment of marginalized peoples in the US. Finally, the students themselves represented a constituency. For a few of the students, this project created an uncomfortable juxtaposition between their "objective" scientific training—they were here to learn an archaeological technique and collect geophysical data—and their "subjective" desire to see social justice for a group of people who in the past had suffered under what would today be seen as unacceptable circumstances. Not all the students were completely comfortable walking on the graves and sticking probes into them. Their discomfort was a challenge for them, but it also reinforced for all the importance of maintaining appropriate respect for the location.

We discussed the issue of these potential disagreements and conflicts as a team on several occasions. The presence of newspaper reporters, photographers, and filmmakers made it essential to develop our own policy. The compromise we reached was an agreement amongst ourselves to stick to educating people about the scientific methods, the history of the Infirmary and park, and the importance of gathering new data to improve our understanding. We chose to listen to others' opinions regarding what should happen while not deliberately making suggestions or advocating for any one outcome ourselves. The students learned there is no such thing as objective, neutral science because the application of the knowledge gained in scientific research can have significant ramifications—social, political, ethical, and economic. The researcher must be aware of this nuanced context while simultaneously striving to be objective. This lesson was tested for the students at the end of their public presentation at the library. When the question of what should be done arose, with one exception, the students held to our policy, despite their own personal convictions. Most understood that even as students in that context—standing in the public library in front of over a hundred residents—they represented one form of authority, and with that came responsibility.

## *Mapping the Cemetery*

In the field, our archaeological data were collected in a precise grid. To analyze the shallow subsurface features, we needed to be able to map them in two-dimensional space and reference them to surface features, like the rectangular patches of vegetation described earlier. The basic concept behind these maps is straightforward. Both the magnetic gradiometer and the resistance meter are mobile units, and as they are moved across our spatial grid we record their locations in terms of a Cartesian coordinate system with x and y values representing an easting and a northing respectively. In addition to these spatial coordinates, the machines record a geophysical reading (a numerical value of units representing either nanoteslas or ohms). The spatial coordinates define a limited and precise area, and in terms of the mapmaking, each area is treated as a pixel within a digital image. Thus, the size of the pixel is determined by the density of samples collected in the field. When samples are taken close together, we have a more fine-grained map of the subsurface features. When samples are widely spaced, then the map—like an old digital photograph—starts to pixelate and is harder to interpret. The trade-off for gathering high-density datasets is that they take much longer to collect in the field. Transects used at Schneider Park were north-south lines following the grid system established at the beginning of the project. The sample interval can be defined as the distance between each reading along each transect. The traverse interval refers to the distance between each transect.

For the magnetic field gradiometry survey, we collected readings with a sample interval of 12.5cm (i.e., eight samples per meter) and a traverse interval of 50cm. Over a 20m x 20m grid, then, we collected 6,400 readings using magnetic gradiometry (8 readings/m x 20m = 160 samples/transect x 40 transects/grid square). As noted earlier, a total of twenty-seven grid squares were collected, so our gradiometry maps display 172,800 data points as individual pixels, provide a fine-grained image of the strength and orientation of magnetic fields immediately at and below the surface of the ground. For the electrical resistance survey, we used smaller 10m x 10m grids for the entirely practical reason that the need to pick up and set down the remote probes is a very slow, laborious process. It is essential to create a stable electrical field before taking the reading, so there is a much longer wait time for each data point to be recorded. Our sample interval was 0.50m, and our traverse interval was 0.5m, effectively creating a square pixel 0.5m on a side. For each resistivity square we collected 400 grid points (2 readings/x 10m = 20 samples/transect x 20 transects/grid square). Over the 40 grids that we surveyed our maps display 16,000 data points which provide a map of the resistance of the shallow subsurface soil to the passage of an electrical current.

After the data were collected, the students downloaded the files to a field laptop computer. The program they used to process the data is a proprietary software application called GeoPlot, proprietary software for the GeoScan magnetic gradiometer and the electrical resistance meter we were using. Data are collected as long strings of measurement values and GeoPlot's download protocol places each value into a spatial coordinate system defined by the user. In effect, the end result of the fieldwork is a vast array of numbers in a spreadsheet with rows and columns representing spatial coordinates and individual cells displaying the readings either in nanoteslas (nT)or in ohms ($\Omega$). While it is possible to immediately display and analyze the raw field data, typically the datasets require considerable processing and manipulation to enhance the features of interest and to eliminate unwanted modern elements and noise from the maps. First, it is necessary to create a composite of all the separate grid files collected over the course of the survey.

Next, the composite file is processed with the general goal of increasing the signal-to-noise ratio. In the case of Schneider Park, the *signal*—that is, the targets of interest—are the possible human graves. The *noise*, which needs to be reduced as much as possible, is modern artifacts and features such as ferrous metal trash, utility lines, cars, fire hydrants, subsurface drainage systems, etc., as well as data defects caused by operator error and machine error in data collection. Especially in magnetic field gradiometry it is very easy to introduce noise into the data collection because the sensors are so sensitive. The operator of the machine must have completely magnet-free clothing, which means eliminating zippers, metal grommets, jewelry, pins, underwires, many types of eyeglasses and sunglasses, shoes with metal supports, and so forth. Some surgical and dental steel is magnetic. Likewise, anyone standing within three or four meters of the operator must be metal-free. Occasional visitors pose a significant problem for the use of magnetometers, including dogs with metal tags and collar buckles! Assuming we can reduce the noise caused by ferrous objects, there are still periodic errors caused by the operators, including walking at an inconsistent pace, swinging the magnetometer slightly as they walk, and by environmental conditions. The magnetometer sensors need to be aligned at several points each day as the machine is jarred or bumped or as the internal electronics heat up as the outside temperature changes. Processing the data in GeoPlot allows the operator to highlight the signal and reduce the noise through mathematical manipulation of the data array. By using different processing algorithms within GeoPlot, it was possible to enhance the imagery for both the magnetic gradiometry and resistivity results, making it easier to plot the location of likely graves.

The geophysical map shown in figure 4-5 represents the twenty-seven grid squares of magnetic gradiometry data as collected using the FM-256. There has been no processing of the data other than compositing the individual grid files collected over the three-week field season into a single image. The grid squares have differing background shades of gray caused by the differences in calibrating the machine several times each day. This effect is easily removed during processing. Each grid square is 20m x 20m in size.

The most striking features of this raw magnetometry map are numerous strong dipoles—seen as white and black features—in which high positive and high negative values are immediately adjacent to one another. These features are almost certainly modern ferrous metal objects, such as a nail, a lost pocketknife, or a buried utility cover. Like all magnets, they have a strong north and a strong south pole, and their size and the orientation of the white versus black signals reflects: (1) the strength of the magnet, (2) the size of the magnet, and (3) its orientation in the ground. Most of these dipole magnets were probably buried immediately

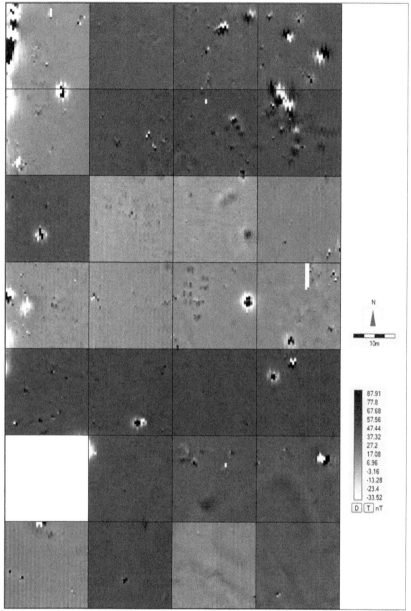

Fig. 4-5. Map of the raw (unprocessed) magnetic gradiometry data from Schneider Park (Map: Timothy Matney)

beneath the surface, as we removed obvious interfering features, such as modern surface trash, before the surveying started. Unfortunately, these features are noise (since they are not the features of interest to us), and they render other, more subtle magnetic signals less visible in the data and may distort our interpretation. At the northwestern corner of the map, a long linear feature of alternating strong positive and strong negative values can be seen. This signal is typical of buried iron pipes and represents modern urban noise.

During the processing of geophysical maps, it is typical to generate hundreds of different maps using varying color palettes, processing filters, and data manipulations. GeoPlot allows the user to customize the process to maximize the signal-to-noise ratio and to focus specifically on the targets of interest. One batch of graves is clearly seen in the very center of the survey area, displayed as weak but distinct positive magnetic features relative to the surrounding background. Processing the data allows us to see far more graves than is possible by just viewing the raw field data.

The magnetic gradiometry map from Schneider Park required numerous enhancements that are standard to processing many geophysical maps. First, the difference in the background values is removed by an algorithm called Zero Mean Grid. This process calculates the mean of the values in each grid and then subtracts that mean from each value, resulting in a background with a mean of zero. Next, it is necessary to remove the strong ferrous metal dipoles as their presence in the map reduces our ability to see the more subtle ancient features. In effect, the modern noise values are outliers within a distribution, while the majority of our target data is in the center of that distribution. By using a function in GeoPlot called Search and Replace, the analyst can replace the original values for those large dipoles with dummy values. While this creates "holes" in the map, removing the extreme outliers causes the distribution of the remaining points to form a more normal distribution and enhances the contrast between the remaining values. Likewise, other data spikes—outliers at the edge of the data distribution—must be removed using the Clip and Despike filters. Finally, the processed numerical readings can be displayed by assigning either any color value or grayscale value to each pixel according to its value in nanoteslas. These values can be seen in the plan key, with black representing strong positive values (with a maximum of 87.91nT) and white representing strong negative values (with a minimum of -33.52nT).

Figure 4-6 shows the processed magnetic field gradiometry data from Schneider Park. The graves are represented by black (magnetically negative) rectangular features. Many more features can be seen in this map than in the earlier drone or satellite images. In effect, we selected the middle portion of the range noted above, between 13.25 and -13.25nT, and expanded the grayscale. Areas that were a uniform gray before processing now have clear features, including over two hundred possible graves. The graves appear as small, magnetically positive (black) rectangles with their long axis running nearly east-west in orientation. They line up into long rows running more or less north-south, although they are not perfectly straight, presumably since they were dug sequentially over decades. The absence of ferrous metal suggests that the bodies were not interred in wooden caskets, as one would expect the presence of coffin nails to be notable. It is our understanding that the practice of the time may have included nothing more substantial than wrapping the body in a winding sheet or blanket. The southeastern corner of the map has several long linear features at least 20m (60 feet) long, which probably represent a modern subsurface construction or soil disturbance.

A section of the processed electrical resistance data is illustrated in figure 4-7. The graves are represented by white (low resistance) rectangular features on the left in (a). These graves are marked in the interpretation map on the right in (b). Other graves are visible only from aerial survey and surface mapping, but not in the geophysical prospection, and two graves were only seen using geophysical techniques.

The subtle features which were so clearly seen in the magnetic field gradiometry are not at all visible in the electrical resistance survey. The basic concepts in processing the electrical resistance data are similar to those for magnetic gradiometry, although some differences exist. The dataset has a large number of dummy values across the entire site, but especially in the centermost grid squares. This is caused in large measure by the dry conditions noted earlier. High surface contact resistance meant that a stable current was difficult to achieve. This meant that either no value or a value at the high or low edge of the distribution (outlier) was recorded. The latter case appears in the map as squares with mixed white

## Science in the Public Eye

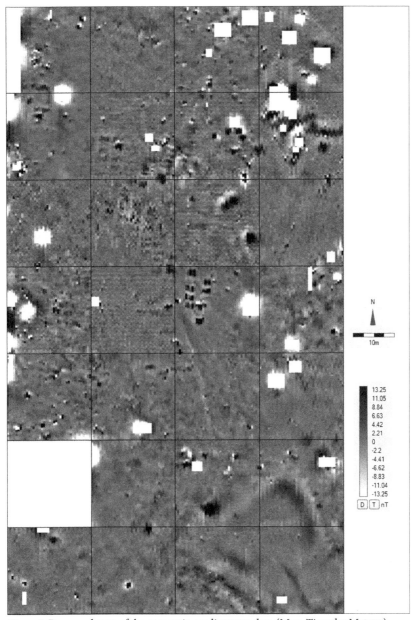

Fig. 4-6. Processed map of the magnetic gradiometry data (Map: Timothy Matney)

and black pixels. Good electrical resistance should have smooth contours of grays with a few white (low resistance) or black (high resistance) data points. This is illustrated in the area in the southwestern portion of the site (except the single grid square in the southwest corner). The grid squares used to collect electrical resistance data at Schneider Park are 10m x 10m in extent.

The graves, fifteen of which were recognized on the electrical resistance maps, appear as small areas of low resistance (white). This is typical of graves and other types of pits because the soil in the graves is less compact and, therefore, holds moisture better. The soil in graves may also have a higher organic content because it was partly filled in with topsoil. The area in the center of the map was, as noted above, covered with a thin layer of sand that had been brought into the park at some point in the past. The presence of a large sand patch also added to the problems we were facing with contact resistance. Unfortunately, the confounding factor of the dry soil conditions rendered most of our efforts to collect electrical resistance data somewhat moot, as the targets of interest (signal) were swamped by the noise introduced by non-archaeological features. We mapped less than half of the survey area using this technique.

### A Curious Public

Journalist, newscaster, filmmaker, public relation specialist, and podcaster are the titles offered by some of the people who approached the team during our time in Schneider Park. These interactions added a public archaeology emphasis to the students' intensive geophysical experience. Revels and Marino, both team leaders in the class and co-authors here, took point on many of these interactions.

Everything we said to any media representative needed to be thought out and well-articulated, as this was a major representation of archaeology and the university to this community. We quickly learned that once an interview was recorded, control of the message was out of our hands. We had to learn what being a public archaeologist really means in the present age of social media and quickly moving news outlets. The term *public archaeologist* is not a new one but has shifted in meaning as science has become more accessible, and local projects like this one interest a public beyond the immediate community. In short, science can quickly become

Science in the Public Eye 123

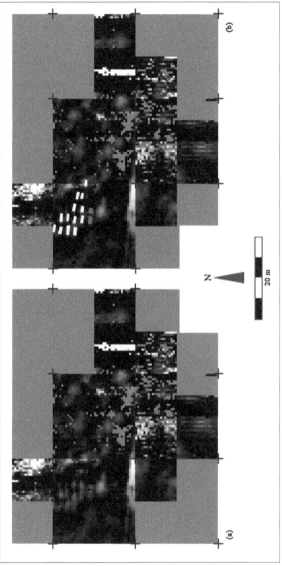

Fig. 4-7. Processed map of the electrical resistance data, selection portion (Map: Timothy Matney)

a consumable commodity. Through television, movies, and social media, what archaeologists and other scientists do is exposed to a wide audience. Public archaeologists find themselves working within a mass media world that requires more inclusive language compared to the archaeological jargon that we are accustomed to using among ourselves.

In the case of Schneider Park, unidentified graves, and no official marker explaining the co-occurrence of an unmarked cemetery and a public park in the same space, had allowed imaginations to run. Sensational, even supernatural stories of mistreated inmates, ghosts, and mysterious fog had accumulated haphazardly across time and been shared largely by word of mouth, although a couple of newspaper articles and some blogging helped expand the number of people who knew something about the park. This presented a challenge since our role is to gather data and seek the clearest possible picture of what happened in this part of the park. We chose to listen to the stories but for our part to focus attention on science and our machines with their differently esoteric tales of electrical resistance and magnetism within the ground. It is true that sensational stories draw and hold public attention. We realized part of translating science to the public involves capturing attention and that the perennial fascination elicited by discovery of hidden graves could be helpful in turning excitement into knowledge of archaeology and science. As reporters asked questions such as "How does being at a place of so much suffering and death make you feel?" and "Do you believe the ghost stories about Schneider Park?", we quickly honed our public speaking skills and figured out how to tackle questions like those and turn them into opportunities to supply clear information about the archaeological work being done. Being clear about this challenge, it is not easy to replace speculation about the likelihood of fog collecting over the forsaken graves with a description of geophysical datasets and shifts in numeric readings of nanoteslas and ohms.

Paraphrasing our responses to the question of whether we get an eerie feeling being in Schneider Park given what we know of the socially marginalized lives and deaths separated from families of support, we replied that as archaeologists we are constantly dealing with past lives; that comes with our job. Yes, we agree tragic things happened in the Infirmary and the infirmary system had significant flaws, not the least of which were the assumptions about human worth based on eugenic pseudoscience. Our work is learning about the individuals who otherwise are not visible in the historical record and bringing information about them to the public. An answer like this one generally was a good way to get into a discussion about historical and archaeological data.

However, this did not always work. Two of the students on the project, including one of the team leaders, were part of an on-site discussion with a journalist. Both of the students were able to give many details about the site itself and how certain aspects of our data from Schneider Park could be explained. At the end of the discussion, both students felt satisfied with how they had explained the archaeology and history of Schneider Park. But when the article came out, they were frustrated by the only quote the journalist had used from one of them: "If there are any restless spirits on Earth, they would be here" (*Akron Beacon Journal* 2017a). Despite all the information she had given about the equipment and site, this small comment meant as levity at the end of the conversation, was the only direct quote. News media is sometimes more interested in grabbing a quick headline than in teaching all of their readers about the science of magnets and electrical currents. However, this type of article is important. Much of our field work is ultimately presented in highly specialized, peer-reviewed journals. To reach members of the public who share an interest in this sort of activity but have no access to (or interest in reading) scholarly papers, public media outlets are a vital bridge.

Another lesson learned in this project is that public archaeologists need to adapt their communication for different types of media. For example: one of the university's public relations specialists came out to Schneider Park and was using Snapchat and Instagram to record what we were doing and saying. We needed to be upbeat, animated, and quick with our explanations using these forms of social media that are watched for ten seconds, and some of which disappear after twenty-four hours. By comparison, when a television news channel came to film us, we needed find the sweet spot for all audiences but were able to increase the level of detail and slow down our explanations to align with the larger amount of time the segment would allot us. The main reason for these changes in approach to different media is the understanding that the viewer demographic for each type is different. Only 14 percent of snapchat users in 2017 were over the age of thirty-five, while those watching nightly news programs are typically between forty-five to fifty-three years old (Pew

Research 2015). Paying attention to audience, we worked to tailor what we said and how we talked about the project to the platform. The goal was to get good at optimizing the effectiveness of our communication to generate the interest, excitement, and engagement across demographic groups.

The project at Schneider Park took on a life of its own thanks to engagement with and the interplay of mass media and interested people in the community. Our public presentation was reproduced in a blog by a citizen. This allowed the students participating to learn and hone valuable, transferable skills that lay well outside of typical field school classes or volunteer projects. Those skills also jumpstarted an understanding of how mass media has played a role in archaeological work in the last decade, a role that is likely to increase in significance in the future so we need to learn to work with it.

*Analysis of Archaeological Data*

Our analysis and interpretation of the Schneider Park data involved examining all types of data gathered. By examining and identifying all potential graves in each of the four survey types, we established a scale to evaluate the likelihood that each feature was correctly identified as a grave. The way this was done is quite simple in concept. First, we superimposed all four datasets onto our base site map and grid. Each potential grave that was seen and mapped in the visible surface survey was scored with a value of 1. Subsequently, those graves also visible in the drone imagery were also scored with a value of 1. Thus, graves seen in both the surface and drone surveys now had a cumulative score of 2, while those visible in only one survey had a cumulative score of 1. This process was repeated for the magnetic gradiometry maps, as well as the electrical resistance maps. The results are shown in Table 4-1.

| Technique | n = | % (of 328) |
|---|---|---|
| Drone survey | 119 | 34.8 |
| Surface survey | 114 | 36.2 |
| Magnetic gradiometry survey | 302 | 92.1 |
| Electrical resistance survey | 15 | 4.6 |

Table 4-1. Number of features mapped with each technique (Table: Timothy Matney)

Using this system, we were able to identify 328 potential graves, each with a score from 1 to 4, as shown in Table 4-2.

| Score | n = | % (of 328) | Interpretation |
|---|---|---|---|
| 4 | 5 | 1.5 | Probable |
| 3 | 90 | 27.4 | Probable |
| 2 | 28 | 8.5 | Likely |
| 1 | 205 | 62.5 | Possible |
| Total | 328 | | |

Table 4-2. Counts and percentages of features organized by score based on the number of techniques by which they were mapped (Table: Timothy Matney)

Because of the poor quality of the resistance dataset, only five graves received the top score. An additional ninety graves were seen in three of the surveys and twenty-eight in two surveys. The majority of the graves were only seen using one of the survey techniques, typically electrical resistance. Since each technique looked at different properties of the earth (i.e., visible surface indicators from both the ground and the air, electrical, or magnetic properties), those places in which positive identifications overlapped are more likely to represent actual graves.

Through the visual ground survey conducted by the students, 114 graves were located. These were each precisely mapped using an electronic total station. Using the drone map provided by Dr. Lancaster, 119 graves were visible. Through magnetic gradiometry 302 graves were recorded and, finally, electrical resistivity was the least effective technique given the field conditions and only 15 graves were detected. In total, 328 graves were visible in at least one survey method. The graves were numbered sequentially and their general location in the northwestern portion of Schneider Park is shown in figure 4-8 relative to the topography and surface features at the park. The thick gray line indicates the location of a buried sanitation sewer, according to the city records. The circles are trees. The small black box is a park bench. The triangles are fire hydrants.

A detailed map of just the graves identified within the geophysical survey area is illustrated in figure 4-9. Note that two of the graves are numbered 329 and 330. Likewise, note that there are no graves numbered

163 or 164. These were graves initially identified by the students, but later determined not to be likely graves.

As a disclosure, in their public presentation students had overcounted the number of graves based on the initial maps generated during the class. They reported 156 potential graves using drone survey and 311 using magnetic gradiometry. Some of these potential graves were later rejected when examined in greater detail, as they appeared to represent natural features such as rotting tree stumps. Furthermore, due to the difficulty of aligning the drone image with the other maps, some graves had been counted twice in the initial assessment. Thus, the student presentation noted 384. That number has been corrected here to 328.

A few general observations can be made regarding this technique for assigning values to the graves. First, although the number of graves seen by the two visible surface techniques were similar (surface survey n=114 and drone survey n=119), there were only eighty-nine graves seen in both techniques. Twenty-five graves seen and mapped on the surface survey were not visible by the drone; most of these were obscured by the canopy of trees at the park and the drone was flown above the tree branches. Likewise, thirty graves were mapped by drone but were too faint to be seen while standing at ground level in the cemetery, or they were isolated from larger groupings. This is also partly explained by the way in which our pattern recognition worked. On-the-ground identification was aided by repetition of graves in a line and the ability of the surveyor to note minor changes in topography. The drone image was analyzed looking for size and orientation. Magnetic gradiometry was by far the most efficient way of finding graves. Of the 205 graves that were only located by one technique, magnetic gradiometry accounted for 181 (88.3 percent) of these. Spatially, the graves uniquely identified via gradiometry tended to be recovered at the edges of the visible graves. In other words, these are graves that are obscured at the surface but probably lie immediately below the surface where the gradiometer can penetrate but no surface indicators remain visible.

## *Conclusions*

Part of the goal of our research project was to identify the edges of the cemetery, which we were unable to accomplish in the few weeks of

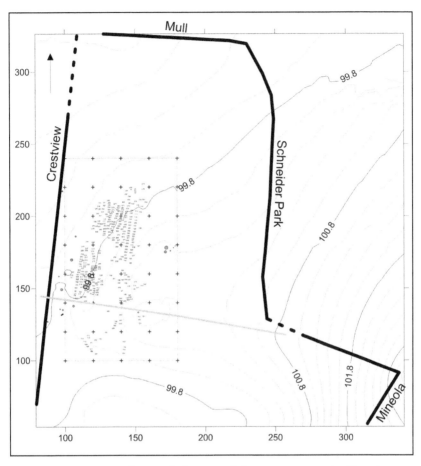

Fig. 4-8. Composite map showing the location of all 328 graves recognized by at least one of the four survey techniques (Map: Timothy Matney)

our summer class. Most importantly, graves were identified very near the southern edge of the survey area, with Grave Nos. 309 and 154 approximately 2m from the southern edge. This suggests to us that the cemetery initially might have extended beyond the limits of our geophysical survey. According to a city utilities map of Schneider Park provided by the City of Akron, the area to the south of our research area was significantly impacted by the construction of a major storm sewer and drainage system within the last few decades. No graves were identified in the 10m grid squares along either the northern or eastern portion of the site, which

130 WHAT REMAINS

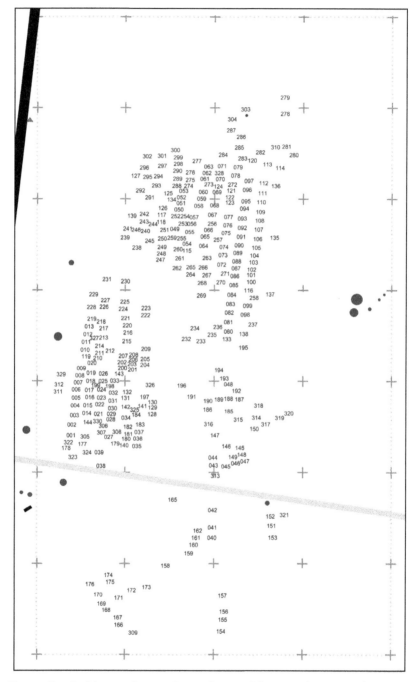

Fig. 4-9. Detail of the map showing the numbering of the graves (Map: Timothy Matney)

may indicate that here we were able to define a boundary for the graves. The neat alignment of the visible graves with additional graves detected during magnetic gradiometry strongly suggests that these features are correctly identified. It is interesting to note that across the entire survey area, there is only one place where a straight east-west line can be drawn and not intersect a grave identified by one of the four techniques. This place is the location of the city sanitary sewer. While further research would be required to demonstrate this with great confidence, the obvious interpretation is that the graves along the line of the trench for the sanitary sewer were disturbed or removed during this work. The absence of graves in the center of the research area is probably related in some way to the large sand patch mentioned earlier and easily visible on the drone and satellite images. Minimally, we would estimate that forty to sixty additional bodies may have been interred in this area, but their fate is unknown since it is unclear whether the area was excavated or the sand was simply dumped on top of the graves.

Further archaeological work in Schneider Park is certainly warranted. Expanding the grid southward may allow us to identify more graves and to define a conclusive southern boundary. Likewise, it might be useful to test other parts of the park as residents reported to us possible graves along nearly the entire eastern border of Schneider Park and to the north of the current survey area. It would also be useful to employ different geophysical prospection techniques, especially ground-penetrating radar (GPR), which is frequently used in the recovery of lost or clandestine graves. This would provide a fifth dataset and would further solidify our interpretation of where the graves are within Schneider Park through the use of another independent method. Finally, further survey using magnetic gradiometry and electrical resistance is also recommended. By extending the probe spacing on the mobile electrical resistance probe frame, data could be collected at greater depth with the RM15-D. Likewise, increasing the sample density by using smaller sample and transect intervals would further enhance our geophysical maps. The magnetic gradiometer also has a stacking function which can be used in data collection with the FM-256. This feature slows down the rate at which the operator can walk, but rather than taking a single data point at each physical location, a series of up to sixteen readings can be taken and then averaged.

This function provides a much cleaner dataset with fewer outliers and is generally useful when looking for especially subtle low-contrast features. All these factors might allow us to better locate graves as well as dismiss anomalies that may otherwise be misinterpreted as potential graves.

    The use of cutting-edge archaeological field methods allowed us to probe and map the graveyard at Schneider Park while not disturbing any human remains that might still be at rest under the surface of the park. Questions of ethics and the broader issue of how to deal with the archaeological data presented here are difficult ones. As has been demonstrated in this chapter, science does not always take place in an isolated laboratory. Rather, there is an inherent messiness in navigating the social, political, and emotional landscapes in which archaeology is practiced. It is our contention that the academic discipline of archaeology is best served when these complex issues are brought forth and discussed frankly and openly with the public.

## Chapter 5
# Who Were They?
## A Demographic Analysis
*Patricia Connelly and Patricia Arnett*

No one refutes that there were inmates at the Summit County Infirmary, that some of them died while in care there, and were buried on the grounds of the Infirmary in the area now known at Schneider Park. Some of those bodies were possibly moved in the 1930s to a new cemetery in Munroe Falls, but there were over three hundred graves, at a bare minimum, and it is almost certain that many bodies still remain buried under the ground. In this chapter, we share what we have learned about the people buried in the Infirmary cemetery and attempt to put that information into social context within the City of Akron by comparing the burial population from the Infirmary cemetery with two other groups of burials, both from Glendale Cemetery located closer to Akron's center. Chapter 2 noted that not only were inmates buried at the Infirmary cemetery, but the City of Akron also sent the bodies of people who were unable to afford private burials there to be interred. The Summit County Infirmary cemetery thus also served as a potter's field. Importantly, an alternate potter's field was set aside as a charitable gesture in the otherwise higher-class Glendale Cemetery. It seems clear that city and Infirmary officials considered known and unknown deceased indigent people and the residents of the Infirmary as a similar category of deceased people.

This analysis looks at three populations: the poor and indigent inmates and non-inmates buried at the Infirmary cemetery and two groups who were buried at the Glendale location. The first group had relatives, friends, or estates with sufficient means to afford private burial in the main Glendale Cemetery. The second group are those interred in the potter's field portion of Glendale. Our specific concern is what we can learn about these individuals, especially about their health and illness based on historical information recorded about how they died using the methods of biological anthropology.

Our dataset is derived from death certificates and other contemporary documents. In the comparative analysis below, we will look specifically at lifespan, infant mortality, causes of death, regional origins, and names included on these different documents. Information gleaned from these demographic comparisons will provide insight into lifestyles of the individuals interred in the different cemeteries and help illuminate the degree of socio-economic disparities more broadly in Akron in the early years of the twentieth century.

## *Biological Anthropology*

Biological anthropology has a subfield called *forensic anthropology* which concerns itself with primary and secondary sources of information regarding causes of human deaths (Buikstra 1997; Larsen 2002; Goodman and Armelagos 1989; Grauer 2018, 2019; Grauer et al. 1998; Roberts et al. 1994, 1998). This is a form of detective work in which we explore data, sometimes incomplete scraps of data, to gain understanding about the causes and contexts of death. Our primary sources are typically the physical remains of the people, and our secondary sources are usually written records that directly described the person or their physical remains, such as an autopsy report. In the case of the inmates of the Summit County Infirmary who were buried in the cemetery, no bodies have been officially exhumed except those that were reinterred at the Munroe Falls Infirmary (about which we have no written records or photographs), so for this chapter we will examine secondary sources, namely death records created by the Infirmary staff and officials working for the City of Akron at the time of death for each person. As we describe, not all records are present, and not all those we did find are complete. However, by examining the records individually and then considering them as a group or population, we can learn about who they were and how they related to the greater population of residents at the time.

Records of diseases and the ultimate causes of death can reveal information regarding social status and economic status in and between populations (Ensor et al. 2010; Gadson et al. 2017; Gregorio et al. 1997; Hart et al. 1998; Kaler 2008; Manderson et al. 2009; Mirowsky and Ross 2000; Pillay van Wyk and Bradshaw 2017; Winkleby et al. 1992). Scholars often measure these "socio-economic" differences in populations correlating wealth or annual income with life expectancy. As one might expect, life expectancy typically correlates positively with income; as incomes increase across a population, life expectancies within that population rise (Mirowsky and Ross 2000; Preston 1975). Recently, some analysts have tried to disconnect wealth from longevity. However, those studies have failed, only reinforcing the original observation that, in industrial and postindustrial consumer capitalist societies like ours, money provides food, shelter, and medical care, so longer life expectancy strongly correlates with favorable socio-economic conditions (e.g., Pillay van Wyk and Bradshaw 2017).

◇◇◇◇◇◇◇

Economic opportunities across the rise of industrialization in the US were more plentiful in urban centers like Akron so, for many people, these cities were an irresistible magnet. However, the strength and longevity of those opportunities did not distribute evenly across all new arrivals. In the late 1800 and early 1900s in Akron, where industrial scale clay pipe production, Quaker Oats, and the beginnings of the rubber industry provided employment opportunities, people arriving with few resources generally had only their physical strength and agility as assets for entering the job market. Higher paid, higher status, less draining or dangerous work went to people with status markers like educational attainment, social connections, or those trained in specific crafts. The less social or economic capital a person arrived with, the more constrained their access to economic opportunities became. Migrants who looked or sounded least like the urban mainstream and elites had the most difficulty gaining an economic foothold. Historically, immigrant groups who had a longer presence in the region, like German-speaking groups, found greater opportunity. There were well established, wealthy German Americans like Ferdinand Schumacher, whose oatmeal company eventually became Quaker Oats, and a sizable blue-collar community with German roots to embrace and assist newcomers. As will become clear from our data, other immigrant groups were more marginalized.

The Summit County Infirmary was used primarily to house people who had no or exceptionally weak support systems of their own, or were unable to work, and thus had to rely on social services. Inmates were formally accepted into the facility, which distinguishes them from destitute people living without that institutional support in the margins of the community; this is important for us since it creates a record of their presence at the Infirmary. It is reasonable to assume that the lives of both inmates and non-inmate destitute people involved stressors that influenced their health. For the inmates, these stressors hopefully were lessened after arriving at the Infirmary, or after their mothers' did, in the case of infants born at the Infirmary. From a biological anthropologist's point of view, this historic urban population of Infirmary inmates can provide insights into the health status of the Akron community overall by revealing common as well as unexpected health challenges experienced by people with the fewest resources. Comparing the inmates at the Infirmary to a population of more economically and socially advantaged people through death records can tell us a great deal about life in Akron over a century ago. Our comparison also includes a third group in the comparison: destitute people who died outside of the Infirmary's system of care.

◇◇◇◇◇◇◇◇

What are some of the indicators of socio-economic stressors that might impact a body in a manner recorded in a death record? Three primary indicators are limited access to food (Kaler 2008, Manderson et al. 2009; Mirowsky and Ross 2000), ineffective shelter or marginal living conditions (McCarrier et al. 2011; Weinick et al. 2005), and limited access to healthcare (Grauer 2019, Pillay van Wyk and Bradshaw 2017). Marginal living conditions typically refer to living closer to factories or other work environments with increased pollution generally or poor air quality specifically (Gotschi et al. 2008). Decreased air quality can manifest itself in a slew of chronic diseases including tuberculosis, a bacterially derived disease that primarily infects the lungs and is spread airborne through coughing and sneezing (Harris 2019). Tuberculosis (TB) thrives in close, crowded living conditions with poor ventilation (see Diamond 1991; Gotschi et al. 2008). This is a debilitating condition that interferes with most types of income-generating work. A common cause of death for a person suffering from TB is respiratory failure. Limited access to food impedes a child's physical growth and development and an adult's ability to work. It also increases women's morbidity and mortality because of the energy costs of giving birth and lactating (Ensor et al. 2010; Goodman and Armelagos 1989; Loudon 1991). Reduced or no access to healthcare has predicable implications for morbidity and mortality (Grauer 2019).

## *Three Populations*

In this chapter, we demographically compare three populations of dead people buried in two cemeteries in Akron. The Summit County Infirmary has been described in detail in earlier chapters. As noted above, for our analysis we also chose to also study two populations buried within one large, formal cemetery in Akron, Glendale Cemetery, as a comparative sample to those buried at the Infirmary. The Glendale Cemetery, now encircled by the expanding City of Akron, was once known as Akron Rural Cemetery, although in this book we will use its modern name. Glendale Cemetery was the first public cemetery in Akron and was designated for the interment of middle- to upper-class citizens (Colopy 1991:3). Most of the people buried in Glendale Cemetery were individuals with publicly recognized names; people who shaped Akron's history, served the state or country, or individuals who came from families of means (Trexler 2014). Colopy (1991) argues the Akron Rural cemetery was not a place for laborers (Colopy 1991:5). Cemeteries for the well-to-do often show a monetary investment in the actual burials themselves; these cemeteries typically have professionally carved stone monuments, headstones, and other forms of recognition for the interred individuals (Colopy 1991).

However, the Glendale Cemetery also included a spatially segregated potter's field—an area where people without resources to pay for formal burial were interred and whose graves, like those in the Summit County Infirmary cemetery, were left unmarked. For this analysis, we divide the two populations buried at the Glendale location as analytically separate; the distinction between them corresponds to the location of the grave within the cemetery. In this chapter, we will refer to three populations as the Infirmary cemetery (meaning those from the Summit Country Infirmary cemetery), the Glendale Cemetery (meaning the middle- and upper-class marked graves at Glendale), and the potter's field population (meaning those buried at the Glendale location in the segregated area for poor and indigent individuals with unmarked graves).

## Data Constraints

This demographic analysis does not access skeletal remains to potentially confirm disease presence or causes of death. Instead, we use death records and death certificates as stand-ins (or proxies) for skeletal material, with the following caveats. Because these records are old (1908–1916), there are issues with terminological consistency and with level of detail. Medical terminology of the period was less standardized than it is now, so different doctors or coroners diagnosing causes of death might differ in cases where today's specialists would use the same term or phrase. Of course, medical knowledge is always evolving, and while there has been an improvement in the precision of medical language over the past century, there are still situations in which terms may be used inconsistently.

Another concern to note is that the records we have vary in the level of detail on each document. Some death certificates have much more information than others. It is not appropriate to assume that minimal or missing information signals that something was unknown. The person filling out the form might not have asked, might have been unsure of translation in the case of an unfamiliar language when gathering information from informants, might have been uncomfortable with recording some information to shield the family of the deceased from social discomfort, or might simply have intended to complete the form later and never returned to it. We cannot interpret the absence of information on these documents, so it is important not to assume that absence of information on a form means anything other than that it is not available for our analysis.

The data presented here come from the Glendale Cemetery ledger books and death certificates (when accessible) and from the Summit County Infirmary's death certificates. The categories of information contained in Glendale Cemetery's ledger books include: name of deceased, "nativity" or place of birth, year and age of death, disease (if known or provided), location of the burial in the cemetery, and undertaker. In contrast, the death certificates, as official state records, contain more information: name of deceased, sex, "color or race," birth date, death date, marital status, birthplace, occupation, father and mother's names and birthplaces, cause of death, doctor or medical signature, undertaker and county registrar signature. Thus, the data garnered from these two sources overlap but are not the same. This creates an imbalance in our analysis. For example, "sex" is recorded in the death certificates, but the Glendale ledger books do not contain that information which, if no corresponding death certificate is available, can only be imperfectly inferred from the first ("given") names of the deceased. This does not produce reliable data, as some names were used for both men and women, and some first names were unfamiliar as translated from foreign languages. We elected not to make such inferences except in a brief note below on correlating sex with accidents/suicides.

Figure 5-1 shows how the data from the Glendale Cemetery were recorded in the Glendale Cemetery entry books. As seen by this figure, the handwritten records, columns, and ink became hard to decipher over time. Further, not every individual has the same data recorded in these entry books; completeness of records likely depends on who made the records and when they were made.

Another limitation of our comparison of datasets is the fact that the Glendale Cemetery ledger books have a field for "disease," which is similar but not necessarily equivalent to the "cause of death" data field on the death certificates. When matching death certificates could not be located for the Glendale ledger books for corroboration, we chose to treat the "disease" data field as listing a cause or contributing factor to the death but not as a definitive cause of death. This comparison across datasets with mismatched data fields also meant that we could not address race. For an exploration of the data on race in the Infirmary's official state death certificates, see chapter 6.

Finally, we are constrained by the uneven distribution of the records through time. The Infirmary's graves, like those of the potter's field, were and remain unmarked by headstone or any other monument. This is unfortunate for our study, since burial markers often contain useful information on the individual's life status, values, and meaningful connections through their inscriptions. Without these, the principal data source that we can use to study the demographics and health conditions at the time

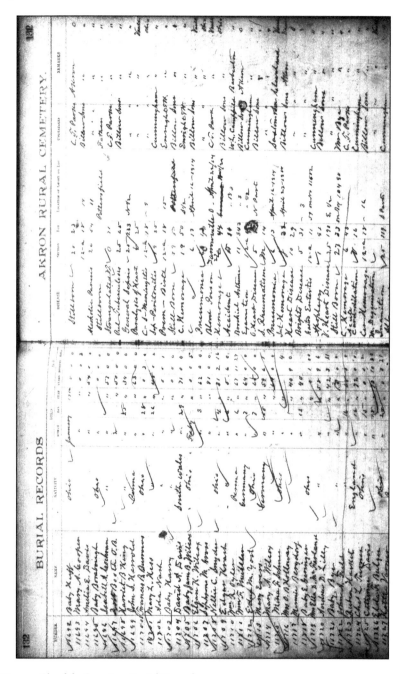

Fig. 5-1. Glendale Cemetery Burial Record

of death for the Infirmary population are death certificates. Existing death certificate records from the Summit County Infirmary date between 1867 and the closing of the Infirmary with relocation of the remaining inmates to Munroe Falls in 1919 (*Past Pursuits* 2006:3). While the records stretch across half a century, the bulk of the Summit County Infirmary's cemetery death certificates date between 1908 and 1916, so our record is skewed toward the later interments. Ohio law only started requiring statewide registration of deaths and death certificates in 1908, so many of the deaths prior to that date have no accompanying documentation.

## *The Documents*

The Infirmary dataset is entirely made up of death certificates. These death certificates represent individuals from the Infirmary who died and were interred in the Infirmary's unmarked cemetery and also indigent or unknown dead that the City of Akron sent to that location as an alternate potter's field. The example in figure 5-2 is a case of the latter. Little Neil Smith died of malnutrition (a particular condition of which is called marasmus) while in care at the Mary Day Nursery, a care facility for working-class children that later evolved to become Akron Children's Hospital. He was sent to the Infirmary for interment in an unmarked grave. The information contained in these forms is much more complete about causes of death, address, and sex of each individual. Appendix A describes all the known extant death certificates for the Summit County Infirmary.

Glendale Cemetery ledger books are available on microfilm in the Akron-Summit County Public Library's Special Collections. These ledgers contain handwritten entries that are sometimes illegible. When the name of the deceased is the illegible data field, it becomes impossible to find the corresponding death certificates in the Ohio Death Records Index. This introduced a level of error into our analysis and interpretation. Therefore, we focus most our comparative analysis to the data fields: age, diseases, sex, and "regional" origins or "nativity."

There are a total of 280 death certificates in our dataset for the Infirmary dating from 1908–1916. Comparative samples of individuals from Glendale Cemetery (2,626 death records) and Glendale's potter's field (222 death records) from the same year range were assembled. These three cemetery populations thus total 3,128 individuals (Table 5-1). Note

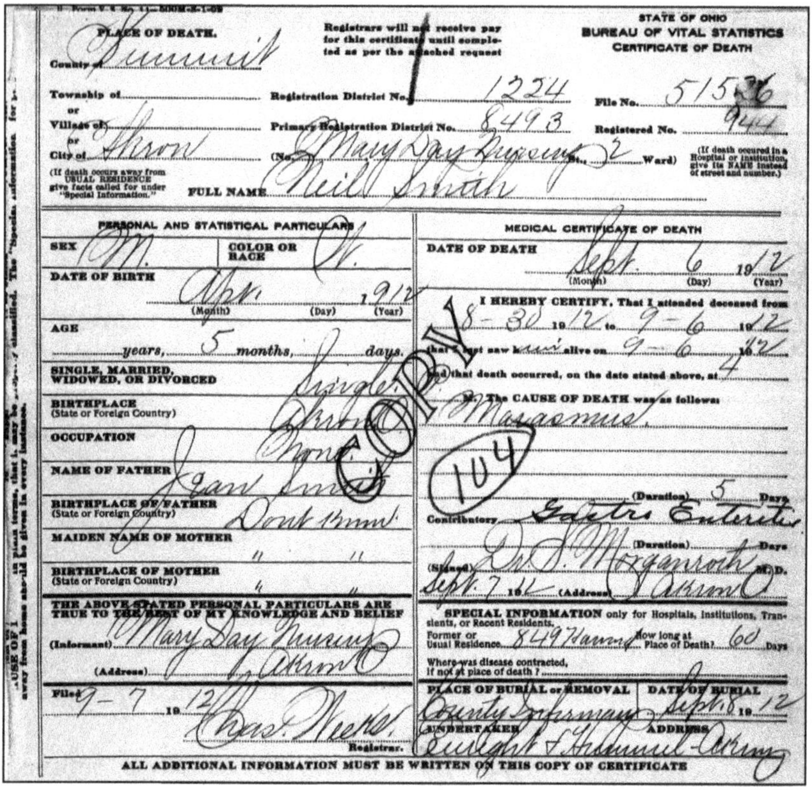

STATE OF OHIO
BUREAU OF VITAL STATISTICS
CERTIFICATE OF DEATH

Registrars will not receive pay for this certificate until completed as per the attached request

PLACE OF DEATH.
County of Summit
Township of
or
Village of
or
City of Akron
(If death occurs away from USUAL RESIDENCE give facts called for under "Special Information.")
Registration District No. 1224
Primary Registration District No. 8493
(No. Mary Day Nursery St., 2 Ward)
(If death occurred in a Hospital or Institution, give its NAME instead of street and number.)
File No. 51536
Registered No. 944
FULL NAME Neil Smith

PERSONAL AND STATISTICAL PARTICULARS

SEX M.
COLOR OR RACE W.
DATE OF BIRTH Apr. 1912 (Month) (Day) (Year)
AGE years, 5 months, days.
SINGLE, MARRIED, WIDOWED, OR DIVORCED Single.
BIRTHPLACE (State or Foreign Country) Akron
OCCUPATION None
NAME OF FATHER
BIRTHPLACE OF FATHER (State or Foreign Country) Dont know
MAIDEN NAME OF MOTHER " "
BIRTHPLACE OF MOTHER (State or Foreign Country) " "
THE ABOVE STATED PERSONAL PARTICULARS ARE TRUE TO THE BEST OF MY KNOWLEDGE AND BELIEF
(Informant) Mary Day Nursery
(Address) Akron
Filed 9-7 1912 Chas. Weeks Registrar.

MEDICAL CERTIFICATE OF DEATH

DATE OF DEATH Sept. 6 1912 (Month) (Day) (Year)
I HEREBY CERTIFY, That I attended deceased from 8-30 1912 to 9-6 1912
that I last saw h... alive on 9-6 1912
and that death occurred, on the date stated above, at 4
The CAUSE OF DEATH was as follows:
Marasmus.
(Duration) 5 Days
Contributory Gastro Enteritis
(Duration) Days
(Signed)
Sept. 7 1912 (Address) Akron
SPECIAL INFORMATION only for Hospitals, Institutions, Transients, or Recent Residents.
Former or Usual Residence 849 ... How long at Place of Death? 60 Days
Where was disease contracted, if not at place of death?
PLACE OF BURIAL or REMOVAL County Infirmary
DATE OF BURIAL Sept. 8 1912
UNDERTAKER
ADDRESS Akron
ALL ADDITIONAL INFORMATION MUST BE WRITTEN ON THIS COPY OF CERTIFICATE

COPY
104

Fig. 5-2. Schneider Park Death Certificate

that the Schneider Park numbers contain how many of each sex; this is because these data are from death certificates, where sex is denoted. The Glendale Cemetery and potter's field numbers are taken from the Cemetery Log Books, and do not reliably have sex listed.

| | Glendale Cemetery | Potter's Field | Infirmary Cemetery |
|---|---|---|---|
| Total n | 2626 | 222 | 280 |
| Adult n (≥18 yrs.) | 1874 | 24 | 218 |
| Subadult n (<18 yrs. ) | 715 | 189 | 58 |
| Female n | Unknown | Unknown | 53 |
| Male n | Unknown | Unknown | 227 |

Table 5-1. Number of burials included in this analysis (Table: Patricia Connolly)

While tallying the causes of death for both death certificates and the ledger book entries, we found many examples of nonstandardized or inconsistent medical terminology, as discussed above. A surprising range of medical terms were used to describe similar phenomena. Further variation and potential sources of errors were added when nonmedical professionals recorded the entries. To address this problem, we grouped the approximately 150 different named causes of death given in the death records and certificates into fifteen broad categories. Table 5-2 shows the categories we used, and the number of ailments subsumed within each category. For example, the category "heart" combines fifty-five different cardiac ailments together. Table 5-3 provides a listing of some of the ailments included in the category heart. A quick perusal of this table shows that some cardiac ailments are very specific, and easily recognizable (e.g., myocarditis, pericarditis, mitral insufficiency, aortic rupture), but others clearly are vague and lacking medical specificity (e.g., heart disease, heart trouble, heart clot, disease of the heart). As we sorted the individual ailments into the fifteen categories, we were careful that no ailment fit into more than one category, and we researched the ailment descriptions that did not align directly with current medical terms to ensure that we understood and correctly sorted those causes of death that relied on outdated medical terminology.

| Cause of Death Category | Number of Ailments included |
|---|---|
| Heart | 55 |
| Lung | 47 |
| Brain | 45 |
| Blood-related | 17 |
| Abdominal Viscera | 105 |
| Disease | 28 |
| Infant | 9 |
| Malnourishment | 4 |
| Infection | 15 |
| Trauma, nonspecific | 55 |
| Cancer | 46 |

| Cause of Death Category | Number of Ailments included |
|---|---|
| Bone-related, not trauma | 11 |
| Accidental | 23 |
| Suicide | 11 |
| Other | 72 |

Table 5-2. Causes of death (Table: Patricia Connolly)

| Category | Ailment Terms Included (not exhaustive list) |
|---|---|
| Heart | Paralysis of heart |
| | Myocarditis |
| | Heart failure |
| | Angina pectoris |
| | Arteriosclerosis |
| | Heart disease |
| | Endocarditis |
| | Cardiac embolism |
| | Cerbocarditis |
| | Malformation of the heart |
| | Mitral insufficiency |
| | Heart trouble |
| | Pericarditis |
| | Enlargement of the heart |
| | Disease of the heart |
| | Heart clot |
| | "probably endocarditis" |
| | Fabroid myocarditis |
| | Chronic heart disease |
| | Cardiac bolus |

| Category | Ailment Terms Included (not exhaustive list) |
|---|---|
|  | Organic disease of the heart |
|  | Trouble of heart |
|  | Rupture of aorta |
|  | Aortic and mitral regurgitation |

Table 5-3. "Heart" Cause of Death ailments (Table: Patricia Connolly)

There were some causes of death that did not easily align with our categories and were left to stand alone, e.g., alcoholism. Likely these difficulties were due to our inability to determine a modern name for the ailment, the lack of the specific ailment in searchable areas, potential misspellings of the ailments on the documents, or mis-transcribing them due to difficulty in reading the handwriting.

## *What We Expected to Find*

What did we expect the data to show regarding longevity and health? Research on other cemetery populations, poorhouses, and potter's fields (Grauer 2018, 2019; Grauer and McNamara 1995; Grauer et al. 1998; Murray and Perzigian 1995; Sutter 1995; Winchell et al. 1995) suggest there are several important aspects of life and death in early twentieth-century Akron that we can examine with these data. Starting with longevity and health, we have three populations. We hypothesized that, because individuals interred in the Infirmary cemetery and the potter's field had fewer resources, they will have suffered from more ailments, especially those that are associated with malnutrition, poor housing, and dangerous work environments and, subsequently they should have died younger than individuals interred at Glendale Cemetery. In other words, we expected to find a correlation between age of death and cemetery location, and also between cause of death and cemetery location. Further, we hypothesized that average age of death would be more similar between the cemetery and potter's field than either was to Glendale Cemetery. A complication arose when we considered that more children were likely to be represented in the potter's field population than in Glendale Cemetery or the

Infirmary cemetery, although for different reasons. The Infirmary at that point housed few children older than infants because the Ohio Board of State Charities had mandated the creation of Orphanages and Children's Homes specifically to remove them from the more general population in Infirmaries, thus we expected fewer children to be buried in the Infirmary cemetery. Meanwhile, the portion of the Akron population making use of the Glendale Cemetery was more likely to have higher quality of life, including access to preventive and supportive medical care, so we hypothesized that their children and young adults might be represented less in the Glendale Cemetery than in the potter's field. In other words, the same pattern (i.e., fewer buried infants) might be the result of different causes (the presence of orphanages or access to better health care).

When comparing the three populations in terms of health, we looked at causes of death. We hypothesized that dead interred in the potter's field and the Infirmary cemetery would more commonly have died from chronic illnesses and accidents related to "harshness" of their occupations. This is supported by other research into nineteenth-century poorhouses (e.g., Grauer et al. 1998). Following that logic, we thus expected more deaths related to aging or "lifestyle excess," such as overly rich diets and lack of sufficient physical exercise, among the Glendale Cemetery population, including more deaths related to heart disease. Finally, we hypothesized more lung-related causes of death among the Infirmary cemetery and potter's field populations because they were more likely to have been employed in, or lived near, sources of localized air pollution like factories and railroads. Air pollution is causally linked to lung damage during life (see Gotschi et al. 2008 for a review).

Finally, we turn to the issues of immigration and nationalities and their correlations with the three burial populations. Akron, like so many US cities, is defined by the successive waves of immigrants who became the "locals" to subsequent waves of newcomers. New Americans and new Akronites experienced various forms of marginalization as their newness or otherness set them apart in the minds of those settled before them. Larger and well-established immigrant groups have more power and can choose to either welcome or marginalize new arrivals. In competition for jobs, housing, and other resources, ties to ethnic and social groups played important roles in how immigrants integrated and survived in bustling turn-of-the-twentieth-century Akron.

Glendale Cemetery contains large monuments and mausoleums. There are burials of families across generations from original immigrants. The surnames of many who flourished in Akron's history are engraved in stone there. While the individuals interred in the potter's field section are unmarked and un-engraved, Glendale's ledger books reveal a great deal about their origins. Based on what we know broadly about the marginalization of newer immigrants and the challenges of gaining an economic foothold without language skills and social capital, we expected to find more recent immigrants in the potter's field and in the Infirmary cemetery than in Glendale Cemetery. Additionally, we hypothesized that the potter's field would contain more individuals who were born locally, either in Akron or in the surrounding region, than in the Infirmary cemetery because the Infirmary would have been a last resort and individuals who had any support at all would have remained near that support. Recent immigrants, especially those with languages different from the strong communities of dual language speakers in Akron, would have been more likely to take that last resort.

Finally, we expected that the marginalized population interred in the Infirmary cemetery would have a higher number of people missing names on their death certificates than either of the other two populations. This prediction follows from Olson's suggestion officials and medical professionals held dismissive and dehumanizing attitudes toward the inmates at the Infirmary, seeing them as unclean or diseased. Additionally, some people seeking treatment at the Infirmary, like people without medical insurance today, may have delayed seeking care, arrived sicker, and succumbed to their illnesses prior to staff obtaining full demographic records. Therefore, we predicted that a high number of people in the Infirmary dataset will have partial or missing names on their death certificates compared to the individuals buried at Glendale Cemetery or the potter's field.

## *Analysis: Testing Our Expectations*

In this section, we set out to examine the relationships between cemeteries, ages of death and causes of death. We describe the three populations using the ledger book and death certificate data, beginning with Arnett's findings from her 2018 undergraduate thesis in the Honors College at the University of Akron. Arnett focused on documented cause of death, age

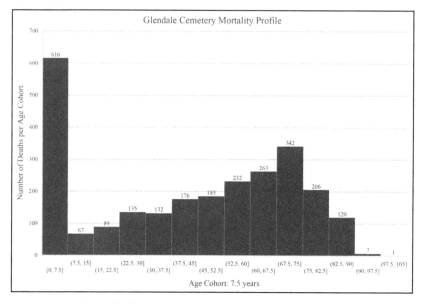

Fig. 5-3. Mortality Profile for the Glendale Cemetery (Chart: Patricia Connolly)

of death, and location of burial and found positive statistical relationships among these variables for each of the three populations. Her analyses support the argument that the Infirmary population generally lived in poorer health than either the Glendale Cemetery or potter's field population. The primary statistical results from Arnett's thesis set a stage allowing us to delve more deeply into the differences between the cemeteries, considering in subsequent sections the status, health and specific causes of death.

*Mortality Profiles*

Demographic patterns in human populations are typically examined through mortality profile analysis. Mortality profiles are used to show when people in different populations tend to die. These profiles allow us to examine if there are sex-related differences in life expectancies or if there are sex- and age-related deaths (e.g., Buikstra 1997; Chamberlain 2006; Yang and Land 2013; Discamps and Costamango 2015). Graphic comparisons will show if there are any spikes or dips in mortality at certain ages within the population. For example, historically and globally, many marginalized populations show high degrees of infant and childhood

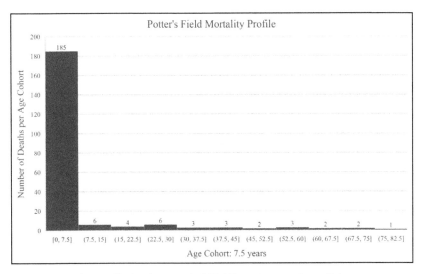

Fig. 5-4. Mortality Profile for the potter's field (Chart: Patricia Connolly)

mortality, then a drop off as individuals get older (Balk et al. 2004). When a society is stratified economically, mortality rates tend to be higher among infants and children from lower socio-economic households and communities (e.g., Gregorio et al. 1997; Mirowsky and Ross, 2000). Populations that demonstrate mortality spikes at middle age might be experiencing harsh work environments or war, especially if those dying at those ages are predominantly men.

In most demographic, paleodemographic, and bioarchaeological research, it is typical to divide a sample population's ages at death into five- or ten-year increments (age brackets or *cohorts*), demonstrating differences in young childhood, adolescent, teen, and adult life stages (Buikstra 1997). For the three cemeteries in this chapter, we used a consistent set of cohorts to construct our mortality profiles. These profiles are shown in figure 5-3, with the numbers at the top of the histogram columns showing how many individuals died in each cemetery by the age cohort.

The mortality profile for the Glendale Cemetery population shows a very typical pattern for the time period: high degrees of infant and childhood (0–7.5 years) mortality accounting for 24 percent of the total, then decreased mortality rates until later life with a peak in the 67.5–75 age cohort (13.3 percent of the total). Infant deaths alone account for 18

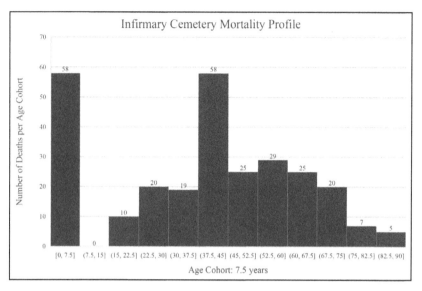

Fig. 5-5. Mortality Profile for the Infirmary cemetery (Chart: Patricia Connolly)

percent of the total sample in this population. Life table statistics indicate infant mortalities over 10 percent are normal for the time period (e.g., Loudon 1991), in line with our dataset for the Glendale Cemetery.

The mortality profile for the potter's field is shown in figure 5-4. This profile is striking for the high number of infants, accounting for 78 percent of the total interments in the sample. Overall, the youngest cohort (0–7.5 years) accounts for 85 percent of the total with surprisingly few older individuals represented.

The mortality profile from the Infirmary cemetery is shown in figure 5-5. This profile depicts a high degree of infant and childhood mortality (21 percent of the total burial), and another spike at 37.5–45 years of age (21 percent). The second spike graphically illustrates Arnett's (2018) statistical analysis that positively correlated low socio-economic status and dying at a younger age.

Collectively, these three mortality profiles show high degrees of infant and childhood mortality, an expected result for the time period, especially given the lack of childhood immunizations against deadly diseases. The Glendale Cemetery shows a more typical mortality profile for an early nineteenth-century population; both the potter's field and the Infirmary cemetery show patterns that differ from the expected norm.

Life expectancy in the United States between 1908 and 1916 averaged about fifty years (Smith and Bradshaw 2006). While the average life expectancies were in the low 50s for this time period, all three cemeteries had individuals who reached much older ages. Overall, the Infirmary population has a lower average age range at death (between 38–48 years), compared to the Glendale Cemetery population (excluding infants, between 60–70 years).

*Causes of Death*

The causes of death by population are shown in figure 5-6. This graph depicts the causes of death by cemetery by the percentages each one contributes to the total deaths examined in this chapter. As shown, the potter's field has an inordinately high degree of infants interred. There are more disease, trauma, accident and suicide as total percentage of cause of death in the Infirmary cemetery.

For ease of comparison, all three populations are shown on this plot. Raw count data were converted to percentages to allow side-by-side comparison of each category of causes of death. Examining the contributing causes of death by location is revealing. It is noteworthy that great discrepancies are not immediately apparent in many of the categories across the three sample populations. However, a statistical analysis of causes of death by population shows that there are associations between location of burial and cause of death (Kendall's Rank-order correlation, $p<0.04$). One of our original predictions was quickly eliminated; populations in the potter's field and Infirmary cemetery were not more like each other than either was to the population in Glendale Cemetery. The primary cause of death category for the potter's field was infant death, including stillborn and premature deaths. These account for over 50 percent of the interments in the potter's field. Neither the Glendale Cemetery nor the Infirmary cemetery had any single causes of death category over 17 percent. The main causes of death at the Glendale Cemetery were heart-, lung-, or brain-related or involved abdominal viscera-related issues. The main causes of death for the Infirmary were: heart-related, abdominal viscera, disease-related, accidental, and suicide. The overall profile of causes of death, when taking into account sample size differences show a higher degree of concordance between the Infirmary cemetery and the Glendale Cemetery, contrary to our expectations.

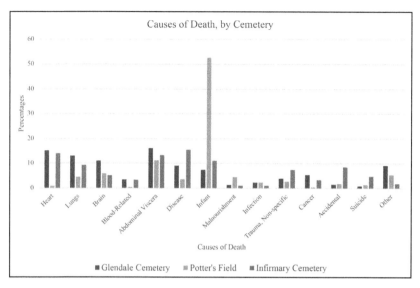

Fig. 5-6. Causes of death, by cemetery (Chart: Patricia Connolly)

We made specific predictions about differences in the causes of death in each cemetery, with arguments that the Glendale populations should show higher rates of heart-related issues than the Infirmary, and that Infirmary interments would show increased lung-related issues. To further examine this issue, we explored four specific categories of cause of death that showed interesting patterns: heart-related, lung-related, disease-related, and accident and suicide. Accidents and suicides are combined here as sudden deaths not necessarily related to degenerative conditions or disease. Each of these categories presents data pertinent to the socio-economic and health status of the people who were interred by the Infirmary. Figure 5-7 shows more clearly heart-, lung- and disease-related causes of death along with accidents and suicides in each cemetery. The numbers at the top of each column show the percentage that each cause of death category contributes to the overall deaths at each cemetery. As shown, the Glendale Cemetery and Infirmary cemetery have similar percentages for heart- and lung-related, but the Infirmary cemetery has higher percentages due to disease, accident and suicide. Those elevated percentages are predicted in marginalized populations. Figure 5-7 shows greater similarity between the Glendale Cemetery and the Infirmary

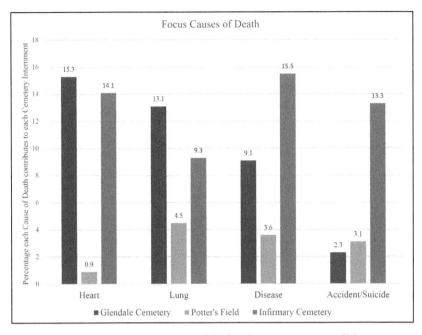

Fig. 5-7. Focused examination on causes of death (Chart: Patricia Connolly)

cemetery for both heart-related and lung-related causes of death. This does not fit with the prediction that these two causes of death would be associated differently with each population.

Could there be an age-related factor in the heart-related and lung-related deaths? Did the individuals interred at the Infirmary cemetery die at younger ages from same causes of death as people from Glendale Cemetery? Table 5-4 shows both the raw number of individuals in each age cohort and the percentage of deaths by age cohort. It also provides the average ages of death by burial location. Table 5-5 shows the average ages of death by cause of death category. There are a few interesting points. First, there does not appear to be much of a difference in heart-related average ages of death across the groups, so our initial prediction that more heart-related deaths would appear in the Glendale Cemetery data does not hold up. Likewise, the average age when individuals died of lung-related causes were similar between the Glendale Cemetery and the Infirmary cemetery.

| Age Cohort (years) | Glendale Cemetery % Deaths (n) | Potter's Field % Deaths (n) | Infirmary Cemetery % Deaths (n) |
|---|---|---|---|
| 0–7.5 | 24 (616) | 85 (185) | 21 (58) |
| 7.5–15 | 2.6 (67) | 2.8 (6) | 0 |
| 15–22.5 | 3.4 (89) | 1.8 (4) | 3.6 (10) |
| 22.5–30 | 5.2 (135) | 2.8 (6) | 7.2 (20) |
| 30–37.5 | 5.1 (132) | 1.4 (3) | 6.8 (19) |
| 37.5–45 | 6.8 (176) | 1.4 (3) | 21 (58) |
| 45–52.5 | 7.2 (185) | 0.9 (2) | 9 (25) |
| 52.5–60 | 9 (232) | 1.4 (3) | 10.5 (29) |
| 60–67.5 | 10.2 (263) | 0.9 (2) | 9 (25) |
| 67.5–75 | 13.3 (342) | 0.9 (2) | 7.2 (20) |
| 75–82.5 | 8 (206) | 0.4 (1) | 2.5 (7) |
| 82.5–90 | 4.6 (120) | 0 | 1.8 (5) |
| 90–97.5 | 0.2 (7) | 0 | 0 |
| 97.5–105 | 0.003 (1) | 0 | 0 |

Table 5-4. Mortality Percentages by Cemetery (Table: Patricia Connolly)

| Cause of Death | Glendale Cemetery | Potter's Field | Infirmary Cemetery |
|---|---|---|---|
| Heart | 60.6 | 56.5 | 57.3 |
| Lung | 44 | 6.8 | 47 |
| Disease | 35 | 12 | 39 |
| Accident/Suicide | 31/48 | 20/25.6 | 41.7/37 |

Table 5-5. Average ages of death for the focused categories: Heart, Lungs, Disease and Accident/Suicide by cemetery (Table: Patricia Connolly)

The two categories where differences are seen are the disease and the combined accident/suicide categories. The Infirmary population includes more people dying of diseases and accidents/suicides than either Glendale Cemetery or the potter's field. Looking just at Glendale Cemetery and the Infirmary cemetery, the average age of death from disease was similar (thirty-five years for Glendale; thirty-nine years for the Infirmary). The percentage of people dying of diseases differs significantly between these two groups (9 percent for Glendale; 15.5 percent for the Infirmary). This percentage of disparity reinforces the hypothesis that Infirmary inmates' health statuses were lower than typical Akron residents. This is good confirmation of research discussed at the beginning of this chapter that there is a positive correlation between socio-economic marginalization and poor health.

Accidents and suicides caused the deaths of a large percentage of people buried in the Infirmary cemetery, accounting for 13.3 percent of the total burial population there, but only 2.3 percent in Glendale Cemetery and 3.1 percent in the potter's field. While the two causes were lumped for earlier analyses, we divided them into accidents and suicides to consider these variables in relation to the age data (see Table 5-5). It is notable that there is an age discrepancy between the Glendale Cemetery and the Infirmary cemetery, for suicide in particular. Collectively, the ages of death for the "accident/suicide" category for all three populations was considerably lower than for any of the other causes of death (heart, lung or disease), as seen in figure 5-7. There was a single murder noted as an "assassination." The attending physician filling out this certificate speculated that the murder was carried out by the Italian Mafia.

People died at younger ages from accident or suicide than from heart, lung or disease-related causes in these cemeteries. The individuals succumbing to accidental deaths are younger in the Glendale Cemetery (31 years) than in Infirmary burials (41.7 years). The reverse is the case for the suicides. Infirmary suicides were younger (average 37 years) than those at Glendale Cemetery (average 48 years). Accidental deaths included being hit by trains, cars or trucks, drowning or falling off bridges, and electrocution. The largest single accidental death cause across these data was "hit by train," with some fairly graphic descriptions preserved in these records. Olson notes that a particularly dangerous railroad track was the line that ran through the heart of Akron, the C&P, which operated through Bluff Street until at least 1921 (G. M. Hopkins and Company 1921). Pedestrians crossing Bluff Street could not see trains coming around the sharp bend to the north. Bluff Street was closed to through-traffic sometime later, perhaps due to the high fatality rate at this crossing (Eric Olson, personal communication). Suicides occurred most often by gunshot, hanging, and some by "cutting." In the Infirmary records there were two suicides listed as "by train."

Are these accidental and suicide causes of death typical of marginalized populations? The repeated implication of the railroad is important. With little to no fencing or other security measures around tracks more individual might have been caught by the trains. The railroad was certainly a site for employment both for work loading and unloading trains and for track maintenance. In addition to hazards related to hitching a ride on a passing train, the tracks themselves likely provided a sort of road for foot traffic—raised, straight, relatively free of mud. They may have been an attractive, if hazardous, route of choice.

Accidental deaths could also be due to hazardous workplace environments. With the number of death records with "laborer" listed as employment from the Infirmary population, and the high degree of accidental deaths, it follows that some of these deaths were likely workplace related. Hofmann et al. (2017) reported that during the early 1900s between 18,000 and 23,000 workers per year in the US were dying from workplace injuries, an approximate rate of 37 deaths per 100,000 workers annually compared to a rate today of 4 deaths per 100,000 workers. Labor laws for safer workplaces were enacted in the mid- to late 1800s, but it was not until much later during the Progressive Era that worker compensation laws and unionization movements began to have real impact. And it took decades for some industries to become less hazardous (e.g., Fishback and Kantor 1998; Hofmann et al. 2017). Because we are only examining a short time frame with these records, we cannot say with any certainty if accidental deaths decreased over time.

When examining the suicides, the main difference between the populations is the younger average age in the Infirmary sample. All of these suicides were male. We do not have the sex for the Glendale Cemetery ledgers, but a rough tally based on likely sex based on first names suggests that Glendale also had all, or a preponderance of, men in the group who are listed as suicides. This sex difference is not surprising, and similar differences are found when examining relationships between suicide, homicide, and accidental deaths by sex during the twentieth century (Holinger and Klemen 1982). The conclusions drawn from these data present a stark reality; that the overall stress and harshness of life may have been too much for many marginalized men during the early 1900s in Akron.

*Infant Mortality*

The ubiquity of the use of "infant" as a cause of death in the potter's field records deserves further consideration. The total percentages of death records listing causes of death listed as infants is 7 percent from the Glendale Cemetery (n=188), 11 percent from the Infirmary cemetery (n=30), and 53 percent from the potter's field (n=117). There were two additional causes of death listed in the ledger books and death certificates that we subsumed into our "infant" category for analysis: "premature birth" and "still born." It is unclear what the actual discerning factor was between premature and stillborn in early nineteenth-century medical practice in Akron. Even in modern medical data, these categories do have some overlap: a stillborn baby can be premature.

Figure 5-8 depicts differences between the two main categories of infant mortality, stillborn and premature birth. As this graph depicts, both Glendale Cemetery and Potter's Field show similarities in percentages; however, there are more premature births from the Infirmary cemetery. This could be indicative of the degree of medical care provided to the mothers or other aspects of socio-economic stress in those individuals, contributing to higher rates of premature births.

While records are not available to tease apart potential correlations between maternal and infant mortality at the Infirmary, this question has been explored by Loudon (1991). The general assumption closely linking maternal and infant mortality and corresponding to socio-economic factors requires consideration of local context. For example, Loudon (1991) found that between 1900 and 1960 there were only slight correspondences between infant mortality and maternal mortality in the US, while other studies suggest links between socio-economic wealth and overall positive health outcomes in many contexts (Ensor et al. 2010). Relating those studies back to our data, it is likely that the Infirmary inmates were economically marginalized before arriving at the Infirmary. Based on what Loudon shares, they likely did not have consistent access to health care as adults and probably did not seek out prenatal care. It is reasonable, based on this information, to assume that the socio-economic

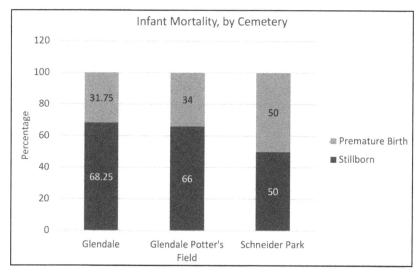

Fig. 5-8. Infant mortality, by cemetery (Chart: Patricia Connolly)

conditions enveloping people who eventually became inmates contributed to a higher percentage of premature births compared to non-inmate residents of Akron.

The next striking point is the sheer number of individuals listed with infant as cause of death buried in the potter's field. We expected that both the potter's field and Infirmary cemetery would have similar percentages of "infant" burials due to presumed similar marginalized socio-economic conditions, however, that is clearly not the case. The answer to the question of why there is such a difference in the potter's field and the Infirmary cemetery could lie in religious affiliations. Until recently, the Roman Catholic Church prohibited miscarried or stillborn babies to be buried in consecrated grounds because they were not baptized (Dinn 1990; Murphy 2008; Nash et al. 2015). Research shows that infants born prematurely or stillborn were buried without ceremony, their grave markers in "undesired" areas often referred to as the ground of the holy innocents, away from church graveyards, but close enough that they were not forgotten. Many but not all of these practices came to an end during the mid-twentieth century (Dinn 1990). One possible explanation for the high percentage of infants being buried at the potter's field is that contemporary religious practices did not permit premature or stillborn infant burials in consecrated grounds. If this is the case, then the infants are not necessarily all of the same socio-economic status as the adults buried in the potter's field, despite both being interred in the same plot of land.

*Recorded Names*

At the beginning of this chapter, we noted that limited use can be made of names on death certificates and other documents because names are not uniquely linked to a single sex. Here we make a simple point using the name data: while the name on a death certificate can be ambiguous, certificates with no names at all tell us something about the relationship of the individual to society. An individual's name is part of their identity. It provides information about family and, with some names, association with regional origins or even religious affiliations. So, what does it mean to have no name listed on death records? In our data, individuals interred in the Infirmary cemetery were more likely to have incomplete names (missing first names) or the notation "unknown" in the name field on the death certificate. One possible interpretation of this is that the staff filling out the form cared less for them as individuals and felt less compelled to record information that would help contact relations at the time of these deaths. Table 5-6 shows how many individuals have missing names in the cemetery records or death certificates. People interred in the Glendale Cemetery and potter's field were more likely to have full names (i.e., both a given and surname) in the ledger book, while those buried in the Infirmary cemetery were less likely to have first names listed on the death certificates and more likely to lack both first and last name (i.e., to be listed as unknown). This observation speaks broadly to the idea that those buried at the Infirmary were more "anonymous" than those buried elsewhere in Akron.

| Cemetery | Last Name (n) | No First Name (n) | No Last Name (n) |
|---|---|---|---|
| Glendale Cemetery | 99.8% (2616) | 0.003% (6) | 0.001% (4) |
| Potter's Field | 99% (219) | 0.013% (3) | 0 |
| Infirmary Cemetery | 88.5% (247) | 83% (233) | 11.4% (32) |

Table 5-6. Names on records (table: Patricia Connolly)

*Regional Origins*

Many of the individuals buried in the Infirmary cemetery were not born in Akron or in Ohio. A large percentage of immigrants were identified in the death certificate data as coming from Hungary, Austria, Ireland, and Italy. Olson has noted that longer-term inmates at the Infirmary were born in Austria, Belgium, England, France, Germany, Ireland, New York, Ohio, Scotland, and Virginia. Shorter-term inmates were born in Akron, Austria, France, Germany, Hungary, Ireland, North Carolina, Ohio, Pennsylvania, Serbia, Sweden, Switzerland, United States, and Virginia. Unclaimed individuals who were not infirmary inmates came from many of the above-mentioned locations, along with Finland, Italy, Poland, Romania, Russia, Slovenia, and South Africa (Eric Olson, personal communication).

Like Akron's population, ours is a country of immigrants. Across the many waves of people arriving in the US, those immigrants already here deemed some newcomers more desirable than others. During the mid- to late 1800s, the notably undesirable immigrants included those from Ireland and Eastern Europe (Mora et al. 2007). These anti-immigrant prejudices shifted over time as those groups acculturated and new groups arrived (Verea 2018). How undesirable immigrants are treated by existing populations is an underlying thread in the history, use, relocation, and ultimate forgetting of the Summit County Infirmary.

In the early nineteenth century, the population in Akron comprised people who had migrated from other states or from different areas of the world, and social bias against these immigrants by "natives" is well documented (e.g., Brown and Warner 1992; Mora et al. 2007; Siener 2008; Garand et al. 2015; Bohmelt et al. 2020). Chapter 3 argues that the initial founding of the Summit County Infirmary derived, in part, from these perceived biases. Immigrants were thought to carry diseases from which the local population must be protected. This was accomplished through strict quarantine practices that stigmatized and further disadvantaged the new arrivals. While it is beyond the scope of this chapter to discuss potential societal prejudices, we can examine the relationship between where individuals were born ("nativity" in ledger books) and the cemetery where they were interred. Were there more immigrants interred in the Infirmary cemetery than in the Glendale Cemetery and potter's field?

*Who Were They?*

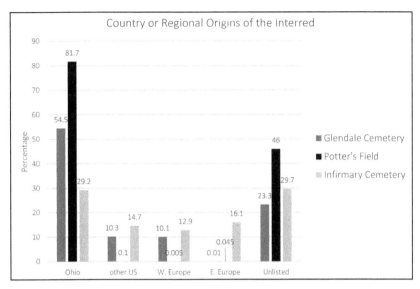

Fig. 5-9. Country or regional origin of the interred, by cemetery (Chart: Patricia Connolly)

As summarized in figure 5-9 and table 5-7, there appears to be a relationship between ethnic origin and burial location, although it is not as clear a correlation as we expected. Figure 5-9 depicts the places of origin listed in the cemetery records or death certificates, with the percentages at the top of each column showing the proportion of individuals from each region of origin. Most of the individuals buried in the Glendale Cemetery and potter's field were from Ohio, whereas the Infirmary cemetery burials contained more people from other areas of the US and more immigrants from both Western and Eastern Europe. While not shown on this figure, the Infirmary cemetery also has the only identified individual from Africa in these data. The diversity of the individuals buried in the Infirmary cemetery supports assertions that the immigrant community in Akron may have been more marginalized than the "local" people.

Table 5-7 lists both the country and region of origin for the individuals interred at each of the cemeteries. These data are given in percent of the total burials and the number of burials. The Infirmary cemetery includes a higher percentage of individuals who were from the US but outside of Ohio, as well as more individuals from both Eastern and Western Europe when compared to the Glendale Cemetery or the potter's field.

According to US Census records (US Bureau of the Census 1922), Akron had a "foreign-born white" population of 19.2 percent in 1910. Notably, 10.2 percent of the Glendale Cemetery interments were first-generation immigrants from Europe, while 29 percent of the Infirmary burials were first-generation immigrants. European-born immigrants were almost three times more likely to be buried in the Infirmary cemetery than in the Glendale Cemetery and potter's field.

| Country or Region | Glendale Cemetery (n) | Potter's Field (n) | Infirmary Cemetery (n) |
|---|---|---|---|
| Ohio | 54.5% (1430) | 81.7% (161) | 29.2% (73) |
| Other US | 10.3% (277) | 0.1% (2) | 14.7% (41) |
| Western Europe | 10.1% (266) | 0.005% (1) | 12.9% (36) |
| Eastern Europe | 0.01% (28) | 0.045% (9) | 16.1% (45) |
| Canada | 0.005% (14) | 0 | 0 |
| Middle East | 0.0007% (2) | 0 | 0 |
| Africa | 0 | 0 | 0.003% (1) |
| Unlisted | 23.3% (611) | 46% (233) | 29.7% (83) |

Table 5-7. Country or regional origin of the burials (table: Patricia Connolly)

## Conclusions

In a broader context, there are also many forgotten populations in cities outside of Akron, Ohio. Unlike the forgotten burials in what is now Schneider Park, many of these other individuals ended up in skeletal collections in museums both in the US (e.g., the Terry Collection at the National Museum of Natural History at the Smithsonian Institution, the Haman-Todd Collection at the Cleveland Museum of Natural History, the Mutter Collection at the Mutter Museum), and elsewhere in the world (see Grauer 2019 and references therein). These skeletal collections are comprised of people whose remains were not claimed. Instead of being interred in potter's fields, they ended up in museums, skeletonized and used for research purposes. Anecdotal information about US skeletal collections shows similarities to the Infirmary inmates at death and how they were perceived and treated by physicians in their time.

As an example, the Terry Collection is derived from medical school dissecting room cadavers from St. Louis, Missouri (Hunt 2017). Medical records of these individuals show tuberculosis as a common cause of death, something also found in the Infirmary population. Examination of the skeletal pathologies of the Terry Collection shows not only individuals with diagnosed or recorded tuberculosis at the time of death with the cause of death listed as pathological tuberculosis, but also individuals whose causes of death were not attributed to tuberculosis or lung-related disease, but whose physical remains show skeletal pathologies (rib lesions) of tuberculosis (Roberts et al. 1994, 1998). This difference in listed causes of death and evidence from skeletally determined pathological disease could indicate differential care given to individuals whose skeletons end up in these kinds of collections. In other words, these individuals are the demographically "unseen" from larger cities, laborers whose jobs are integral to the functioning and growth of societies, but whose appearances are rarely noted in the cities themselves. Numerous publications analyzing museum (i.e., dissecting room) samples show this pattern: marginalized people in society, lacking or with reduced access to good health care, end up sickened from diseases that are treatable or potentially misdiagnosed as a result of medical biases against certain populations. Bias results in differential treatment.

◇◇◇◇◇◇◇◇

Analyses conducted for this chapter indicate that both age of death and cause of death are factors related to where a resident of Akron was buried. Contrary to our original hypotheses, the cemetery that shows the greatest difference from the other two for mortality profiles and causes of death is the potter's field. Causes of death were distributed more similarly between the Glendale Cemetery and the Infirmary cemetery. Individuals interred in the Infirmary plot generally died at younger ages, with disease and accidents comprising a higher overall percentage of deaths than the Glendale Cemetery or the potter's field. The Infirmary burials also contained a higher percentage of premature births within the "infant" death category than the other two cemeteries. Additionally, the individuals interred at the Infirmary were more likely to be foreign-born immigrants to the Akron community. Collectively, our results are concordant with other analyses of poor houses and potter's fields during this time frame.

The differences between the Glendale Cemetery and Infirmary cemetery could potentially be attributed to a longer life expectancy for people of higher socio-economic status than those of a lower socio-economic status (Mirowsky and Ross 2000; Gregorio et al. 1997). However, it is likely more complicated than just money or "lower positions in social hierarchy" (Gregorio et al. 1997:1472). Multiple analyses have examined the interactions between social and material discrepancies, unhealthy living conditions, and workplace hazards (e.g., Gregorio et al. 1997, and references within). All of these factors are likely contributors to the increased mortality rates at younger ages in the Infirmary cemetery population. Their residential locations likely had increased pollutants, leading to decreased air quality. This was one reason why we hypothesized increased deaths due to pulmonary ailments in this population. Likewise, historical data and death certificates record more employment as "laborer" for the Infirmary burials compared to the Glendale Cemetery and the potter's field. Traditionally, manual labor jobs are considered harsher for the worker than other types of employment and lead to increases in mortality rates among those holding such jobs (e.g., Sorlie et al. 1995, Gregorio et al. 1997).

The confounding factor for correlating workplace harshness with longevity is childhood health status. Studies have shown that low birthweights, malnutrition, and generalized socio-economic stress at young ages ultimately lead to lower life expectancies and increased morbidity and mortality at later stages in life (e.g., Hart et al. 1997, and references therein). In examining the overall health status of the people buried in the Infirmary cemetery, as estimated by only death certificate data, it is very difficult to ascertain a single causative factor that resulted in the mortality profiles. It is very likely that a multitude of factors individually contributed to that profile: socio-economic stress at younger ages, a marginalized adult population that gained employment differentially as laborers, and potentially a lack of medical care. All of these factors have been shown to contribute to increased mortality at younger ages in other contexts (e.g., Gregorio et al. 1997; Hart et al. 1998).

Hahn et al. (2002) surveyed funeral directors in the mid-1990s regarding the ways they acquired and recorded information on death certificates. Anecdotal answers to some of Hahn et al.'s survey questions about death certificate data demonstrate that "ethnicity" or "race" was still occasionally *assigned by the funeral director* based on examination of the body and effects. Given that such practices still occurred in the 1990s in the United States, it seems highly likely that similar guesses at regional origins were prevalent during the early 1900s and greatly influenced by biases among the individual filling out the forms. Chapter 3 recounts at least one documented case at the Summit County Infirmary that illustrates this bias. Death records of three infants of Eastern European descent, the Kleten triplets, were among the Infirmary death certificates. The triplets died within days of each other, but the physician filling out the forms assigned them to two different countries of origin.

Perhaps the main factor to consider is employment; during times of urban industrial expansion in the US, employers hired immigrants to do much of the needed manual labor (Chang and Fishkin 2019; Dearinger 2016). In many places, immigrants were differentially hired into jobs that native-born people were unlikely to take, and with these jobs came marginalizing conditions like low wages, limited access to health care, and other factors contributing to overall health problems among these workers and their families (McCarrier et al., 2011; Weinick et al. 2005).

These differences in causes of death between each of the cemeteries correlates with health status and socio-economic status of the individuals interred. The Glendale Cemetery is most directly associated with the wealthier families of Akron, and the Infirmary with the least. This supports the original prediction that the overall health status of individuals buried in different cemeteries is reflective of socio-economic stratification and that the presumed lower income or status individuals suffered more health problems and died younger than the individuals of the more affluent socio-economic levels. This chapter demonstrates that carefully delving into cemetery records can provide insight and pictures of past populations.

## Chapter 6
# Reframing Akron History
*Carolyn Behrman*

This chapter extends the historical context of the Infirmary, tracing events and ideas that influenced the understanding of marginalization and variations of experience among Akronites from the closing of the Summit County Infirmary in 1919 to present-day Schneider Park. Despite its length, this section necessarily makes some broad generalizations. An interested reader will find a wealth of literature to explore, a sampling of which is referenced here. The wide-angle context for this chapter is national and international, highlighting ideas embedded in Progressivism and the Eugenics Movement. These ideas both framed and filtered the ways Americans in general, and Akronites specifically, thought about marginalized, "unemployable," and indigent people. In the light of social and cultural history, the people whose voices were strongest in the historical record—civic leaders who were largely white, male, and native English-speakers—framed what was considered central and what was peripheral, as well as whose voices and perspectives were privileged in the weaving of social memory. Ideas like progressivism and eugenics filtered the view and offered terms, variables, and explanations to help people understand why their own location in the shared story had different significance and different potential outcomes from other people's.

The experience of Black Akronites in the mid-nineteenth century and early twentieth century is considered in detail below. Black Americans participated in broad American culture in that era but also built guarded or sheltered economic, political, and social institutions, protecting themselves to a degree from effects of race-based structural and individual violence. This was certainly the case in Akron. Looking at a wealth of information from other scholars and historical documents, including the 308 death certificates, I offer a few thoughts on the relationship between Akron's vibrant Black community and the Summit County Infirmary. That section of the chapter is followed by a short history of disability rights as a movement that continues to evolve in the US. My disabilities discussion serves as a bridge to the book's final chapter, a description of creative work by members of the community who seek to shift the social memory of Schneider Park.

## *From Better Babies to Eugenic Engineering*

The late nineteenth and early twentieth centuries were times of dramatic change in American life. Industrialization, begun in the early 1800s, roared after the end of the Civil War. The "growth in productivity, in output, and in wealth was unprecedented in human history" (Bernstein and Leonard 2009:178). Swelling economic possibility and prosperity across the nation accompanied intertwining currents of activity. Workers, with or without their families, migrated for better employment; for many this involved leaving the farm for the city. City limits bulged and expanded; new buildings and houses were constructed. Research and development in existing industries increased, while what today we would call *start-ups* pitched their ideas to venture capitalists. New forms of collaboration sprang up among powerful people in government, business, and a range of scientific fields, necessitating new thinking about both opportunities and government regulations. There was a flowering in arts, music, and entertainment from lavish amusement parks to ragtime and then jazz joints, to splendidly appointed art museums. This period saw significant attention to social infrastructure from innovative public school systems to earnest civic dialogues on the quality of social safety nets.

◇◇◇◇◇◇◇

An expanding sense of what is possible often leads people to consider how an innovation in one space might be usefully repurposed in another. This applies not only to physical technology (like the mill wheel's function using river water to turn gears that grind grain being reimagined with the addition of the steam engine, to propel boats in a river) but also for systems of thought. Lakoff and Johnson's work (2003) shows that new ideas are more persuasive when they echo or mirror things already understood to be valid. Another way of saying that is that we humans find a sort of soothing intellectual harmony when a set of relationships we believe to be true in one context is repurposed into another. The repeated logical pattern encourages us to trust the validity of the analogy. A very simple example of this is linguistic. We often associate the concept of "up" with positivity and "down" with negativity, as when we say, "I am feeling up today" or "It was a downer." We make an additional positive relationship between up/good and "more" and their reverse, down/bad and "less." Therefore, we are comfortable with these grouped notions repurposed to, say, the logic of school grades. Higher is better, and together they mean a larger number. In a math class, students reasonably expect test grades to be calculated from some specified number of points, with a score of 100 percent being the best and 0 percent being the worst possible outcome. It would be jarring for students if a teacher announced that a perfect grade on an exam was 0 percent. Even if she explained her logic, saying that the zero represents the absence of error points—the absence of unacceptable work—the students would struggle with this reversal. It would feel like an upending of the natural way of thinking about grades. The students, and the rest of us, are comfortable with the repurposing of the up/good/more analogy to the arena of school evaluation. This repurposing can fuel incredible innovation and scientific advancement. As you will see below, however, the same process of being comfortable with a repurposed analogy can be used to promote deeply troubling ideas, including those that emerged regarding human diversity during the Progressive Era and ultimately filtered through to the treatment of inmates at the Infirmary.

One thread in the evolution of these troubling ideas starts in New England. The earliest record of an agricultural county fair in the US dates to 1807 in Massachusetts, long before the founding of the Infirmary. The practice of annual fairs became widespread by the mid-1800s (Mastromarino 2002) as a way for farmers and other agricultural experts to share information on improving farm yields of both crops and livestock. Businesses selling farm materials, educational institutions interested in both the science of agriculture and public health, county officials whose communities depended on the economic success of family farms, and the producer-families themselves all shared aligned interests. Of course, long predating US county fairs, there were harvest festivals in agricultural communities around the world. They operated for similar reasons and included competitions with prizes for the best examples of husbandry and craft (Mastromarino 2002:170). These competitions were added in Massachusetts and subsequently to county fairs around the country. A system of judging and prizes arose that ranged from excellence in the nurturing of capacious pigs to perfection in the production of pies and quilts. County fairs spread and grew, becoming important opportunities for others, including government and health officials, to connect and share information directly with rural residents.

In 1911, two health officers tasked with promoting infant and child health through nutrition education, Mary T. Watts and Dr. Florence Sherbon, were at an Iowa county fair. They did their work under the banner of Better Babies competitions. This program promoted health education by getting mothers to bring their babies in for examinations and infant care-focused interviews designed to share best practices drawn from the latest science of nurturing with mothers. During these interviews, parents of especially healthy infants and toddlers were encouraged to enter their children into competitions. There they were judged on a set of criteria that would not surprise any of the farmers displaying their livestock. There was a focus on physical qualities indicating healthy development. These competitions enjoyed great popularity at fairs and were seen as excellent point-of-contact educational tools by state public health officials (Selden 2005).

Watts and Sherbon related this story in several different ways over the years, but one version of it is that while on a break from their work at the fair, they overheard a farmer comment that he thought it was good to be so publicly focused on raising healthy infants. However, he went on to suggest that attention also ought to be on the bigger picture: successful breeding over generations takes into account parentage and other family members' qualities. Whether this story is true or not, Watts and Sherbon's work placed them in the mainstream of a civic dialogue focused on public welfare and how to manage unproductive members of society. The broader discussion was known as the American Eugenics Movement, led by many highly educated health and legal professionals. The primary goal of the movement was to develop ways to measure and then control human heritable traits. Selective breeding seemed like a good way to increase positive qualities and eliminate negative ones. The focus was primarily on white people, specifically the management and safeguarding of what they imagined as a distinct, discrete, white gene pool (Selden 2005).

Watts and Sherbon were ready to accept the farmer's notion of repurposing animal breeding concepts to humans. The transposition of this way of thinking from farm to human social engineering was already part of eugenics discourse at its highest levels, and Charles Davenport, a preeminent eugenicist and director of the Eugenics Records Office (ERO) in Cold Spring Harbor, New York, actively communicated with Watts and Sherbon. With his support, they developed Fitter Family for Future Firesides contests. These contests encouraged families to consider their genealogies as pedigrees, keeping track of both good and bad traits and thinking in terms of their own and family members' relative worth as human specimens and their fitness to reproduce (Selden 2005).

It does not come as a surprise that the competition format of Fitter Families encouraged people to think comparatively, judging others as well as themselves. This repurposing of animal breeding strategies coincided with a sentiment beginning to take hold in rural America. There was a growing sense of nostalgia tinged with anxiety in the countryside over rural population loss. Farming communities were experiencing a deterioration in their identity as descendants and representatives of frontier and heartland family values. The evident trend of people leaving the family farms for urban, industrial work—along with the visible allures offered by urban life from newspapers, books, and cinema screens—reinforced the concern (Lovett 2007).

It took Watts and Sherbon nearly ten years to develop and launch Fitter Families as research strategies and data collection forms were negotiated with Davenport. By 1920, when they were ready, there had already been a number of developments in the American Eugenics Movement. The ERO was thriving. Efforts to focus white America on the science of breeding for greater human flourishing (positive eugenics) were increasingly overshadowed by articulated concerns about procreation that promulgated undesirable traits in the "race" (negative eugenics). Animal breeders knew how to gradually breed out undesirable traits in livestock (e.g., aggressive behavior, susceptibility to disease). Eugenicists repurposed that approach and began studying and describing undesirable traits in humans so they could be identified for elimination from our shared gene pool. Believers in eugenics saw comforting logic in the repurposed animal-breeding analogy. Here we can clearly see one of the Eugenics Movement's most troubling ideas rise to visibility. Moving beyond the physical traits alone, they linked physical impairments in bodily form and function to mental ones, and either or both of those to criminality and "moral degeneracy" in humans (e.g., Carlson 2001; Black 2012).

These poorly developed ideas took hold in the public imagination; pseudoscientific eugenics displays usually appeared alongside the Fitter Families contests at fairs. Eugenicists developed categories of unfitness or degeneracy, with hierarchical terms to sort people, such as the series "idiot," "imbecile," and "moron" to distinguish people in the "feeble-minded" category. As public discourse on eugenics advanced beyond the county fair and into civic dialogue, people biased against lower-income and non-English speaking immigrants began insisting that some of these undesirable traits were overrepresented in the genes of these subpopulations.

In the early 1900s, the ERO and eugenicist lawyers were at work creating a model eugenic sterilization law. The template for these laws sought to establish that select authorities at the state level could mandate forced sterilization of individuals deemed unfit to procreate. The first such law passed in Indiana in 1907, and eventually thirty-seven states adopted their own versions. Ohio legislators made five failed attempts to pass legislation between 1915 and 1963. The closest Ohio legislators came to passing a eugenic sterilization law was in 1925, when it passed the State House but was vetoed at the governor's desk. The last attempt, in 1963, took place when most states with such laws had stopped the practice of sterilization in state-run institutions (Paul 1968).

Less obvious, but still present, in mainstream public discourse was another ominous element of eugenics movement ideology, namely the idea that non-white people were irrelevant except as potential sources of

Fig. 6-1. Poster illustrating the perceived connection between mental disability and "vice, crime, and pauperism." (Courtesy of the Ohio History Connection)

contamination of the white stock. Practices such as involuntary sterilization were applied to women of all races over time with devastating impacts for Native American (Lawrence 2000), Latina (Novak et al. 2018), and Black women (Washington 2007). Parallel European movements were underway and shared information with the ERO and the American Eugenics Society. German eugenicists relied heavily on these idea exchanges. Some of the ideas developed in the US would eventually form the foundation of the

Nazi party's platform regarding the genocide of physically and mentally disabled people (Black 2012). Eugenic thinking when applied to white populations in the US was framed in terms of improving the "race." When applied to non-white people, negative eugenic practices served as forms of social control but without the implication that there was some core stock that was valued and needed to be preserved and improved. The American Eugenics Movement claimed its tools were intended to eliminate undesirable "biological" traits, but faulty repurposing of ideas meant that they targeted social statuses including poverty, ethnicity, and culture in the US. A few years later the Nazis would add being Roma, gay, or Jewish to the mix.

Sensational activity on the part of some eugenicists stirred up debate both for and against their ideas and helped spread their messages more widely. One example of this sensational activity unfolded in 1915. A Chicago physician, Harry Haiselden, refused to operate on an infant with a physical deformity, instead allowing him to die. He explained to the press that the little boy's survival would involve a life-long physical impairment, which Haiselden felt would likely be accompanied by intellectual and moral degeneracy. A furious public debate followed. Haiselden was acquitted of any wrongdoing in court but lost his license to practice medicine. His actions were condemned by the likes of Jane Addams and G. K. Chesterton and praised by others, including Clarence Darrow and Helen Keller. Haiselden went on to produce and perform in a feature-length film, *The Black Stork*, which taught eugenic lessons through a dramatic cautionary tale. This film toured the country for many years across the time Watts and Sherbon's work on Fitter Families was expanding. Haiselden's film boldly asked viewers: "Are you Fit to Marry?" Watts and Sherbon's stated goals were:

> to "stimulate" the "interest of intelligent families" and arouse a "family consciousness by which each family will conceive of itself as a genetic unit with a definite obligation to study its heredity and build up its health status. (Lovett 2007:35)

What one sees from county fairs to cinema houses across the nation, is a slide from a public health focus on better babies through hygiene and nutrition and a nascent understanding of the role of genes in heritable health conditions to a focus on supposedly heritable traits like criminality

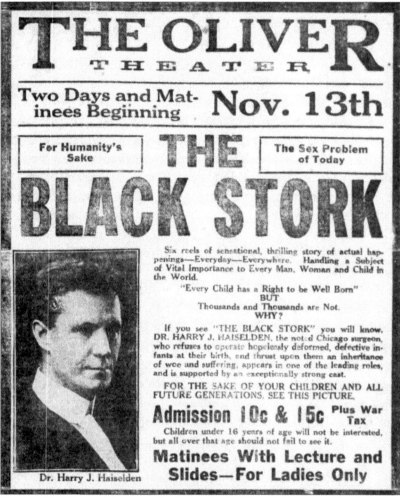

Fig. 6-2. Advertisement for a eugenics lecture by Dr. Harry J. Haiselden. (*South Bend News-Times*, November 9, 1917, Hoosier State Chronicles, Indiana State Library)

and upstanding moral character. The goal of eliminating undesirable heritable traits and an effort to breed humans toward superior traits would eventually be called "race hygiene."

◇◇◇◇◇◇◇

More soberly, economists, captains of industry, and legislators were focusing on maintaining a strong workforce to sustain their own prosperity. Their efforts included defining and supporting employable workers while sidelining the "unemployable" with appropriate home-based, institutional, or social service supports. The unfolding framework of their thinking laid emphasis on the potential for productivity and saw dependency as a drain on society. The eugenicists among these strategists advocated for reliance on institutions like infirmaries for support of inmates, but they also saw them as a potential means to ensure the separation of the unfit from productive society. Webb and Webb defined the unemployable as:

> ...children, the aged, and the child-bearing women, the sick and the crippled, the idiots and lunatics, the epileptic, the blind and the deaf and dumb, the criminals and the incorrigibly idle, and all who are actually "morally deficient".... and [those] incapable of steady or continuous application, or who are so deficient in strength, speed, or skill that they are incapable...of producing their maintenance at any occupation whatsoever. (Webb and Webb 1920, cited in Bernstein and Leonard 2009)

Across the 1920s and 1930s, as houses rose and streets were bricked and paved around Schneider Park, eugenic ideas continued to impact lives across the country. Sterilization bills made their way through state houses, and a strategic challenge took the practice to the Supreme Court. The *Buck v. Bell* decision in 1927 confirmed the right of states to sterilize people identified as feeble-minded. It was in this case that Oliver Wendell Holmes penned his famously damning line "...three generations of imbeciles are enough." The evolving Progressive Era and intertwined Eugenics Movement began before and continued beyond the life of the Summit County Infirmary. We see their influence on the shaping of it as an institution as well as the community into which it emerged. During and after the institution's lifetime, we can trace the impact of the culture, politics, and economics of wildly blooming capitalism as well as malformed notions of humans with their combined power to judge, elevate, marginalize, memorialize, and erase citizens.

## A Focus on Black Akron

The broad public engagement with ideas about what it meant to be human and to contribute to society described above took place at the same time as two particularly large migrations to urban areas. These ideas and the migrations directly affected Akron. The first migration, touched on at several points already in this book, stemmed from industrialization.

In chapter 2, Olson discusses the economic and social impact of Irish and other immigrants arriving to work on the Ohio and Erie Canal starting in 1825. Industrialization, beginning in the 1820s, is credited with a profound transformation of US cities, including a shift from approximately 6 percent urban residence in 1820 to 40 percent by 1900. Chapter 5 describes the work options for immigrants, particularly non-English speaking Europeans coming to Akron, which tended to be physically demanding and low wage.

The second migration, known as the Great Migration, was stimulated by the Civil War and Reconstruction periods. The Great Migration comprised primarily Black Americans moving from the South to industrial centers in the US Northeast, northern Midwest, and West. It took place from roughly 1910 to 1940, with a second wave following World War II and continuing into the 1970s. Prior to the Great Migration, Akron had a small but steady number of Black residents, hovering around 1 percent of the overall population (US Census data for Akron reported in McClain 1975). Just as there was economic and social flourishing for many U.S.-born whites and, notably, German-born immigrants in Akron during the time that the Infirmary burials took place, there were also successes in education, health care, arts and culture, politics, business, and industry for Black Akronites.

McClain (1975) lays a foundation for understanding the mindset of Black people who settled in Akron in the early and mid-1800s by describing the colonization and antislavery movements as they related to Akronites. She paints a picture of persistence, self-respect, goodwill, and sturdiness in the face of repeated challenges. McClain's meticulous dissertation is well worth reading, but these are some of her key points. Addressing the original Black settlers in Akron, she notes they were subject to oppressive, if not always enforced, Black Laws, one of which required them to register themselves and their children and acquire documents attesting to their free status, often at significant cost. These laws were repealed just as the Fugitive Slave Act of 1850 came into effect, giving people little relief. McClain's data indicate that those who settled in Akron had occupations such as laborer, blacksmith, sailor, boatman, and barber.

By the 1850s, Black residents of the area had created civic organizations and convened broad gatherings. One example was the Summit and Medina Counties Convention of the People of Color in 1859, which considered the merits of proposals that free Black Americans become colonists in West Africa or Central America. Individuals and Black civic groups in Akron wrote letters, held meetings, hosted speakers, and engaged in a wide range of actions on antislavery, Black colonization, women's rights, temperance, peace, and other reform movements across the middle of the nineteenth century. Akron was the site of the famous oration from Sojourner Truth but also quietly sheltered active abolitionists while regular citizens lived in fear of being kidnapped and conveyed south by putative slavecatchers. During this time, Akron made history with its innovative public school plan that became the model Akron School Law of 1847. The model of a centralized school system with neighborhood elementary schools feeding spoke-and-hub style into upper schools was a model that spread nationally. However, the 1847 law expressly excluded Black children from that public education in Akron. The State of Ohio amended this to allow for separate public schools for Black children in 1849 (Knapp 2009).

From the 1860s to the 1890s, as the Summit County Infirmary was being built and the Ohio Board of State Charities (OBSC) was regulating the development of its services, Black Akronites, like white Akronites, were founding churches, establishing social clubs and political societies, and expanding their range of employment. Thus, Akron was a destination for Black Americans during the peak of the Great Migration starting in 1910 in part because there was already a small but well-established Black community present. The population of Black Akronites was 525 people in 1900. It increased from 657 to 5,580 people between 1910 and 1920, or from 1 percent of residents to 2.6 percent, according to the US Census. This percentage would nearly double again by 1930. However, Akron also had its drawbacks for Black migrants. Despite burgeoning employment opportunities in the hot industrial marketplace, Black workers were confined to only the lowest-paid positions which involved grueling physical labor and exposure to lung-clogging particulates and toxins. Making Akron even less desirable, it was rapidly becoming the seat of what would be the largest chapter of the Ku Klux Klan in the US. By 1925, the Akron-area chapter boasted an astounding 52,000 members (Maples 1974:2).

Leon Gordie asserts in the opening to his 1922 *Akron Negro Year Book*:

> We have acquired personal property, church property, some land—and bank accounts; we are succeeding in profitable enterprises which require great skill and executive ability to direct and control, namely. Grocers, bakers, barbers, caterers, hotelkeepers, undertakers, builders, contractors, printers, decorators, tailors, insurance agents, real estate agents, millers, druggists, lawyers, doctors and poets, and the majority of the people do not know it, and as a consequence, those who are doing these great things are not receiving at the hands of the public, that respectful recognition to which their advancements entitle them. This Negro Year Book is endeavoring to enlighten the public on these vital industrial developments and to show our industry, thrift and economy which are everywhere in evidence. (Gordie 1922:1)

Gordie's Year Book includes profiles of important community members along with information about organizations, businesses, and houses of worship. The volume's intended readership included Black Akronites but also members of the non-Black community. As he indicates, the contents "embrace respectability in an effort to reverse negative racial stereotypes." It also offers a view into Black feminism of the period. Mrs. W. E. Mayo writes in her essay *Women of the Hour*:

> One of the outstanding facts as a result of this great World War is that woman has found her economic independence. She has become a separate factor in civilized life with individual ideals of her own.
> ...For many, many years society has suffered a great loss because a large number of women of magnificent mental endowment, who were equipped by nature for service in various lines of endeavor, have been suppressed and forced into doing other things which they were not born to. But this great new-woman movement has cut loose these shackles which bound her and feminine leaders, organizers, captains and generals are rapidly becoming created throughout the world into a vast unified army of progress which will make their movement irresistible.... She is beginning to think for herself, and thinking is bringing to her freedom."

She then offers up a long recitation of impressive, entrepreneurial Black women's work-lives and organizations in the City, for example, "Mrs. Mary Upperman, whom you cannot meet without feeling the atmosphere of courage and authority that radiates from her. She is sole owner and manager of one of the largest grocery stores among our people in Akron. Along with this she conducts an Employment Bureau, a hand laundry and a large rooming house." (Mayo *in* Gordie 1922:3–21)

The main reason for sharing this information from Gordie, McClain, and others is to sketch at least a little of what Black Akron residents built while also dealing with racism's challenges. But it is also noteworthy that Mayo emphasized participatory citizenship *proved through industry*. This is in keeping with Progressivism; successful Black and white Akronites, and Americans in general, found this vision compelling. While the optimism of Progressivism was shared, the two groups differed in their relationship to the ideas underpinning the Eugenics Movement. White eugenicists deployed both positive and negative approaches (protecting and refining whiteness through selective breeding and legislated serialization) while Black leadership, when it approached the subject, emphasized nurturing positive qualities and celebrating successes that challenged racist stereotypes rather than seeking to eliminate the reproductive potential of those with undesirable traits. Du Bois and many other leading Black intellectuals fiercely opposed the core concepts of a racialized worldview and the *biological determinism* of eugenics, calling out scientific racism. But Black communities also held better babies-style competitions, and the NAACP journal *The Crisis* printed hundreds of babies' portraits starting in the 1920s specifically to subvert notions of inferiority. This positive eugenic emphasis does not contradict the underlying principle that expressed heritable traits—phenotypes—are attached to inherent worth in specific ways (Lombardo 2011).

## *Race, Gender, and Social Service*

This section focuses on how Ohio's charitable and social service institutional system evolved with attention to Akron within that systemic growth. The system functioned from the start to manage and remove people deemed undesirable from mainstream view. Two other attributes of identity—being non-white and female—also carried lower status in society, and this chapter will consider the intersection of race and gender as it relates to social services like the Infirmary. The death certificate data from the Infirmary cemetery will be examined again with this intersection in mind. Finally, the chapter will close with a discussion of disability rights as they evolved from people's experiences with federal and state institutional systems.

*Institutionalization: the Ohio Board of State Charities*

Poor farms existed across the Ohio landscape in the eighteenth and nineteenth centuries. These farms, owned by counties, towns, or individuals, housed elderly or disabled people without other means of support. Public or charitable funds, raised locally, along with the paupers' own labor supported these residential arrangements, which were essentially unregulated and of vastly varying quality. In Ohio, as elsewhere, across the mid and late 1800s, a concerted effort unfolded at the state level to bring these elements of a rudimentary social safety net under an umbrella of regulation and management. Initially, the state created Infirmaries that housed anyone without other support—the chronically ill, the elderly, physically, emotionally, or intellectually challenged, wayward boys and girls, the insane, unwed mothers, orphans, and so on. Gradually, the State of Ohio began creating a system of care through organizing, regulating, and creating new facilities. As this process unfolded, subpopulations in this system of care were separated into specialized settings such as children's homes, industrial schools, reform schools, homes for unwed mothers, and institutions for the feeble-minded (intellectually impaired and neuro-atypical people). The Summit County Infirmary entered the picture before this separation, at the start of this evolving state management of a social safety net when the Ohio Board of State Charities (OBSC) was formed.

The OBSC's first director, A. G. Byers, personally inspected the Akron facility three years after its founding, when its new building was completed in 1868. As you read his description of the facility, consider how he thinks of the Infirmary as charity—serving people as dependents vs. social service—serving people to increase their capacity. Also note the lumping of intellectual, physical, and disease-related incapacities.

> The buildings are new, display foreign architectural taste, are commodious, well arranged, and in very many respects, comfortable and attractive. Unfortunately, in securing fine architectural effect in the external appearance of the building, the comfort of the interior is greatly lessened. The insane department is a rear projection from the building, and is, in

fact, a part of the whole rather than separate from it. This connection of the two departments, while it adds nothing to the convenience of either, materially affects the comfort of both. There were quite a number of filthy insane, idiotic and epileptic inmates. Those occupying the apartment for the insane rendered it (imperfectly situated as it is) quite offensive, and the relation of the two apartments is such that when the doors are open a draft is created by which the offensive air of one is unavoidably drawn into the other. At the time of my visit, in the latter part of August, the effluvia generated in the insane department pervaded the entire building, rendering it quite disagreeable. Here there is no room for reflection upon the management.

There was a manifest disposition to do everything possible to render the Infirmary a comfortable if not really a pleasant place. That there had been a mistake in the construction of the building was fully realized, and determination to remedy the defect as soon as possible was expressed.

There were an unusually large number of very filthy inmates, and, under the impression that it was best, several of them were kept outside of the building in rude board pens, a board partition separating the sexes.

In one of these was an insane man whose hip and knee joints were entirely anchylosed (a kind of inflammatory arthritis). He was entirely naked and performed locomotion by sliding about on his posterior with the aid of his hands. This man was once—so said—an intelligent and ingenious machinist and draftsman, but beyond this tradition his history, save what his appearance reveals, has been entirely lost. In the other pen were four females: one a miserable driveling idiot, eating its own filth; and the other three insane. They were also all of them entirely naked, and their condition was indescribably pitiable. Since my visit there, a letter from W. Cunningham Esquire of Akron, one of the directors who accompanied me, and whose interest in the institution, as well as his gentlemanly courtesy, entitle him to honorable mention, informs me that they had subsequent to my visit clothed all of the insane. (OBSC Bulletin, 1868:55)

Two years later, nearly every county in Ohio had an infirmary—many replacing poor farms. Each facility reported to the OBSC (later to become the Ohio State Board of Charities and Corrections). At this point, in 1870, Byers again inspected and reported on Summit County's Infirmary in Akron. Here he recounts a terrible event at the facility and is at pains to confirm the Infirmary management's lack of culpability. Consider how his words and those from the newspaper account he shares reflect notions of charity, social service, organization, class, and gender.

> The Infirmary of Summit County, is among the better class of institutions of its kind. There was a wise and humane care manifest in its management. The Superintendent and matron are intelligent and seemingly quite attentive, surely acquiring important experience in the discharge of their duties. William M Cunningham Esquire of Akron is among the more experienced and efficient directors of Infirmaries to be found in the State.
>
> Here too during the year, another of those dreadful tragedies occurred so common among the irresponsible classes of our infirmaries not, however, in this instance, as appears, from any want of attention or care upon the part of the management, as will be seen from the following statement published by the directors of the Infirmary in the Summit Beacon [newspaper].
>
> *Infirmary tragedy—a statement from the directors.—the directors of the Summit County Infirmary, in view of the late homicide, committed at said Infirmary, deem the following statement to the public, right and proper:*
>
> *Ellen Boyd has been an inmate of the Infirmary for quite a number of years, and is perhaps, hopelessly insane. She has never been considered dangerous, nor has she ever before this occasion, with one slight exception, attempted violence upon any of the inmates.*
>
> *Her confinement in her cell, most of the time, has been to keep her from running away, for it has been her practice, ever since she has been at the Infirmary, to make her escape from there whenever she could.*
>
> *Not unfrequently, before being so confined, would she escape and go into the city and hire out to do housework, She would do well for a week or two, or until she would get some whiskey. Then she became furious, and would be taken to the jail and from thence to the Infirmary again.*
>
> *During all the time she has been at the Infirmary, she has been in the habit of doing her own washing, and frequently doing other work besides, only requiring watchfulness to keep her from running away.*
>
> *The Infirmary has a hired man, in addition to the Superintendent, whose sole business it is to look after and take care of the insane of the institution, and of their apartments. This man was at his post of duty when this tragedy occurred.*

> As usual, in the case of Ellen, a fire had been made and water prepared, and everything ready for her washing, at the place in the backyard, and within perhaps two rods of the door of the hall leading to her cell. Ellen went to work at her washing as usual, and nothing unusual in her conduct or temper was observed. Mr. Polly, the hired man, concluded while she was engaged with her washing, he would change her bed, and for that purpose started with it to the barn, to fill it with fresh straw, leaving the back door of the hall leading to her cell, open.
>
> The Superintendent, Mr. GW Glines, was in the office, and was so situated where he could have his eye upon Ellen at the wash-tub. Soon, he noticed her start suddenly and pick up an old axe, and go in the direction of her cell. He, thinking that while the hired man was away with her bed, she intended to go into the cell and break up her bedstead, dropped his writing and made all possible haste through the house and into the hall of the insane department, at the opposite end from where Ellen had entered.
>
> He arrived within, not to exceed 3 minutes, from the time he saw her take the ax. Yet Ellen, in that time, had entered the hall, drawn her victim from the door of her cell, inflicted 3 blows on the head, and made her escape out, and was washing the blood off the axe, as Mr. Glines saw her through one of the hall windows. He immediately ordered Ellen into her cell, she readily complied. The wounded Mrs. Lyons was immediately cared for, and everything done which medical skill and kind care could do. But the wound was fatal.
>
> Had Ellen ever before attempted any violence of the kind, there would have been no excuse, and blame might have attached to the officers of the institution; but from the fact that it was her first attempt, and also from the fact that she has been allowed to be out of the cell every few days since she has been here there, and to do her washing and other work in the Infirmary, and being in the habit of mingling with other inmates while so out; never having before made any demonstration of the kind, there was no reason to expect or look for anything of this kind, and hence no blame can attach to the officers of the institution.

The story is a dramatic one, but in its telling, the narrative conveys a sense of the workings of the Infirmary—coordination among staff and their interactions with residents; residents' own work and social activities, as well as their engagement with the outside world in terms of employment and with the legal system.

Over the sixty-five years of *Bulletins* reviewed for this chapter, we can see the development of a strong set of beneficent institutions overseen by smart, well-informed, and well-organized leadership. Across those years, prose accounts like Byers' give way to more short reports, spreadsheets, and lists of bureaucrats' and inspectors' names. The spreadsheets have columns for—among other things—reporting inmate data. Gender was a data field from the start, and Summit County reported roughly a 4:1 or 5:1 male-to-female gender ratio in most years. In the 1890s, a column was added for race, but the Summit County Infirmary never reported in that column. The quotes above highlight male and female inmates and male management and staff, but there were female staff members at infirmaries, including a head matron at each institution.

We can see a little more about gender by looking at the people who worked within the system. Institutions shared the names of the people working with and for them reprinted in OBSC's *Bulletins*. These roles were points of pride, and many prominent white Akron family names are visible here (see fig. 6-3), including Marie and Oscar Olin, the latter of whom gave his name to the building housing the Anthropology Department at the University of Akron.

Ohio's system of institutions supporting people in need adapted each year based on new information from its facilities and new medical and social science. Reading through the reports in these *Bulletins* one is impressed with the varied voices of the superintendents and matrons. They share experiences, professional recommendations, and organizational innovations. In doing so, their goodwill, balanced generosity and efficiency, and shared sense of mission to alleviate suffering are evident.

However, these *Bulletins*' references to eugenic ideas steadily increase and develop greater specificity regarding action. Along with an emphasis on the desire to mitigate suffering, the *Bulletins* began to address ways to actively prevent hereditary causes of unfitness or unemployability. From its inception, alert to the disparate needs of their subpopulations, OBSC had been systematically creating separate facilities for children, people with epilepsy, and people considered to be lunatics or insane. In 1896, Ernest Percy Bicknell, a newspaper reporter from Indiana recently appointed to that state's Board of Charities, shared his report, "Feeble-mindedness as an Inheritance," using information he compiled

## 92 OHIO BULLETIN

Nina Dressler................................Akron
Grace C. Fendner...........................Akron
Dr. E. B. Foltz...............................Akron
   Member State Commission for Relief
         of Needy Blind
Mrs. A. K. Fouser...........................Akron
        County Visitor
Julius Frank..................................Akron
      County Commissioner
J. C. Goodwin................................Akron
Roscoe Graham..............................Akron
C. Elise Houriet..............................Akron
J. A. Hulse....................................Akron
Mrs. J. A. Hulse..............................Akron
L. M. Kauffman.............................Clinton
      County Commissioner
Kate Kendig...................................Akron
M. Ella Kilmer................................Akron
Walter F. Kirn................................Akron
J. M. Kleckner...............................Akron
   Assistant Director of Public Charities
R. F. Koplin..................................Akron
   Superintendent County Infirmary
Mrs. R. F. Koplin...........................Akron
   Matron Summit County Infirmary
Russell H. Kurtz.............................Akron
Amy Larned..................................Akron
Sarah S. Lyon................................Akron
O. E. Lytle....................................Akron
     Judge Juvenile Court
Mrs. C. F. Meese.............................Akron
L. J. Michel...................................Akron
Mrs. W. W. Milar............................Akron
Robert E. Myers.............................Akron
  Assistant Superintendent County Infirmary
Kathryn L. Newbauer.......................Akron
Ethel Niermeyer..............................Akron
Marie E. Olin.................................Akron
Orear E. Clin.................................Akron
   Professor Economics and Philosophy,
        Buchtel College
Ira A. Priest..................................Akron
Bessie Quine..................................Akron
A. Ross Read.................................Akron
     State Representative
Rev. J. O. Reagle.............................Akron
Mrs. H. A. Robinson........................Akron
   Secretary Home and School League
Mrs. F. W. Rockwell.........................Akron
Rev. H. J. Rohrbaugh........................Akron
Mrs. O. L. Sadler.............................Akron
F. D. Saunders...............................Akron
   Superintendent Children's Home
Mrs. F. D. Saunders.........................Akron
    Matron Children's Home
Nellie C. Saunders...........................Akron
   Visiting Agent, Children's Home
Mrs. C. W. Sieberling........................Akron
E. W. Simon..................................Akron
Nora Sippy...................................Akron
T. A. Steele........................Cuyahoga Falls
    County Commissioner
Rose K. Steinmetz............................Akron
   Superintendent Children's Hospital

Mss. A. W. Sillito............................Akron
Anna Tier.....................................Akron
Florence T. Waite............................Akron
  Assistant Secretary Charity Organization
         Society
Anna Wear....................................Akron
Mary Williams................................Akron
Mrs. J. S. Wilson.............................Akron
Percy H. Wilson..............................Akron
Adjutant A. Winter..........................Akron
    Volunteers of America
Mrs. A. Winter...............................Akron
  Matron Girls Home Volunteers of America
Edith Wise....................................Akron
Mrs. J. B. Wright.............................Akron
Margaret S. Wright..........................Akron

     TRUMBULL COUNTY
C. A. Root...................................Warren
   Superintendent County Infirmary

    TUSCARAWAS COUNTY
G. W. Kelley...........................Canal Dover
   Superintendent Children's Home
Mrs. G. W. Kelley......................Canal Dover
    Matron Children's Home
Apollo Opes........................New Philadelphia
   President Social Service Union
Mrs. Apollo Opes..................New Philadelphia
      County Visitor
W. H. Stoutt..........................Uhrichsville
    Trustee Children's Home
Mrs. F. H. Waldron...................Canal Dover
      County Visitor
F. M. Wills........................New Philadelphia
      County Visitor
Mrs. F. M. Wills..................New Philadelphia
   Matron County Infirmary
Mrs. Harry Winch.................New Philadelphia
   Secretary Social Service Union

      UNION COUNTY
Mrs. Mate L. Braun.....................Marysville
      County Visitor
R. A. Linn..............................Marysville
   Superintendent County Infirmary
Mrs. R. A. Linn.........................Marysville
   Matron County Infirmary
Mrs. Luella A. White....................Marysville
      County Visitor

    VAN WERT COUNTY
D. P. Dunathan..........................Van Wert
      County Visitor
Edmund G. McGavren....................Van Wert
      County Visitor
John Stevens.............................Van Wert
   Superintendent County Infirmary
Mrs. John Stevens........................Van Wert
   Matron County Infirmary

      VINTON CONTY
N. C. Darst.............................McArthur
    Trustee Children's Home

Fig. 6-3. Akron delegates to the Ohio Board of State Charities, 1914 (*Ohio Board of State Charities Bulletin* 1914:92)

from data collected at facilities around Indiana. His failure to consider variations in the ways others had gathered the data he compiled, including how methods for classifying people varied across the many organizations that gathered the data, his own hit-or-miss research methods, and his lack of background in education, psychology, or health care made his findings exceptionally dubious. Bicknell asserted that 80 percent of the offspring of feeble-minded adults were also mentally deficient. He also reported that women were 12 percent more likely than men to inherit degenerate traits. The number-rich report seemed reasoned and scientific. It recommended isolation of people variously termed unproductive, degenerate, unfit, or defective for at least the duration of their reproductive lives. Because it was reprinted in the annual *Bulletin* of the OBSC, this report made it into the offices of every social service professional and shaped OBSC actions going forward (OBSC *Bulletin* 1896:63–68).

Ideas about human diversity and human worth in the US continued to evolve into the new century. Rhetoric in the *Bulletins* became more insistent in its focus on heredity and the prevention of future "degeneracy." The terms "unfit" and "unemployable" accompanied emphases on race and protecting racial integrity by preventing genetic degeneracy. An example echoing much from the dominant discourse on eugenics comes from the annual address of Starr Cadwallader, the president of the Ohio Board of State Charities and Corrections. In his speech, printed in their 1916 *Bulletin*, he focused on the perennial challenge for the social servant of serving both the individual in need and also the greater good; however, this meditation is threaded with references to that dominant discourse.

> The goal of the race lies not in the ruthless exaltation of a super-man, but in the evolution of a super-mankind. (Cadwallader in OBSC *Bulletin*, 1916:6)

He explains that this:

> means the improvement, if possible, of the character of life, at least the preservation of that which has proven good in our own country, and the perpetuation of what we call our race. To attain these ends we endeavor to care for the weak and the defective, to protect society from the anti-social, to extend means of living to the many in order that all and not only the few may have the opportunity to develop intellect and

in character up to the limits of their ability. (Cadwallader in OBSC *Bulletin*, 1916:6)

"Man's intelligence" he continues:

> has always been in revolt against nature's crude methods. Civilization cares for the unfit. But never has civilization gone far enough to make it impossible for the unfit to reproduce their kind. The successful efforts to improve the conditions of life make necessary the effort to improve the quality of life. To what end are such strenuous efforts made to save the lives of babies, if it be practically certain that they are destined to lives weakened by disease, hampered by defect, worn out by underpaid labor and blighted by poverty without hope. (8)
> ... The state up to this time, like the private agency, views social service first of all as the care of the unfit. The organization of the Board of Administration marks an advance in that the prevention of dependency, delinquency, and defectiveness, is recognized as of equal importance with the feeding and clothing of state wards. (Cadwallader in OBSC *Bulletin*, 1916:9)

Returning to the larger societal perspective as he closed his speech, Cadwallader said, social servants':

> ... interest in humankind must be combined with sufficient knowledge to bring the social point of view to the solution of industrial, educational and social problems as well as helping in individual cases. In other words, social service is not to be undertaken lightly, nor pursued unintelligently; for upon it may rest not only individual welfare but also community development and possibly the integrity of the race. (10)

Regarding gender, as president, Cadwallader also shared the board's thoughts on the distribution of available funds for institutional care.

> The board is of the opinion that the state should eventually provide accommodations for all those who need institutional care. This cannot be done at once, and, in the meantime it urges the provision be made for the most dangerous classes, which are:
> First, girls or women of childbearing age who are almost certain to reproduce their kind or to become prostitutes;
> Second boys and young men who develop harmful traits either of delinquency or dependency (10).

The *Bulletins* also shared professional women's views—in the form of reports and advice columns. Mrs. Fannie McDonald, Matron at the Clinton County Infirmary, shared her thoughts in the Section for Infirmary Matrons. She begins by recognizing gender inequality.

> It has been said that "This is a man's world." Whether this be true or not, we will have to admit that there is a strong leaning that way in a county infirmary. (OBSC 1916:92–93)

She goes on to describe some of her adult female inmates in terms of their economic and marital trials, physical challenges, and small pleasures. Her report is kind and cheerful. She encourages her fellow matrons to do the best with what they have under the gender constraints that keep women inmates confined more than their male counterparts. However, she also uses phrases such as "you all know the type" to sum up her description of one woman's hygiene and "so many of them are just like children" when talking about the group's behavior.

The effect of this orientation was to focus on making people comfortable at best and not to reintegrate them into society. This is visible from the top of the OBSC, down through the ranks, and across the system of facilities of which the Summit County Infirmary was a part. The important care work continued, but the system also continued sectioning off and creating facilities for subsegments of the unfit. At the time of its closure, the Summit County Infirmary cared primarily for elderly indigent people, long-term or permanently physically disabled indigent adults, people with a range of mental health challenges that did not rise to a diagnosis of insanity, and people considered "feeble-minded." "Outdoor Relief" was the term used for carry-away supplies and financial support for the not-quite-indigent. It was assumed that people who came for these resources were self-housed and employable but did not have access to work that was sufficient to meet household needs. Outdoor Relief ballooned as a proportion of Ohio counties' social services budgets across the 1910s. It seems reasonable to think that all Akronites facing hard times would have wanted to stay away from the Infirmary's beds, conferring as they would the stigmas of unfitness or unemployability. These terms suggested permanent rather than reversible statuses even if the mental or physical health challenges arose from temporary situations like work exhaustion and the lack of safe and sanitary housing of World War I's wartime economy, or the unemployment and underemployment stresses of the postwar depression. Continuing to trace the intersection of race and gender across this time and place, I turn now to consider what we can know about the white and Black women from our sample of death certificates for the Infirmary cemetery.

## Race and Gender in the Infirmary's Cemetery

In chapters 2 and 5, Olson, and Connelly and Arnett, describe the countries of origin, causes of death, and age distribution of the inmates from the Infirmary and the unclaimed corpses from the city morgue whose death certificates are in the Infirmary cemetery dataset (compiled by Michael Elliott of the Akron-Summit County Public Library, see Appendix A). Again, these represent burials in the eight-year period from 1908–1916. We chose to focus on these 308 not because they were the only evidence of burials—there is another set from preceding years, but they contain less information and are less comparable because of the way deaths and burials were recorded before 1908 in Ohio (Elliott, personal communication). Burials in the cemetery ended in 1916 when plans emerged to move the Infirmary from West Akron.

The 308 are a subset of the actual number of burials the park has held. That total number is unknown. In chapter 4, we learned that geophysical survey or subsurface mapping of the park in 2016 identified 328 burials in one subsection—roughly 10–15 percent. The 308 recorded certificates do not necessarily match any of the 328 from the geophysical survey. Can we *estimate* the total that could have been buried there? The site was in use as a poor farm in the early and mid-1800s, but we do not know for certain that the poor farm used this site for burials (although it is extremely likely). Using the conservative start date of the founding of the Infirmary in 1865, there is a fifty-one-year stretch (1865–1916). If an average of 308 burials occurred every eight years, that would be approximately 1,964 people.

These death certificates contained fields for recording a person's "color or race" as well as gender. This table (6-1) contains a breakdown of those data by race and gender.

| Specified Race | Specified Gender | Number |
|---|---|---|
| White | Male | 209 |
| White | Female | 54 |
| Black or Colored | Male | 13 |
| Black or Colored | Female | 2 |
| unidentified | Male | 27 |
| unidentified | Female | 2 |
| Total | | 308 |

Table 6-1. Race and gender distribution in death certificates from the Infirmary (Table by C. Behrman)

So the reader can get a sense of both the people and what the data offer, below is a small sample of what the full death certificates report for a few individuals.

> Eliza Kilbourn, a White woman born in Ohio, was at the Infirmary for 23 years and died of apoplexy with arterio sclerosis as an underlying cause at age 87 in 1909.

> Isaac Dunlop, a Black man born in Virginia and barber, was at the Infirmary for a year before dying in 1910 of chronic valvular disease of the heart—probably aortic stenosis.

> Martin Sherman, a White man born in Germany, was at the Infirmary 8 years and died of pneumonia in 1910 at the age of 55.

> 3 White babies, all girls, died in the winter of 1915–16, two of pneumonia and one of cholera.

Approximately 5 percent of the certificates in this dataset are identified as Black people. That is roughly double the representation of Black people in the overall population of Akron across this time period (Gordie 1922). Only two Black female deaths were recorded, both as perinatal deaths with age at death listed as "0," so there is an overrepresentation of Black men in this sample and possibly no Black women. I say *possibly* because there are two women for whom racial identity is missing. Their names are Eliza Richards and Netta Martindale. A search of publicly available records brought up a Netta Martindale from northeast Ohio whose parents, Luther and Annette, are both listed as white in the 1870 census and Netta's age aligns with the death certificate. This is likely the same person. Eliza Richards has proved elusive thus far. It is a common name and ancestry searches found a fairly large number of people named Elizabeth or Eliza Richards born around 1857 who resided in Ohio at some point—a White Lake Ojibwa woman, a woman married to a cabinet maker with two children whose parents were born in England, and so on. For now, Eliza Richards remains an ambiguous figure regarding the intersection of race and gender in these data while we consider the absence of other Black women. It seems like there is a limited set of possibilities to explain this and an interesting set of potential explanations. If there were Black women inmates at the Infirmary or women who were buried by the city in the Infirmary cemetery if they died destitute, maybe no Black woman happened to die between 1908 and 1916. Or maybe someone was at the Infirmary but died and was buried elsewhere. Or their death certificate was lost. Or Eliza Richards was Black, and this sample size is very small by chance.

If Black women were not in the Infirmary as inmates or were not buried by the city in that cemetery, that also could be by chance. It may have been that systems of support outside the county and state institutions protected Black women from needing to access their resources. It may have been that ideas about support, service, and charity in this small community of Black residents shielded women in particular from the sometimes tolerant, but more often inhospitable civic arena. There were concerns of free African societies in Newport, Rhode Island, Philadelphia, and Boston as early as 1770 to ensure proper burial of their dead. "Given the difficult and uncertain conditions of their lives, free blacks' concern for proper burial was a means of seeking some degree of dignity, security, and remembrance—if only in the form of a respectable place to be buried" (McHenry 2002:47).

But how can the mismatch between Black men and Black women in the data be explained? It may be that few Black men or women from Akron's core community used these social services. If that is the case, the Black men in our sample might be less connected to that core—more recent migrants or outsiders of some other sort. It is also important to consider that work options for the least abled-bodied men may have been less available for Black men than for non-Black men. The overrepresentation of Black men in the cemetery (~6 percent of men in the sample compared to 2.6 for the general population) may be associated with the dangers of the lower-status work in the rubber industry available to Black men. This included not just physical strain but also the toxic environment of raw or crude rubber production (Nelson 1988:54). White and Black men in the Infirmary cemetery data died for similar reasons: work-related accidents, other accidents, illnesses including tuberculosis, homicide, and suicide. They undertook similar work when active; most of the men represented among the Infirmary death certificates had once been laborers of some sort, a few had trades. Some were married, most were single, and a few widowed. It seems worthwhile to consider further Akron's long-standing Black community, paying attention now to how it interfaced with local social services and how it approached the less fortunate among its numbers.

*Akron after the War*

Before World War I, Akron's industrial output rose, and for the last decade of the 1800s and the first decade of the 1900s, labor recruiters from Akron were active in the US South. Over one hundred years earlier, as the structure of the Republic was built following the American Revolution, free Black people were isolated, guaranteeing their exclusion. There were concerted efforts to organize within free Black communities through mechanisms like mutual aid societies and, somewhat later, literary societies (McHenry 2002:42). Just before and during the First World War, demand for rubber in the form of tires among other rubber products boomed. The city's population swelled, housing was scarce, and sewers and refuse disposal could not keep up. The city's population swelled, housing was scarce, and sewers and refuse disposal could not keep up. Boarding houses' sheets never cooled since the men slept in three eight-hour shifts per day, quipped Cleveland businessman and writer, Don Knowlton in 1926 (in Johnson 2006). After the war, unsurprisingly, industrial production and particularly tires for military use, fell off; Akron's rubber production fell to a dramatic 20 percent of its wartime output (Blackford and Kerr 1996).

Thousands lost employment in the industry (Johnson 2006). At the same time, the working population was decreased by morbidity and mortality losses due to the influenza epidemic of 1918–1920.

Concerns about drifters, loiterers, crime, and unsafe living conditions that had arisen during the boom years lingered during the postwar depression of 1920. The racism evident in Akron by the huge presence of the KKK led to racially divided relief efforts for the newly unemployed. This is evident, for example, in the news that prominent Black lawyer, George W. Thompson, who had been working on programming for Black residents with the Young Men's Christian Association (YMCA), transferred to the Charity Organization Society to oversee relief efforts for the Black portion of the population in need (Sulik 2020; Gordie 1922). The Infirmary, now located in Munroe Falls, is rarely mentioned in the newspapers and other public-facing documents of the period. This relative silence seems to imply that its services were unobjectionable and accepted but also set aside. There is no evidence yet that the public saw these inmates, or their care, as requiring engagement. The challenges of the postwar era in Akron in the 1920s appear to have pushed the drift of the Infirmary's population to the outer edges of social consciousness.

With attention focused on relief for the able-bodied unemployed, both white and Black, George W. Thompson was in the thick of it. Here, in the third person, he describes the public-private partnership, Charitable Organization Society, that recruited him. Then he comments on his longer-term vision and goals on behalf of the Black community as he returns to the YMCA.

> Early in 1920...the community began to feel acutely the effect of a general depression.... As an emergency measure, the secretary of the Y was transferred to the Charitable Organization Society, that he might develop and administer relief to colored people. This work continued from January 11th to June 1st, at which time the secretary, turned the work back to the COS and made recommendations concerning the permanency of this type of service. The work is now being continued along lines of those recommendations.
>
> Under the leadership of the board of managers, the Y is carrying out a non-equipment program, utilizing the school buildings and many of the churches. Night classes for adults—a community course in home

economics, recreational and athletic activities are being promoted. In addition to the above the organization conducts room registration and free employment bureaus. For the past three years all cases of juvenile delinquency affecting colored children, and many of those pertaining to ruptured domestic relations, have been managed.

This branch of the YMCA stands for positive amicable relations between the white and colored groups, and is working to bring about the greatest development of Christian character in our youth. (Gordie 1922:11)

W. S. Bixby, the white General Secretary of the Charitable Organization Society also described Thompson's work in his article *Out of Work in Akron* for an academic journal. The article touted The Akron Plan as a model response to the postwar depression. The Plan involved seventeen members of the Better Akron Federation of business and community organizations. They each pooled 40 percent of their budgets and directed that wealth toward relief efforts in an innovative public-private collaboration. The effort had three prongs: loans to homeowners, a reemployment scheme for working men, and relief support for the Black community. Here he describes the last of these.

With regard to the colored group: in 1910 Akron had a colored population of 667. In the early part of 1920 there was an estimated colored population of 10,000. During the winter months some 3000 left the city. Of the 7000 remaining approximately 18% have been dependent upon charity and of this number 90% are illiterate....

The large increase in applications [for relief] led to the establishment of two branch offices in outlying districts, the loan office above referred to and an office for the colored people. Among the social workers... was a college trained colored man of even temper and good judgment who had seen service with the YMCA, in France during the war, and who had been placed in charge of the Akron colored department of the Akron YMCA. To this man was given the responsibility of supervising the charity office for colored people and also the authority to select helpers from his own race. He engaged the staff of eight workers 4 men and 4 women. They have made a remarkable demonstration of how well the colored worker can care for their own people, of how up to date they can keep their office records, including dictation, and of how economically they can use appropriated funds. (Bixby 1921:88)

Fig. 6-4. Photograph of Leon Gordie from the *Akron Negro Year Book*, 1922

Bixby goes on to explain that the Salvation Army and Y were both essential to the success of Thompson's work and that homeless men were housed, sick men cared for, and families offered relief "according to the usual family social work methods." He noted that a "colored physician and dentist who had the welfare of their people at heart established a free clinic charging for materials used" (1921:89). Bixby concludes that "*dependency among the colored was thus recognized from the first time as a community problem* [emphasis added] and the responsibility for positive results was placed upon members of that group" (Bixby 1921:89). It is notable that no women, white or Black, are specifically mentioned by Bixby or Thompson, other than Bixby's indication that Thompson hired four women as social service workers. The focus is on men as earners despite what we know from Mrs. Mayo's long recitation of successful women in business. It may have been the case that neither man thought to specifically note women as recipients of services. It may also be that the assumption was that such women would be exceptions, and for the most part, no single women of color needed help.

This glimpse into how Akron's Black community organized social support for its most vulnerable members scarcely scratches the surface. There is a wealth of material and excellent scholarly torchbearers for someone interested in further exploration. For purposes here, we now have a sense of some of the people and organizations that addressed social services for Black Akron. We also have a hint that the experience for white and Black women of few means in Akron varied in significant ways. More broadly, the Salvation Army and the YMCA both played significant roles across the nation for white and Black people. Innovative local leaders responded to crises with options like *The Akron Plan* and the steadily organizing public apparatus of the state, represented by the Infirmary and the other state-supported charitable institutions, continued to evolve.

It is important to note that lack of publicly facing focus on, or engagement with, the Infirmary does not mean that municipal authorities were unaware of the institution and its inmates. OBSC publications make it clear that prominent citizens, along with city and county administrators, were regularly involved in oversight and management issues. In addition, across the boom years of the 1880s–1910s, developers had begun eying open land for new housing. While socially diminished or sidelined as people of less worth, the value of the ground beneath the inmates' feet was increasely coveted. Desire for more and better housing in West Akron grew due to both a housing shortage in the 1910s and the fact that the air pollution of rubber production made the east side of the city less desirable for the expanding ranks of wealthier residents. Before Schneider was ready to develop the Sunset View community, the Infirmary must have been a topic for city government, local materials producers and contractors, representatives of the Presbyterian church in Akron, and dinner-table talk for the wealthier families who had reason to be thinking about buying a tonier house.

◇◇◇◇◇◇◇◇

An article in the *Akron Evening Times* from 1919 interviewed and also described some of the remaining inmates soon to be moved from the Summit County Infirmary to the new County Infirmary building in Munroe Falls (*Akron Evening Times*, May 9, 1919). It is a jovial article in which the primarily elderly, white men interviewed explain their fondness for and attachment to the old Infirmary that had been their home for many years. They are either described as disabled by accident or committed for inability to work or care for themselves independently.

Fig. 6-5. Interviewers with the Infirmary residents. *Akron Evening News*, May 9, 1919

The article highlights the ways the inmates work for the institution. It dwells particularly on one man, Johnnie Pepples, who was "too proud" to burden a nephew who had offered support, preferring the meager measure of independence and self-reliance that living in the Infirmary allowed. Quoting Pepples: "I do enough chores around here to pay for my keep." The article also notes internal social divisions, which echo external ideas of the time. The people who had been maimed tend to group together, and the aged but sound-bodied form another group. Both these shy away from "young men, knocked over by indulgence in stimulants or other bad habits, from the ladder leading to success and an honest livelihood—the saddest group of all." (*Akron Evening Times*, May 9, 1919). The article closes noting that there were four married couples among the inmates, they struck the reporter as filled with "felicity and cheer." The overall message of the article is that these people have been fine, and they will be fine. It "is not the worst existence in the world," the article concludes; society does not need to be concerned.

As discussed in chapter 2, the Infirmary's land was transferred to Schneider. The buildings were torn down. The First Presbyterian Church of Akron bought the corner site on Exchange Street in 1919 and eventually built the magnificent Westminster Presbyterian Church over the footprint of the old Infirmary. Houses went up in Sunset View on the extensive fields once farmed by inmates, and Schneider Park was established.

Schneider, the city, the county, the churches, the builders, and local people who bought the houses knew that some bodies remained in the cemetery; they could not have been unaware.

## *Science, Society, and Bias*

In bringing this historical section to a close, I highlight two currents in the history of the twentieth century: the evolving ethics of academic research and the broader development of disability rights after 1920. Many good texts trace the evolution of regulations guiding academic and medical research with vulnerable and historically mistreated populations (e.g., Stark 2011; Bryen 2016; Washington 2007). Each of these histories emphasizes the negative consequences of too great a separation of institutions that create knowledge from the lived experiences of people. In addition to clinical research, social scientists in nonclinical settings gathered data about the general population that proved important to policymakers overseeing our energetic, developing country. At universities, students and professors have long made it their mission to use the skills from their home disciplines to frame questions, gather data, and conduct analyses with the goal of advancing knowledge and understanding of a given topic. The knowledge generated ideally will not sit on a shelf gathering dust but will instead be useful in improving life in the broadest sense. While some scholarship is remote from everyday life, academic work is often intended to be part of wider community engagement with the topic. In the case of understanding human diversity, the knowledge academic research generates becomes part of the entangled political and economic systems of the era.

By the turn of the twentieth century, undergraduate and graduate students from many state and private universities, under the guidance of professors, often in collaboration with state agencies, were sent to gather data about the heritability of degenerative human traits using methods that assumed eugenic ideas were correct (e.g., Goddard 1911; Sessions 1918). Because the assumptions underlying the methods were flawed, these research findings circularly reinforced ideas about how traits like criminality and physical disabilities co-occur and the degree to which these supposedly linked biological traits pass down genetically. Although there was no external ethical oversight of research at the time, academics nevertheless questioned each other's work, including biases like those of eugenics.

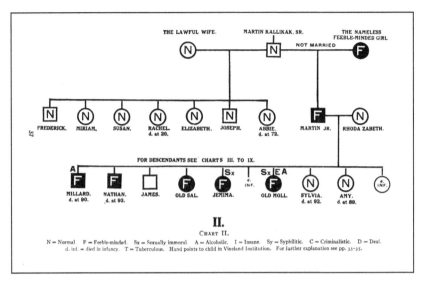

Fig. 6-6. A eugenic family tree, from Goddard's Kallikak study (Public domain image)

For example, anthropologist Franz Boas and his students at Columbia University responded to a call from New York policymakers for data on immigrants living in Manhattan's crowded tenements. Aware of and concerned about anti-immigrant bias as well as the assumptions underlying eugenics research, Boas designed a study focused on body measurements such as head circumference to test the validity of ideas about heritability of lower intelligence based on smaller head size. The team gathered and analyzed data that definitively demonstrated that immigrants, their foreign-born children, and grandchildren born in New York differed in terms of several traits, including cephalic index (head size). Their conclusions clearly refuted eugenic notions of trait co-occurrence and reduced the role of heredity, demonstrating instead the powerful influences of environmental factors like improved nutrition on human growth and development. The politicians and policymakers, embedded as they were in the political, social, and economic complexity of New York in the 1910s, did not receive Boas' results warmly. They had hoped for data that they could use to limit immigration of specific ethnic groups through Ellis Island, and so they set aside his findings. Boas' conclusions were shared among academics at the time, who found they fit well with growing knowledge of the role of environment on growth, called *phenotypic plasticity*. This work contributed significantly to understanding human neurological and physical variation (Boas 1912; Gravlee et al. 2003). The Boas example is important, but it is also an exception.

Overall, across the first half of the twentieth century, knowledge of human variation that moved from academic to public spheres was filtered through dominant ideas that diminished the personhood of non-white people, some immigrant groups, uneducated and poor people, women, and people with physical and mental irregularities. Critical voices from within and outside institutions like universities and government agencies gradually rose in response to harmful research, demanding external ethical guidance. Eventually, the US passed the National Research Act of 1974 and published the *Belmont Report: Ethical Principles and Guidelines for the Protection of Human Subjects of Research* (1978).

## Disability Rights after 1920

Civil rights for people with disabilities also evolved slowly across the twentieth century. Eugenically oriented policymakers argued for separating and sterilizing people seen as disabled, citing the financial drain on society's resources. This cost-centered argument fed into a larger concern about welfare in the US. Recognizing the strain of social safety nets on states and charities following the Depression of the 1930s, Roosevelt's administration revised the nation's welfare system, fusing a federal layer of support onto the structure of states, local governments, and private charities. Other industrialized countries' governments, including Germany's Third Reich, also took on the challenges of social welfare following economic depression (see Lombardo 2011). By the beginning of the Second World War, the once monolithic institution of the Infirmary was fading. The process of dividing the marginalized population into more specific categories and separating them physically, begun for the Ohio Board of State Charities in the late 1800s, was nearing completion. Orphanages, mental health facilities, and senior care centers were siphoning off select groups of inmates and, in the process, eliminating the need for a county infirmary system (Cottrell 1989; Grismer 1952).

Following the Second World War, Americans, appalled by the atrocities that included experimenting on and killing people identified as feeble-minded, grew critical of eugenics. Publicity-oriented events like those surrounding the euthanizing of congenitally deformed babies ceased. The film *The Black Stork* disappeared from theatres. Governments and social service providers reenvisioned their work. We can see this reflected in institutional names; for example, "developmental centers" replaced "institutions for the feeble-minded," at least in name. Policies and practices did not change as quickly. Eugenicists reformed and renamed their organizations but still endeavored to pass and implement involuntary sterilization laws. As noted above, Ohio's last attempt to pass a eugenic sterilization law was in 1963. Likewise, there was a notable softening of dehumanizing language across the second half of the twentieth century, with words like *defective*, *unfit*, and *degeneracy* fading from use. However, many women deemed unfit to bear children (Black, Puerto Rican, American Indian, and white) were involuntarily sterilized well into the 1970s. As recently as 2008 and 2014, the eliding of childbearing out of financially stable wedlock, under-education or unemployment, and reliance on welfare has led some politicians to suggest sterilization be a normalized part of publicly funded assistance (*Times-Picayune* 2008; MSNBC 2014).

The state of institutional care had long been a concern for industrialized societies. Even before Dickens highlighted it early in the Industrial Revolution in England, and Nellie Bly exposed the terrible conditions at a New York asylum for women, leaders and citizens alike were aware and motivated to improve conditions. The OBSC closed the Akron Poorhouse and created the Summit County Infirmary specifically in hopes that regulated practices would eliminate abuse of inmates. The cost of running these institutional systems rose steadily as segments of the inmate population were rehoused in more specific care facilities. This added a different sort of pressure for administrators and policymakers. For decades after the Second World War, one institution after another was exposed for safety violations, abusive conditions, or closed for financial reasons. The 1940s through 1970s saw a series of new federal programs and reforms intended to help people stay out of institutions (e.g., Old Age Assistance, which later became Social Security, Aid to the Permanently and Totally Disabled, which became Supplemental Social Security Income in 1972) leading to the social safety net we know today.

Institutional facilities rethought the types of inmates who remained in their care (Paulson 2012). We can see all this playing out locally for the Infirmary inmates moved to the new facility in Munroe Falls (called the Summit County Home), which served as a hospital, surgical center, and a home for many disadvantaged groups over its time. After the Infirmary failed a fire safety inspection, the inmates were reassigned to other facilities, and the location closed in 1970 (Lown 2006). It seems important to point out that the simplicity of the last point hides the experiences of those who lost their homes and social community in this process that dispersed people, unlike the removal of inmates in 1919 from one facility to another.

Ronald Reagan is the politician most associated with deinstitutionalization in the US (Lerman 1985; Mennel and Spackman 1980). Under Reagan, the process involved closing the remaining state hospitals. Beginning as governor of California in the 1960s and during his presidency in the 1980s, Reagan worked to shift the population requiring significant institutional care toward smaller group settings or pharmacological management of their illnesses. The primary criticism of this approach was that the health care system was not prepared: there were not enough beds in these other locations, and psychiatric pharmacology was still in early stages. Homelessness and incarceration of formerly institutionalized people rose significantly following deinstitutionalization. Meanwhile, adults with developmental disabilities who had been institutionalized without psychiatric diagnoses were further consolidated into the few remaining residential facilities like the Apple Creek Developmental Center in Wayne County, Ohio.

Parents and families of children with developmental disabilities were gaining momentum for a deinstitutionalization of their own, focused on the same sort of small group residential model or homecare with educational mainstreaming. Both deinstitutionalization trends boosted the development of small group and halfway housing along with innovations in pharmaceuticals and therapeutic programming. Eventually, facilities like Apple Creek closed, as they were deemed both too costly and less helpful than the new options in small group settings or home-based support (Johnson 2006). Moving out of institutions made people simultaneously more and less visible, with real consequences for their vulnerability. Because they were no longer behind large, closed institutional doors, they were less vulnerable to institutional abuse and neglect. However, as scattered individuals, they were less powerful and thus vulnerable to societal abuse and neglect in public spaces and behind smaller, closed doors. From the mid-1980s forward, the families and allies of disabled people have recognized the need to organize and advocate for their rights. Many important agencies, policies, and movements were successful, like the Americans with Disabilities Act of 1990, and together they have radically transformed the experience of individuals who a century ago might have spent their lives within the walls of an infirmary.

# Chapter 7
## Closing and Openings
*Carolyn Behrman*

Chapter 1 discussed social memory and considered how memory and forgetting are essential tools humans use to create and maintain our individual and collective identities. People receive and weave together knowledge of the past to make the stories we tell ourselves about ourselves. Relying on the known facts, we build stories that suit our sense of who we are and who we want to be. Past and future are in mind as we do this. These two overlapping processes (shaping the past and imagining the future) do not happen to us; we actively undertake them. For the most part, they also do not happen in isolation but within social groups, hence social memory. What photographs and memorabilia go into a wedding album, while allowing for individual preferences, is organized by the ritual template and the shared ideas of what a pictorial memento like an album should contain. These ideas are negotiated in families, communities, or societies. Then they are commonly held to be "the right way" to do things. In other words, we actively make our stories, but we do not entirely control their production. We are limited and influenced by dominating ideas of particular places and times. We shape and are shaped by our histories. This is a significant part of the groundwork of a living community. We rely on the outcomes of the overlapping story-generating processes to help us say who we are and to help us decide how to act as we strive to live in right relationship with each other.

The preceding chapters contain data and analyses about the Infirmary and the burials under Schneider Park. Traditionally, books, especially academic books, separate researchers and authors from readers and communities, "experts" from "audience." However, this is a book of and from Akron. Our researchers and authors are from the same place as the community in which the work was done. Even more importantly, the processes of memory and forgetting explored in this book are processes the authors are participating in even as they try to gain an analytic or academic perspective on them. Therefore, the authors developed a *community-engaged teaching and research* approach to the production of the book. This approach prompted the authors to reconsider and work to overcome that separation between researchers and community members, to recognize kinds of expertise, and to attend to variations of experience across the community that led to the generation of local knowledge.

Chapter 4 offers a clear, specific example of community-engaged research as it relates to social memory. Matney, Marino, and Revels' historical and archaeological information launched a community-researcher dialogue. Students and residents found themselves searching for the right ways to make meaning of the data and to fit them into a coherent narrative that accommodates the way each understands their roles and relationships to the park, to education, to history, and to those bodies. What that chapter recounts was sometimes uncomfortable. Attempts to construct narratives bumped into each other, and some ideas and explanations were contested. Rather than a simple act of remembering or forgetting, or of academia generating and imposing a single authoritative narrative, the process of social memory turned out to be complex—combining, overlapping, privileging, and sidelining elements of the past to weave a new, coherent-to-us, contemporary version of the story.

Set in the 2020s, this chapter describes three examples of community-engaged scholarship and considers the usefulness of each for whatever may come next in Schneider Park. The first of the three examples addresses storytelling about Schneider Park in a general sense and how people dwell in or inhabit places with difficult histories. The second and third are connected to each other and focus specifically on the nature of difficult history as it relates to disability rights.

The term *community-engaged scholarship* is used in a specific sense here. The community-engaged portion refers to intentional collaboration among people from different groups in the wider community, one element of which is the university. The scholarship portion refers to a particular way of approaching a topic or concern. It is the approach of the respectful and genuinely interested student. In other words, community-engaged scholarship assumes that team members (university and community partners) and residents teach each other by generating local knowledge together. There is an expectation that the team will give deep and sustained consideration to facts, qualities, and dialogue. In each of the examples, the people involved collaborated across differences and placed themselves in a scholarly relationship to the topic of the Infirmary and burials.

## *Two Unclasses, a Film, and a Play*

Unclasses are an invention of the EXL Center for Experiential Learning at the University of Akron. They are undergraduate classes that allow faculty, students, staff, and community partners to pursue a question or issue of shared concern together with unusual freedom. These are intentionally interdisciplinary and do not begin with a structured syllabus or class plan. Instead, the participants build the plan together, establishing goals and setting expectations for what will constitute successful completion. As one might imagine, this makes for a messy process but also gives people in an unclass a sense of shared responsibility and control over their educational experience.

The first unclass to address Schneider Park, entitled Unearthing the Paranormal, was led in the spring of 2018, by Anthropology faculty member Dr. Mira Mohsini. At its core, this unclass asked what role ghost stories and ideas about the paranormal serve in society. Applying social science research and interviewing tools, the unclass participants explored this question. Some of what they learned directly relates to Schneider Park, and with Dr. Mohsini and her student Veronica Bagley's permission, I describe their work here along with relevant testimonials shared on social media following their unclass's completion. Bagley's undergraduate paper, written for the unclass, provided a clear description of the process and results developed by the instructor, students, and community partners (Bagley 2018). These materials give a sense of the variety and depth of public engagement with the fleeting memories of the inmates and the burials that hover like wisps of thought not only in the neighborhood of the park but outward, through social contacts, into the greater Akron community. Bagley explained that the course "wasn't about whether or not ghosts exist, but more about what we can learn by taking ghost stories seriously." Bagley's team in the unclass developed and conducted interviews with people who had lived or were living near Schneider Park.

> Gradually our research focus shifted. Our goal became not to go ghost hunting or prove that people had paranormal experiences, but to look at how their experiences relate to their perception of the park. We shifted away from dissecting the ghost stories and looked more closely at the way the ghost stories fit in with interviewees' sense of Schneider Park [as a public space in their community]. (Bagley 2018)

Bagley's group reported that their interviewees saw the park in its contemporary form as a "happy place" used for sports practices, activities with their children, walking dogs. This sentiment is seen in the following excerpted anonymous quotes from current and former residents:

> "I mean my kids grew up having soccer practice there, having tee ball practice there. We've flown kites there. It's a very nice green space in the area, for everybody to, you know, play in. It's not owned by anybody; it's not touched by anybody, which is a nice neighborhood park."

> "...the rugby club now has practices they do there, and there's homeschool soccer association that uh, that plays there. They put temporary nets and take them down. So, but, it's a great thing."

> "Just like, it's a very happy place, you know. I have great memories there with my kids. And you know, and also now, like when it stops snowing, if it does stop snowing and raining, my husband and I walk almost every evening. We walk around Schneider and come back, you know, it's something, it's a go-to happy place there. And not just us. When we walk around, we don't get a full workout because we're stopping every two minutes or three minutes because we see so many people we know there."

These descriptions of contemporary use coexisted in the minds of the interviewees with impressions of Schneider Park as a "spooky" or unsettling place:

"There were times where you'd get like a cool breeze or a chill when it's 50, like kinda creepy."

"It's just a weird feeling when you walk through there at night."

"We lived on [a street perpendicular to the park] many years ago. My little brother was out one night with his buddies and saw a ghost disappear behind a tree in that park! He is sixty-one years old now and swears to it!"

"The ones who are probably still buried there probably, you know, can't rest, I would think sometimes."

"Growing up and living across the street from Schneider Park, we walked home from [school] in the 1980s sticking to the path, and never walking alone. My bedroom overlooked the park, and on misty mornings, quick glances, you would swear you would see 'beings' in the park. Occasionally, late hours or early mornings, we would huddle under our covers, hearing faint screams only to be told it was our imaginations. We all speculated on the strange 'coffin' shaped patches of earth, that the grass never grew the same there, as we had soccer practices and never dared dribble or kick the ball by. But we were just sensitive kids with overactive imaginations. No one would make a park where they buried people."

"…my friends and I having knowledge of the graves and what they meant to us as boys in the early 1970s. When I was a boy, I went to [school]. Although I lived many blocks away near Copley Road, most of my friends lived within a few blocks of the school. Once we boys were old enough to roam around at night, we frequented the park. The graves were well known to all of us, but we were not aware that some of the bodies had been exhumed. I have vivid memories of autumn evening wanderings, especially around Halloween in both 7th and 8th grades, when my friends and I made a point to visit the graves. As you know, the ground where some of the bodies were exhumed is recessed. We would dare one another to lay down in them. Our imaginative minds, having watched all the classic Universal and Hammer horror films, and having been indoctrinated into the frightening doctrine of good and evil as Catholics believed it to be, envisioned the twisted, decaying, grasping hands of corpses reaching up through the ground to pull us into the graves! The first time, in 7th grade, I was too frightened to take the dare, but two other boys did. In the 8th grade, I was a bit more courageous. As I lay in a grave, I imagined that by tempting fate, I would indeed be pulled into the abyss of hell! My bravery lasted but a few seconds before I bounded up and away, all of us running as fast as we could until winded and distanced enough to feel safe."

These quotes reflect how residents have actively constructed social memory and shared forgetting regarding the burials. Information and impressions regarding the burials are accompanied by and transformed in associations with childhood relationships and wider secular and religious culture.

News coverage of Matney's and then Mohsini's students' engagement with residents and the park in the *Akron Beacon Journal*, on June 28, 2017, and February 22, 2019, respectively, caused further ripples of dialogue through the online newspaper's Comments sections. In this social media-style series people again combined their new and old understandings of the Infirmary and park history with the more ephemeral sense of the space as emotionally important and/or disturbing:

"Whenever I would drive past the park at night when it was foggy (you know how it gets), I always have the feeling that someone will walk out from the fog, like I'm seeing people in my peripheral vision."

"I just strolled upon this post from three years ago. I grew up immediately across the street from the park. I remember the 'rumor' stories and eventually as I got older. I learned more about the truth. I always thought there were obvious graves there that settled or were disturbed at some point."

"Brings back memories.... Had no idea about any of this. It was a weird park. I used to climb trees there. Grew up 2 blocks away."

"Wow. I've walked and driven around this park all my life. Never knew any of this. A little spooky to know the history now."

"My dad as a young kid (he's now 87) said they used to get paid by the city for every bone or artifact they found."

"Great memories from childhood climbing the crab apple trees! Plenty of soccer practices there too. The WAKR annual kite fly was a favorite. Into high school it became a nighttime favorite after school dances."

"I, too, was a victim of the strange bike path with deep grooves in some areas. Every time I visit Akron I drive by and am flooded with memories. I never knew the dark history of the park before today. It certainly does make those early morning fogs that hover the ground of the park more mysterious!"

There is a noteworthy contrast between what we know of the Infirmary inmates' lives and deaths and the happy, if sometimes waggish or spooky experiences of the park shared by the unclass interviewees and online commentators. Are the mysterious elements in the stories part of the process by which communities transition uncomfortable truths into wispier tendrils of meaning; are they forms of recognition we can live with?

Bagley summed up her teammates' main conclusion as follows:

> Our theory, then, was that the memory of Schneider Park's historical significance was not initially preserved because of a *strategic forgetting* of the suffering that occurred at the County Infirmary. This leads to the disjointed and patchy knowledge about the space and history in the present. We contrast this with other historic sites of the period such as Akron's nearby Stan Hywet Hall. Built in 1900, it, flourished as a residence for Goodyear Tire and Rubber's founding family, the Seiberlings, fell into disuse and disrepair, and then was reincarnated as an architectural, landscape, and horticultural showcase. In its new form, Stan Hywet weaves artifacts and stories of the prominent family with contemporary community engagement from Alcoholics Anonymous' Founders' Day and an annual autumn craft festival.
>
> The prison known as the Ohio State Reformatory in Mansfield is another example. Built before 1910, it closed in 1990. The intention of the State of Ohio was to remove it. A private nonprofit group, however,

saved the building and repurposed it for historical tours, somewhat ghoulish paranormal programming and Halloween entertainment. Two things distinguish the Infirmary/Schneider Park from these opposing examples. First, the Infirmary and its inmates were neither as noteworthy as the Seiberlings nor as notorious as the prisoners in their own time. And second, the physical location of the Infirmary was specifically desired for reconceptualization as high-end housing at a point when a booming economy motivated and was well equipped to wipe away the Infirmary's remains. (Bagley 2018)

The conclusions from Mohsini's unclass leave questions. Was it the intention of those in power at the end of the Infirmary's days to disappear the evidence of the remaining bodies through a process of strategic forgetting? It is hard to argue against the idea that there was benefit to Schneider and the residents in the early twentieth century in reframing the open space at the heart of their new neighborhood as someplace where fresh, happier memories could be made. How are we to understand the forces that led neither to a memorial, nor to a marked cemetery, nor to a concerted effort to locate and remove all the graves to Munroe Falls, but instead to a gradual dissipation, a wandering of attention away from people and an institution that were always intended to be marginal and toward the elements of community that were situated as central when Schneider developed the space—homes, gently curving roads, green space? Among these forces certainly were economics, logistics, and politics. But what of the strong ideas that shaped the thinking of the time about whose lives matter, whose deaths warrant memorials, whose names belong on parks, street signs, and buildings? How are these sorts of forces operating on us as we contemplate the park today?

> "What struck me most about this article is that it was a spot/institution where people with disabilities were put. One specific story in the article is of a man who used his hands to propel himself around the ground while scooting on his bottom. That's how my twelve-and-a-half-year-old son with Down syndrome gets around. I don't think it's creepy as much as really fascinating and neat. My son is amazing and I'm glad he can live at home with people who love him and not be put in a home or kept in an outdoor enclosure like that man in the story." (anonymous comment in the *Akron Beacon Journal* in response to the coverage of the University of Akron classes, 2017)

I came across the comment above among the online responses to the articles written in response to Matney's and Mohsini's courses. This personal, but also essentially humanitarian, comment about disabilities and history aligned with my growing desire to draw students and community partners into a deeper consideration of the questions above.

◇◇◇◇◇◇◇

My own academic work and teaching have incorporated the history of eugenics as part of understanding the foundations of social science in the US. I came across references to the Summit County Infirmary years ago and included material on it in my introductory *Human Diversity* course. I listened to Matney's and Mohsini's students with particular interest. After watching two thoughtful films exploring other complex historical and social issues by local filmmaker Josh Gippin, I saw the potential to enrich this flow of community-engaged scholarship. In my capacity as co-director of the EXL Center, I reached out to leadership in the University of Akron's School of Communication and Department of Anthropology, who were receptive so we pooled resources. Then I asked Gippin to consider leading an interdisciplinary team in a year-long filmmaking unclass. Gippin, a kindred spirit, readily agreed and tapped EXL's Akron Community Internship Program (ACIP) to hire Communication student Payton Burkhammer. Together he and Burkhammer spent the summer of 2019 building the course and a film production plan.

Across two semesters in the fall of 2019 and spring of 2020, the unclass team undertook the technical and creative work of producing a full documentary film from background research to postproduction. They began with materials from Matney's archaeology class and Mohsini's paranormal unclass. They imagined they would ultimately be addressing the question of what sort of memorial, if any, ought to exist in the park. They dove into archives and interviewed professors, subject experts, and residents. And then, because Akron is a small enough city that these sorts of serendipitous connections can happen, Wendy Duke, codirector of the nonprofit Center for Applied Drama and Autism (CADA) shared that she and members of CADA's Theatre on the Spectrum project had been mulling over the newspaper article on the archaeology class's presentation. Many of the actors felt that the Infirmary inmates' story of being erased from history because of physical, cognitive, or behavioral differences might have been their own had they been born a hundred years ago. These actors with their range of disabilities were working on a creative engagement with the history of disabilities. It was a small thing to introduce Duke and Gippin, but the consequences of their collaboration changed the path of Gippin's unclass and their film.

Duke's engagement with these topics started decades ago when she volunteered at the Apple Creek Development Center (formerly the Apple Creek Institute for the Feeble-minded, near Wooster, Ohio) as a teenager before becoming a middle school drama teacher at Akron's Miller South School for the Visual and Performing Arts. As a teacher she collaborated with intervention specialist Laura Valendza, exploring how theatre experiences benefit children with disabilities, particularly those diagnosed with autism spectrum disorders. After retiring from the public school system, Duke cofounded CADA with Valendza, who remained an intervention specialist with the Akron Public Schools. Both her familiarity with Apple Creek and the response of the actors spurred Duke to encourage the Theatre on the Spectrum troupe to begin writing a play.

The filmmaking unclass participants stretched their vision beyond the question of a possible memorial monument to include the Theatre on the Spectrum troupe members as they conducted their own research into eugenics and infirmaries and explored their reactions to the information they unearthed. A generous collaboration emerged in which the Theatre troupe and Gippin's class of fledgling filmmakers used the intersection of their activities to capture some of the troupe members' reflections. Below are four quotes from the final cut of the film produced by Gippin's students, *Forgotten Dead* (Gippin 2020):

> "All of us, able-body and disabled, have something to add to the experience of life. All of us experience the same joys and sorrows that life has to offer. All of us are people. I feel like disability rights now have improved so much over the past few years, but there's always more battles to be fought and won." (Brian Cogar, actor)

> "I realize that what makes me different, what makes me unique, is what drives my creativity, which makes me the better me. And it's something I feel like more people should embrace. And we should be able to talk

about that more. Something that really annoys me is when you get put into boxes. Like we are more than just a disability and we are more than just one thing. We're able to do so much more. We live outside the boxes. We live in multiple different boxes. We can excel in music; we can excel in our speech. Our thoughts are special. There's more to us than just that one thing. And I wish people would try to see that more." (Jordan Euell, stage manager and co-actor)

"I began volunteering with CADA two years ago and their project, Theatre on the Spectrum. But like most people, I was shy at first. It can be difficult to get used to the way autistic people communicate. But after a while I kept coming and coming, and I began to talk with them. And I'd realize that they're just like I was. They went to the same movies I did, they had homework like I did. They had all the same thoughts. See, autism isn't a disability or a handicapped. It's more like a different language, a different dialect." (Jude Yovichin, actor)

"I am physically disabled. I have a congenital heart defect, which leaves me with half a functioning heart. Mental disability or physical disability, disability in general, nothing to be stigmatized, nothing to be hidden away. The differences should be shared, differences should be celebrated, because in the end, that's what ties us together is our differences." (Brandon Meeker, co-actor and musician)

In addition to these four perspectives, the film includes other actors' voices, an introduction to CADA, Theatre on the Spectrum, and some of the early content of their play (see Appendix B for the play's script). It also contains broader information about the Infirmary, eugenics, and Akron history. What *Forgotten Dead* does not contain is a discussion of the experience of the unclass participants and their own reflections on this community-engaged scholarship. Addressing this, unclass student Claire Pugel created a short film on the unclass itself, *The Forgotten Dead Documentary: Behind the Scenes* (Pugel 2019). Each of the participants—unclass filmmakers and actors alike—encountered their topic both intellectually and personally. They responded to the Infirmary material by acknowledging the broad societal implications of the institution's story while also recognizing their own place in the historical picture their efforts revealed. In their discussions and in the film itself, the university students highlighted the powerful nature of memory and forgetting as these forces impact people then and now. When asked to reflect in Behind the Scenes, they addressed their own roles and empowerment as part of the filmmaking process.

> "The unclass will actually be really beneficial for me in my career because I have to look at things through different lenses and this was exactly that. It showed me, yes, the anthropological data-side, and the pictures [image research techniques] but also taught me the leadership role and how to communicate with others so much better." (Heather Jandecka, unclass research team)

> "We're going out experiencing things. Really learning how to get good film and build a documentary from the ground up." (Payton Burkhammer, unclass production team)

Like members of the Theatre on the Spectrum troupe, but from their own angles, the students focused on agency—the ability to be seen, heard, and to have a positive impact on the world. *Forgotten Dead* (2020) aired on PBS of the Western Reserve in 2021 and was an official selection for the 2021 Conquering Disabilities with Film International Film Festival.

Duke, Valendza, and the troupe continued developing the play after their interaction with the unclass. They earned Knight Foundation, Ohio Arts Council, and GAR Foundation funding for the work. In the process, they collaborated with San Francisco-based musician, songwriter, and disabilities activist, Jeff Moyer. The scope of the play encompasses "a timeline of the history of disability, a timeline that starts in Schneider Park, our original source of inspiration, then moves back in time to the earliest disabled human remains found in Neanderthal caves. From that point [they] move forward in time, stopping to examine how a variety of cultures have treated their disabled citizens" (CADA 2021). Ultimately, nine original songs by Moyer contributed to the soundtrack of the play entitled *Along the Graveyard Path: A History of Disability*. The play, along with some supplementary videos, can be found on CADA's YouTube channel. An early version of the script is in Appendix B. The online production is the troupe's final version, displaying the results of careful development and revision.

## A Wider Storyline

Together, the authors of this book have traced the threads of a story of marginalization, memory, and forgetting. The chapters here have shared some of the frames and filters that made decisions and practices of the past reasonable, charitable, and logical, even as they led to the burials, the ways the buried people are remembered, and the ways they are forgotten. Recognizing that social memory-making is a shared process, intentional and powerful, people can and do remake social memory as the world changes and adaptation is required. The book's goal has not been to arrive at a set of recommendations about what to do now that more is known about the burials. The unclasses, film, and theatre work described above attest to the fact that the processes of consciousness-raising and memory-making are ongoing. This book's role has been to produce a strong fabric of knowledge about the burials, drawing together all the threads we have available now and logically connecting them. It is the authors' hope that this iteration of knowledge, now shared, will stimulate reflection and further dialogue. It may lead to changes to the physical space of Schneider Park, to an effort to find DNA, to systematically trace ancestry from death certificates to further creative work, or to collaboration and engagement not yet imagined.

◇◇◇◇◇◇◇

The Summit County Infirmary's story is not unique globally or even locally; telling its story adds to a rising tide of unearthed pasts and community conversations. There are too many known and buried histories of unwanted peoples. They have prompted social scientists, activists, and artists to engage the public in dialogue about buried histories, memory, and forgetting in a myriad of compelling ways. George Orwell (1949) imagined the notion of the "memory hole" in his novel *Nineteen Eighty-Four* in which the dystopian State, personified by Big Brother, eliminates historical records that do not support the dominant narrative. Forensic anthropologist Erin Kimmerle and her largely student team used threads of documentation, local stories, and ground-penetrating radar to unearth the bodies of fifty-one boys in Florida. Their work exposed the racism and abuses threaded through the history of the Dozier School, a boys' reformatory. Kimmerle's findings were shared first in academic journals and newspaper articles. These inspired National Book Award-winning author, Colson Whitehead, to write his novel, *The Nickel Boys* (2019). Whitehead won a Pulitzer Prize for this work, which emphasized the intersection of the Jim Crow era with the history of eugenics and institutionalization. Recently, Kimmerle (2022) published a nonfiction account of her community-engaged scholarship, which reads like a social science companion piece to Whitehead's fictional account and RaMell Ross's film adaptation of *The Nickel Boys* earned the 2024 Oscar for Best Picture (2024).

Outside the realm of perverted charity and behavioral control represented by the Dozier School, there are examples driven by commerce. Ordinary New Yorkers' lives were overturned, and their pasts buried as real estate and industrial magnates played out a high-stakes Monopoly game competing to develop the five boroughs of New York City from the 1850s forward. Urbanus related some of the history of Brooklyn's Barren Island and Dead Horse Bay (2018). He explained that this landmass, home to a community whose livelihood was built on the practice of horse-rendering in the mid-1800s, became a favored location for industrial debris dumping, nominally a landfill, for the next hundred years. Trash, rubble, and other debris accumulated. Whole neighborhoods of homes, primarily belonging to low income and immigrant New Yorkers in other boroughs, were demolished to make way for new buildings and highways. The bulldozed remains of dwellings were dumped on and around the Island and into the Bay. It is now a partially mounded and partially submerged wasteland from which remnants of past lives erode or rise and wash ashore.

In addition to the dystopic version of a natural environment this has constructed, archaeologist Robin Nagle commented:

> ... the objects on the beach along Dead Horse Bay will continue to be a tangible reminder of an intangible past—both of the families whose homes were destroyed and of the alienated community and industries that once resided on Barren Island ... We have a tendency as human beings to forget, and that's understandable. Our lives are full and the demands are many.... But in that forgetting we also lose a sense of who we are. (Nagel, cited in Urbanus 2018:63)

Nagle's words align with thought-provoking questions from unclass students during a reflection session. "Who do we include as our ancestors?"

"Who can we claim? Which claims are contested? And who goes unclaimed entirely?" "How do things look if we stop thinking in terms of dividing people into who counts and who doesn't, like schoolyard team-picking scenarios which our own experiences as kids told us were short-sighted and generally wrong?" One student asked, "Why open this up at all?" In other words, why raise to scrutinize these past lives now? To which other students replied that, once known, it would be wrong to deny knowing. But there are many things we know that don't help us. Is knowing this good? Is it good for us as a community, or is it just more unearthed trauma that further divides us with blame and sadness?

But it is also a more complicated question. There is something ghoulish about being so interested in forgotten miseries and atrocities; something disturbing about how deep wrongs clamor for ears and eyes to feast upon despair. In addition to potentially causing pain, does raising this history constitute some sort of prurient entertainment? To these worrying thoughts, political activist and author, Anne Lamott, replies that the concerns are real but whether to raise and reflect on the history it is not entirely up to us. Truth, she says, wants expression. It is healthy and productive to reckon with what we come to know. "Unacknowledged truth saps our energy" (Lamott 1995:166).

Kazuo Ishiguro's novel *The Buried Giant* (2015) tells the story of an elderly couple, a man and a woman, struggling in a land where literal mists of forgetting have taken away their memories. They are not able to recall entirely either the good or the terrible events of their past. Instead, they are confused and teased by vague glimpses. Through his buffeted characters, Ishiguro lures and nudges us to consider what we fear about what has been buried and forgotten. He presses us with the sense that it might be soothing to give up being able to know. How easy it would be to fall asleep to the past; remembering is hard and frustrating, and its reward might be painful. There might be remembered pain and suffering, but also guilt or shame, or new losses suffered as old wounds reopen and old divisions rekindle. Beatrice, the woman, speaks for both as they push through the inertia to regain their humanity.

> "Axl and I wish to have again the happy moments we shared together." She goes on, "We'll have the bad ones come back too, even if they make us weep or shake with anger. For isn't it the life we shared?" (Ishiguro 2015:141)

Ishiguro, through Beatrice, encourages his readers to strive, to work toward understanding our own, specific, messy, contingent pasts. Not only do we need to strive to know, to remember, but we need to struggle against settling for selective memory that selects in favor of those most like us. As one unclass participant observed, "We need to grow an appreciation for a wider deviation from the mean—to recalculate, in social terms, standard deviation."

◇◇◇◇◇◇◇

A hundred years ago, a different war raged in Europe, a different pandemic ravaged the globe, and in Akron, living residents of the Summit County Infirmary were removed to a more distant facility while many deceased residents were left behind in unmarked graves. Each of these challenges—wars, pandemics, and the questions of how to deal with "undesirable" people—presents us as humans with a complex tangle of geographies, economics, politics, and science that together threaten our ability to flourish as a species. *What Remains.* Our ambiguous title can be read three ways. It can stand as an honest question about what lies under the ground in Schneider Park—a question about what can be known leading up to, surrounding, and following those burials. It also can be read as a disingenuous rhetorical question, a quip from a less conscious public who have moved through and around the park, preferring not to acknowledge the burials there. Or, uncomfortably, it can be understood to encompass both, serving as a label for this book's effort to answer the first of these questions while not avoiding the second. Put another way, these particular, physical spaces enable us to change how we think about the past—these efforts help encourage us to make more complete and honest tellings of community, including the processes of segregation, isolation, and integration.

At the time of this book's publication, Schneider Park is a mute monument to a history informed by eugenics and a racialized worldview. A history that excludes portions of the population from the dominant narrative, the stories we tell ourselves about ourselves. It is an indignity for the dead there to go unacknowledged, but pushing to understand who is there and who is not is a process. It is not a simple or unidirectional process, but it is one through which spaces can be rehumanized and transformed for present-day and future community.

## Epilogue

Jane Greenland has lived in West Akron her entire life. She retired from her thirty-five-year career in Customer Relations at the US Postal Service on Grant Street in 2013. This work and her childhood in Akron gave her a strong sense of place and love for community. She remembers walking to their home on Chitty Avenue (between Merriman Road and Aqueduct Street) from St. Vincent's Grade School with her four siblings. On their way they would stop at their favorite store, Kistler Donuts, at the corner of Aqueduct and West Market where, for ten cents they could buy a dozen day-old donuts, fill themselves, and leave the leftovers along the Mount Peace Cemetery fence for the birds. Her mother could never understand why her own flock weren't hungry after their long walk home from school.

Greenland is a widow who raised her three children, first on Neal Court for eighteen years. Then, in 1994, the family moved to Crestview Avenue, the road running along the western side of Schneider Park. An observant and active citizen as well as a kind neighbor, Greenland noticed that people attempting to walk or roll strollers by the park were forced to use the roadway. Passing cars were frequently speeding. There was no sidewalk or reliably dry path along that edge of the park. This struck Greenland as both uncomfortable and dangerous. So, she reached out to the city to see if a walking path might be added on the park's western margin but was told that when Philip Schneider donated the land to the city, he had stipulated that no permanent structures be built there. City officials at the time felt that paths constituted permanent structures since they would involve both digging and the addition of durable materials. As a concession, the city added a stop sign and blocked a portion of the road to make walking the park's edge safer.

One day in 2017, Greenland saw people working with small flags and equipment in the middle of the park. Heading out to investigate, she met Matney and his university students as they were beginning their geophysical survey. They told her about the old graves they were attempting to map. She already knew some of the park's history. She had walked the well-trodden footpaths school children had beaten through the park toward St. Sebastian's School and Simon Perkins School. She remembered the ground was swampy and that bones had been found there. She had also witnessed the work the city undertook when they placed an underground drainage grid in the southern part of the park, helping to finally dry out the wettest portions of the greenspace, enabling the picnickers, pick-up football games, and soccer practices of recent decades.

Her discussion with Matney that afternoon left her focused on how the history of the Infirmary and burials were reshaping her understanding of the community. She later attended the presentation Matney's class gave at the Akron-Summit County Public Library's Highland Square branch and watched the film Josh Gippin and his UA unclass students produced for PBS of the Western Reserve. She thought about the fact that neither the name, Schneider Park, nor any marker in the park itself, identified or commemorated the history of the Infirmary and its burial ground for some of Akron's poorest residents.

In the late spring of 2023, Greenland again noticed new activity involving small flags and equipment in the middle of the park. She stepped out and engaged with the workers. This time she found City of Akron employees, who explained to her that they were going to construct a network of permanent walking paths around and through the park to improve its walkability and enhance it as a recreational space. In light of what she knew, she reached out to then City Council member, Russel Neal, filling him in on the history, the burials, and Philip Schneider's stipulation against building structures in the park. She emphasized the humanitarian perspective that these underrecognized burials needed, in her view, to be respected. Neal responded immediately, connecting Greenland with John Malish, the City of Akron's arborist. With Neal and Malish's assistance, the plan for the park was revised so the paths would avoid crossing over the spaces where graves had been identified by the university team. The result is a beautiful, peripheral walking trail.

These efforts have improved the park while raising awareness of the history, but Greenland does not want to leave the matter there. As this book goes to press, she is working with Council member Jan Davis to have the name of the park officially changed to Schneider Memorial Park and to have a plaque added so that visitors who come to benefit from the park's surface can also begin to understand the layers of Akron history beneath their feet.

## Appendix A
# Death Certificates from the Summit County Infirmary

Below are the details from the death certificates referenced in chapters 2, 5, and 6. The data fields on the original death certificate form are as follows: Last Name, First Name, Race, Sex, Age, Death Year, Place of Birth, Place of Death, Marital Status, Former Residence, Cause of Death, and the Death Certificate File Number. In some cases, the certificate contains additional notes. These have been included just before the file number. As you will see, not all fields were completed for each person.

    The records are organized alphabetically by last name. We have numbered the entries for convenience. For race we have followed the notations from the original certificates ('w" for white, "c" for Colored, and "b" for Black). Sex is abbreviated "m" or "f" when known. Ages are in years with "o" referring to a neonatal death. We have distinguished between place of birth, place of death, former residence using "(b)" (place of birth), "(d)" (place of death), and "(r)" (former residence). In a few cases, the names of the parents of the individual were given. Parental names are written in parentheses in the place of birth field. Although they do not appear in quotation marks, comments by the person filling out the certificate are reproduced here as completely as possible. Since the records were handwritten, there may be errors in transcription. We have not made changes to the spellings provided in the original documentation.

1 **Adams, Parker**, c, m, 52, 1915, (b) Virginia, (d) Infirmary, single, laborer, exhaustion, pulmonary tuberculosis, 5310.

2 **Alberson, Charles**, m, 59, 2154.

3 **Allman**, w, f, 0, 1916, (b)Akron, Ohio (Wilford Allman and Ruth Huff, West Virginia), (d) 193 Bluff St., bronchial pneumonia.

4 **Allman, Dora**, w, f, 0, 1916, (b) Akron (Wilford Allman and Ruth Huff, West Virginia), (d) 193 Bluff St., bronchiti.

5 **Amick, Delila**, w, f, 71, 1914, (b) West Virginia, (d) Infirmary, pareyolymation nephritis, arterio sclerosis, 47496.

6 **Andrews, Perry**, w, m, 29, 1912, (b) Austria, (d) Infirmary, laborer, pulmonary tuberculosis, 60856.

7 **Andy, Joe**, w, m, 60, 1912, (d) 1169 Moore St., laborer, acute lobar pneumonia, 192223.

8 **Anson, Steven**, w, m, 86, 1914, (d) Infirmary, widower, shoe maker, senile arterio sclerosis, exhaustion, 52725.

9 **Antolik, Andy**, w, m, 20, 1915, Infirmary, single, (r) 918 Grant St., Akron, laborer, street work, tuberculosis of lungs, empyema, 18824.

10 **Arkoneilo, Jacob R.**, w, m, 50, 1914, (b) Italy, (d) Williams St., laborer, shotgun wound in neck fired by an assassin, 47444.

11 **Babcock, Harriet**, w, m, 38, 1915, (b) Ohio, (d) Infirmary, (r) Willington [Wellington] Ave., Portage Twp, laborer, parenelymalin-nephritis, 46456.

12 **Bajaci, Andy**, w, m, 56, 1915, (b) Hungary, (d) Franklin Twp., widowed, (r)Barberton, laborer, homicide from gunshot wounds.

13 **Baker, Edward**, w, m, 60, 1915, (b) England, (d) Infirmary, widowed, laborer,, lobar pneumonia, heart failure, 18819.

14 **Banks, Sarah Ellen**, w, f, 20, 1916, (b) Tennessee, (d) Newton Heights, Tallmadge Twp., married, housewife, pulmonary tuberculosis.

15 **Barnes, Mary**, w, f, 67, 1913, (b) Ohio, (d) Infirmary, widow, none,, arterio sclerosis, exhaustion.

16 **Batz, Christopher**, w, m, 0, 1914, (b) Akron (Christopher Batz, German and Emily Schmidt, Pennsylvanian), (d) 171 Abel St., Akron, (r) 171 Abel St., Akron, premature birth, 36414.

17 **Batz**, w, m, 0, 1914, (b) Akron (Christopher Batz, German, and Emily Schmidt, Pennsylvanian), (d) 216 E. South St., (r) 216 E South St., Akron, premature birth (6 months), 69080.

18 **Bauaghan, Frank P.**, w, m, 40, 1911, (b), Texas (French parents), (d) Train depot[?], 2nd ward Akron, married, laborer, shock following crush of face, broken legs and arms as result of being struck by a C. A. and O. Passenger train,, 61699.

19 **Beon, Steve**, w, m, 77, 1916, (b) Italy, Infirmary, widower, stone cutter, lobar pneumonia.

20 **Boamble, George**, w, m, 23, 1912, (b) Kentucky, (d), Infirmary, married, none, ecustism carditis.

21 **Bodich, Mary**, w, f, 20, 1914, (b) Serbia, (d) City Hospital, married, puerperal septicemia, child birth, 11626.

22 **Bonham, Thomas**, w, m, 72, 1909, (b) Ohio, (d) Infirmary, widower, (r) Akron, editor, Artio sclerosis, paresis, 27684.

23 **Bosier, Steve**, w, m, 60, 1912, (b) Hungary, (d) Infirmary, pulmonary tuberculosis.

24 **Brady**, w, m, o, 1914, (b) Akron (George Brady, Austria, Rosie Klaujoki, Austria), (d) near 307 E. North St., (r) 307 E. North St., Akron, child was dead when I got there, it may have been stillborn. It was all over when I got there, 41817.

25 **Brick, John**, w, m, 67, 1916, (b) Ohio, (d) Infirmary, teamster, organic valvular disease of the heart, 21663.

26 **Brown, Everett**, c, m, 21, 1914, (b) Virginia, (d) Infirmary, single, farmer hand, Dilation of heart following mitral regurgitation, 5708.

27 **Brown, William**, w, m, 77, 1916, (b) Ireland, (d) Infirmary, laborer, arterio sclerosis, nephritis, dilation of heart.

28 **Bryant, William**, w, m, 55, 1911, (b) New York, (d) Infirmary, single, mason, chronic nephritis, 45622.

29 **Buden, Gus**, w, m, 45, 1914, (b) Germany, (d) Infirmary, married, brick layer, pulmonary tuberculosis, 25226.

30 **Bumgardner, John**, w, m, 60, 1915, (d) Infirmary, single, none, lobar pneumonia, insanity, 18821.

31 **Burton, Harry** , w, m, 45, 1916, (b) New Hampshire, (d) Infirmary, run over by auto-truck, accidental, broken back at 5 dorsal vertebrae, peritonitis, 52673.

32 **Calvire, Luigi**, w, m, 33, 1914, (b) Italy, (d) City Hospital, married, laborer, lobar pneumonia, 11629.

33 **Cevkosic, George**, w, m, 23, 1912, (d) City Hospital, pulmonary tuberculosis, 68910.

34 **Cleveland, Joseph**, c, m, 70, 2221.

35 **Collins, Edward**, w, m, 38, 1912, (d) B.&O. Railroad yard, 2nd ward, fracture of skull while walking on D. A. & O. RR bridge and falling.

36 **Conrad, Emma**, w, f, 39, 1910, (d) Infirmary, married, (r) Barberton, laborer, anaemia, confinement, 52432.

37 **Crebs, Edgar**, w, m, 0, 1915, (b) Ohio (Wayne Bowman, Ohio, Violet Moye, Pennsylvania), (d) 74 S. Broadway, (r) 12 Steese Court, Akron, prematurity, congenital syphilis.

38 **Czmon, Steve**, w, m, 35, 1914, (d) City Hospital, epidermis[?] Cu[?] [illegible], 36434.

39 **Dajgi, Boleslaw**, w, m, 38, 1915, (b) Russia, (d) People's Hospital, ward 4, single, barber, shock, right leg crushed by car.

40 **Daugherty, Dorothy Agnes**, w, f, 0, 1915, (b) Ohio (Daniel J. Daugherty, PA, Nellie Beers, PA), (d) 130 S. High St., (r) 130 S. High St., Akron, accidental death by suffocation.

41 **Davis, Susie**, w, f, 20, 1885, (b) Cleveland, Cuyahoga County, (d) Infirmary.

42 **Dawson, Elizabeth**, c, f, 0, 1915, (b) Akron (George Dawson, VA., Mamil Epps, VA.), (d) People's Hospital, (r) 13 Manns Court, Akron, lobar pneumonia.

43 **Dawson, Frank**, w, m, 45, 1913, (b) Pennsylvania, (d) Infirmary, single, coal miner, pulmonary tuberculosis.

44 **Dennis**, w, f, 88, 1889, (b) Ireland, (d) Infirmary.

45 **Diefenbach, Henry**, w, m, 67, 1910, (b) Germany, (d) Infirmary, retired, apoplexy, 69423.

46 **Dojcigy, Joca**, w, m, 43, 1911, (b) Hungary, (d) 323 S. High St, Akron, (r) 323 S. High St., Akron, laborer, acute nephritis, 67130.

47 **Doomid, Mary**, w, f, 0, 1916, (b) Ohio, (d) Children's Hospital, measles.

48 **Dopplemyer, Fred**, w, m, 64, 1914, (b) Germany, (d) Infirmary, single, painter, tuberculosis of conils, 18720.

49 **Dosher, John**, w, m, 38, 1915, (d) 1107 S. Main St., (r) 1107 S. Main, Akron, general laborer, acute dilation of heart, chronic myocarditis, 69548.

50 **Douglas, Harvey**, m, 70, 1902, Infirmary, paralysis.

51 **Droulette, Louis**, w, m, 100, 1866, (b) France, (d) Infirmary.

52 **Duffin, Russell**, w, m, 40, 1913, (b) Ireland, (d) 204 E. Market St., single, (r) 204 E. Market St. Boarding House, Akron, laborer, self inflicted gunshot wound, right temple, boarded with James Ray (Irish, scotish parents), and Mary Ray (German, German parents), 63344.

53 **Dunlap, Isaac**, Black, m, 63, 1910, (b) Virginia, (d) Infirmary, single, barber, arterio sclerosis, chronic valvular disease of heart.

54 **Eager, John**, w, m, 65, 1916, (b) England, (d) Infirmary, laborer, lobar pneumonia.

55 **Emmons, Catherine**, w, F, 84, 1909, (d) Infirmary, widow, (r) Richfield, Artio sclerosis, 43578.

56 **Esakor, Mike**, w, m, 0, 1914, (b) Ohio (Mike L. Esakor, Austria, Zorka Pradodo, Austria), (d) Children's Hospital, Akron, athrepsia [marasmus], inability to assimilate, 57762.

57 **Evans, David D.**, w, m, 1901, (r) Summit Building, 407 S. Main St., Akron, professor.

58 **Farnsworth**, w, m, 0, 1914, (b) Akron (Calvin Farnsworth, WV, Gertrude Mailes, WV), (d) 85 W. Crosier, 7th ward, (r) 85 W. Crosier, Akron, stillborn, 41789.

59 **Fekete, Stephen**, m, 30, 1911, (b) Hungary (Stephen and Kathleen (Yukas) Fekete), (d) Infirmary, (r) W. Exchange St., laborer, pneumonia following a cold.

60 **Fisher, Joseph**, w, m, 28, 1915, (b) Austria, (d) Hudson, Stop 63 ABC line, dairy farm laborer, accidentally killed by A.B.C. car, fracture of skull and a broken neck.

61 **Flagle, Jesse B.**, w, m, 66, 1911, (b) Pennsylvania (mother German, father from Maryland), (d) Akron, (r)Cuyahoga Falls Boarding House (James Ray), chronic interstitial nephritis, 67120.

62 **Fragar, Washington**, Black, m, 50, 1914, (d) Infirmary, single, cardiac dilation, mitral insufficiancy, 47498.

*Appendix A*

63 **Frenkler, Joe**, w, m, 53, 1911, (b) Austria, (d) Infirmary, single, (r) Akron, laborer, carcinoma of the heart, 61707.

64 **Gajdos, Antol**, w, m, 40, 1915, (b) Austria, (d) 1167 Andrew St., married, (r) 1167 Andrus St., Akron, rubber factory laborer, intussusception, obstruction, 11478.

65 **Garner, O. S.** [possibly Oliver], w, m, 70, 1915, (b) Rhode Island, (d) Infirmary, widower, gardener, senile dementia, 25196.

66 **Garry, James**, Black, m, 50, 1911, (d) Infirmary, single, laborer, lobar pneumonia, 11633.

67 **Gash, Stephan**, w, m, 50, 1913, (d) City Hospital, syphilitic meningitis, 49179.

68 **Genoskyic, Marie** [or Mamij], w, f, 0, 1914, (b) Ohio (Michael Genoskyic, Russia, Mary Zockinsky, Russia), (d) 651 Edgewood St., (r) 651 Edgewood St., Akron, premature birth at about 7 months gestation, 47422.

69 **Gento, Lewis**, w, m, 22, 1910, (b) France, (d) Infirmary, single, Akron, laborer, pulmonary tuberculosis, 10964.

70 **German**, w, f, 0, 1916, (b) Akron, Ohio, (d) City Hospital, (r) 9 Arch St., Akron (Irma German), neonatal asphyxia, 21534.

71 **Goodis, Julius**, w, m, 55, 1913, (d) City Hospital, peddler, suicide from carbolic acid.

72 **Gorman**, w, m, 40, 1914, (d) City Hospital, lobar pneumonia, 18717.

73 **Gos, Joseph**, w, m, 48, 1916, (d) People's Hospital, (r) 401 Livingston St., Akron, paper mill laborer, intestinal obstruction, valvular.

74 **Griffin, Edw**, m, 67, 2225.

75 **Grill, Philip**, m, 67, 1889, (d) Infirmary.

76 **Grovisky, John**, w, m, 43, 1912, (b) Hungary, (d) Infirmary, married, tuberculosis of the kidney.

77 **Gruber, Benedict**, w, m, 84, 1915, (b) Germany, (d) Infirmary, widower, laborer, broncho-pneumonia, arterio sclerosis, 5311.

78 **Haijval, Paul**, w, m, 54, 1915, (d) Infirmary, laborer, cancer of the stomach, exhuastion, 18817.

79 **Hanney**, w, m, 70, 1915, (d) Infirmary, single, exhaustion, refused to eat, 30877.

80 **Harry**, w, f, o, 1912, (b) Akron, Premature birth.

81 **Hartome, Frank**, w, m, 61, 1913, (b) Germany, (d) City Hospital, single, lobar pneumonia.

82 **Hasemann, Henry**, w, m, 28, 1912, (b) Germany (Fred Haseman, father), (d) City Hospital, fireman, fracture of skull as result of being struck by a B.&O. Train.

83 **Hatfield, Martha**, w, f, 30, 1916, (d) People's Hospital, single, (r) 552 S. High St., Akron, septicemia following septic endometriosis.

84 **Hazeldon, William**, m, 74, 2082.

85 **Hearns**, w, f, o, 1916, (b) Akron, (r) 23 S. High St., Premature birth.

86 **Helfrich, Peter**, w, m, 70, 1911, (b) Germany, (d) Infirmary, single, Akron, laborer, arterio sclerosis, 24271.

87 **Hibach, Elizabeth**, w, f, 45, 1913, (d) City Hospital, unknown, 42928.

88 **Hines, John**, w, m, 76, 1912, (b) Ohio, (d) Infirmary, single, carcinoma of stomach, exhaustion.

89 **Hink, Jacob**, w, m, 75, 1913, (b) Ohio, (d) Infirmary, widower, aortic regurgitation, myocardial degestion, arterio sclerosis contribution.

90 **Hodovan, Peter**, w, m, 40, 1913, (b) Hungary, Dusnok, (d) Infirmary, (r) with John Rogotch, Akron Ohio, married, alcoholic cirohsis of liver, 31062.

91 **Hoffman, Anna**, w, f, 33, 1912, (b) Hungary, (d) City Hospital, married (John Hoffman), housewife, hemorhage from renal artery, pyelonephritis.

92 **Hoffman, Frank**, w, m, 40, 1915, (d) City Hospital, single, (r) Emma Dean Farm, farm laborer, typhoid fever, 18763.

93 **Horworth, Joseph**, w, m, 42, 1914, (b) Hungary, married, (r) 1055 S. High St., Akron, laborer.

94 **Hose, John**, w, m, 60, 1916, (b) Ohio, (d) Infirmary, single, common laborer, lobar pneumonia.

95 **Huffer, Margorie M.**, w, f, o, 1914, (b) Pennsylvania, (d) died on train near Akron, convulsions, gastroenteritis, 31497.

96 **Hurl, Eliza**, w, f, 64, 1910, (d) Infirmary, widow, (r) Barberton, paralysis, 5268.

97 **Husselton, Robert Leroy**, w, m, o, 1914, (b) Portage Twp. (Eva Husselton, Ohio), (d) Fouse Ave., (r) Fouse Ave., Akron, hemophilia, 52727.

98 **Huston, Matilda**, w, f, 77, 1915, (b) New York, (d) Infirmary, single, domestic, paresis, syphilitic.

99 **Inaka, James**, m, 50, 2360.

100 **Ingram, Virginia Ruth**, w, f, 0, 1916, (b) Akron (Charles Ingram, W.V., Edna Warren, W.V.), (d) 371 W. Chestnut St., (r) 371 W. Chestnut St., Akron, gastroenteritis, improper feeding, 63071.

101 **Jarvas, Robert**, w, m, 0, 1915, (b) Akron (Roy Wright and Emma Mary Jarvas, West Virginia), (d) Infirmary (county hospital), premature birth, 25195.

102 **Johnson**, w, f, 0, 1915, (b) Ohio (Harvey Johnson, Colorado, Ruth Harthy, Ohio), (d) City Hospital, premature birth, fever 12 hours, 30811.

103 **Johnson, Peter**, w, m, 69, 1910, (b) Sweden, (d) Infirmary, single, laborer, chronic rheumatism, chronic nephritis contributing, 23790.

104 **Johnson, Susie**, w, f, 33, 1914, (b) Virginia, (d) City Hospital, married (Sam Johnson), (r) 214 E. Market St., Akron, puerperal septicemia, abortion, 34492.

105 **Johnson, James**, w, m, 0, 1913, (b) Ohio, (d) 193 Bluff St., enterocolitis.

106 **Jones**, m, 0, 1917, (b) Infirmary (Miss Jones, mother), (d) Infirmary.

107 **Jordan, Alice**, w, f, 45, 1916, (b) West Virginia, (d) Kenmore, married, housewife, lobar pneumonia.

108 **Josmovic, Nikefor**, w, m, 45, 1912, (b) Hungary (Yosca Josmovic, Hungary, and Saveta Josmovic, Hungary), (d) Infirmary, married, (r) 204 N. Howard St., Akron, tailor, suicide from strangulation, tied belt spring around neck and tied to beam in shed, mental depression, 57077.

109 **Jospaith, L. J.**, w, m, 38, 1913, (b) Austria, (d) Infirmary, married, meningitis, 66343.

110 **Kearns, Alexandre**, w, m, 69, 1912, (b) Ohio, (d) Infirmary, widower, (r) 410 N. Maple[?], Akron, carpenter, chronic myocarditis.

111 **Keen**, c, f, 0, 1915, B. Akron (Alexander Keen, W.V., Aetheia Salton, West India), (d) People's Hospital, ward 4, premature birth, 25150.

112 **Kessler, Andrew**, m, 50, 1907, 2047.

113 **Ketchler, John R.**, w, m, 65, 1912, (d) City Hospital, cerebral hemorhage, arterio sclerosis.

114 **Killbourn, Eliza**, w, f, 87, 1909, (b) Ohio, (d) Infirmary, single, apoplexy, arterio sclerosis.

115 **Kirk, Mary**, w, f, o, 1916, (b) Ohio, (d) 459 E. North (other side of river), cholera infection, 46350.

116 **Kleten**, w, f, o, 1914, (b) Ohio (John Kleten, Hungary, wife unable to locate family, Hungary), (d) 854 Washington St., (r) 854 Washington St., Akron, inanition, small sized and feeble at birth, 41803.

117 **Kleten**, w, m, o, 1914, (b) Akron (John Kleten, Romania, Eva Kleten, Romania), (d) Washington St., (r) 854 Washington St., Akron, inanition, weak at birth, triplets.

118 **Knibbs, Thomas**, w, m, 72, 1915, (b) England, (d) Infirmary, widower, (r) Akron, hemorrhage from stomach, gastric ulcer, 30875.

119 **Kolas, Mike**, w, m, 47, 1916, (b) Austria, (d) Infirmary, carpenter for railroad construction, mitral regurgitation, 10172.

120 **Kovacevic, Vilim**, w, m, 35, 1914, (b) Hungary, (d) Mogadore, laborer, shock and hemorrhage fractured ribs hemorrhage of abdomen, murdered, 57836.

121 **Kust, Stefen**, m, 24, 1912, (b) Hungary, (d) Lock 6, accidentally drowned at Lock 6, 35867.

122 **La Belle, Hugh**, w, m, 64, 1915, (b) Ireland, (d) Infirmary, single, laborer, typhoid fever.

123 **LaCourt, Philip**, w, m, 75, 1915, (b) Belgium, (d) Infirmary, valvular heart disease, asthma.

124 **Laftus, Mike**, w, m, 54, 1915, (b) Ireland, (d) City Hospital, single, paver, accidental death from hemorrhage struck by street car, 25433.

125 **Langly, Julius**, w, m, 28, 1912, (b) Hungary, (d) 409 Washington Ave., Barberton or Cuyahoga Falls, laborer, gunshot wound of right temple, suicide.

126 **Lappin, Mynar**, w, m, 53, 1911, (b) Ohio, (d) Infirmary, single, retired, chronic myocarditis, contributing broken compensation, 61709.

127 **Laterbach**, m, 25, 1889, (d) Infirmary.

128 **Lattimer, Lewis**, w, m, 70, 1909, (b) Ohio, (d) Infirmary, single, (r) Akron, laborer, lobar pneumonia, senility, 16421.

129 **Lautenhizer, Daniel**, w, m, 69, 1911, (d) Infirmary, (r) Barberton, none, chronic nephritis/chronic endocarditis, 30024.

130 **Leslie, Charles**, w, m, 76, 1910, (b) England, (d) Infirmary, widower, (r) Hudson, bookkeeper, shock from operation for hernia, constricted hernia, 58026.

131 **Lessick, Frank**, w, m, 39, 1913, (b) Pennsylvania, (d) Infirmary, single, none, alcoholic cirohsis of liver.

132 **Lewastras, Chester**, w, m, 0, 1913, (b) Akron, Ohio (Ida Lewastras, parents born in W.V.), (d) 900 E. Exchange, cholera infection, 55089.

133 **Ley, Lewis**, m, 55, 1908, (d) Infirmary, epilepsy.

134 **Logan, William**, w, m, 36, 1912, (d) City Hospital, traumatic pnuemonia after being struck by a B.&O. train fracturing 5 ribs of right side.

135 **Lower, Aaron**, w, m, 62, 1915, (b) Pennsylvania, (d) Infirmary, single, common laborer, oedema of lungs, organic disease of heart, 18822.

136 **Lyden, John**, w, m, 48, 1911, (d) Infirmary, pulmonary tuberculosis, 34948.

137 **Madison, Joe**, w, m, 66, 1916, (b) Italy (Luther Martindale and Annette Palmer), (d) Infirmary, married, (r) 158 Furnace St., Akron, common laborer, pulmonary tuberculosis, exhaustion.

138 **Makow, Frank**, w, m, 37, 1913, (b) Romania, (d) Infirmary, single, (r) Akron, none, pulmonary tuberculosis with gangrene of lung, 36807.

139 **Martindal, Nettie O.**, f, 71, 1919, (b) Mentor, Ohio.

140 **McCain, Thomas**, w, m, 45, 1913, (d) Erie RR yard, accidentally struck by an Erie Train, entire body mangled, 36756.

141 **McGee, James**, w, m, 43, 1909, (d) Infirmary, single, (r) Munroe Falls, tetanus, frost bite, 64295.

142 **McGee, Joseph**, w, m, 52, 1915, (b) North Carolina, (d) Infirmary, single, expressman, locomotor ataxia.

143 **McLindslay, John**, b, m, 78, 1916, (b) Virginia, (d) Infirmary, married, (r) Richfield Summit road, Richfield Twp, common laborer, arterio sclerosis, mitral regurgitation from mitral insufficiency, pneumonia.

144 **Mehan, Edward**, w, m, 45, 1916, (d) Cuyahoga Falls RR, fractured skull struck by train on Cuyahoga Falls RR, 46397.

145 **Mekein, Alexander**, w, m, 46, 1911, (b) Pennsylvania, (d) Infirmary, widower, (r) Akron, laborer, erysipelas, 24270.

146 **Mellvern, Thomas**, w, m, 44, 1914, (b) Ohio, (d) Infirmary, single, (r) Stow, farmer, shock following amputation of leg for necrosed bone, frozen feet, 41863.

147 **Mesaros, Joe**, w, m, 37, 1914, (b) Hungary, (d) Infirmary, married, (r) City Hospital, laborer, mitral valvular disease of heart, 18739.

148 **Miller, Violet**, w, f, 0, 1913, (b) Akron, (d) 21 E. Crosier St., Premature birth, 24995.

149 **Miller, John**, w, m, 48, 1914, (b) Germany, (d) Infirmary, single, barber, mitral regurgitation, 34287.

150 **Mitchel, Charles W.**, w, m, 52, 1913, (b) Pennsylvania, (d) Infirmary, single, porter, lobar pneumonia following delirium from chronic alcoholism, 72232.

151 **Mulroy, Thomas**, w, m, 72, 1915, (b) Scotland, (d) Infirmary, married, (r) Barberton, common laborer, cerebral hemmorhage, 46460.

152 **Nagy, John**, w, m, 40, 1915, (d) City Hospital, suicide from gunshot wounds, 18810.

153 **Nichols, Jas**, m, 75, 2180.

154 **Nick, Jr., Rhyan Edgar**, w, m, 0, 1916, (b) Kenmore (parents Italian and Paris, France), (d) Kenmore, Premature birth.

155 **Nodenair, Joe**, w, m, 50, 1913, (b) Slovenia [?], (d) Infirmary, married, laborer, unknown stomach.

156 **Noltee**, w, f, 0, 1916, (b) Akron, Ohio, (d) 394 Livingston St., Akron, stillborn.

157 **Nune, Pete**, m, 20, 2143.

158 **Nutter, Harry**, w, m, 44, 1916, (b) England, (d) Infirmary, widower, laborer, paresis cause not known.

159 **Obentsch, Mike**, w, m, 40, 1916, (b) Austria, (d) City Hospital, widowed, laborer, organic heart disease.

160 **Obradovich**, w, m, 0, 1915, (b) Ohio (Bozo Obradovich, Serbia, Katy Radojoh, Hungary), (d) 73 Ira Ave., (r) 73 Ira Ave., Akron, premature birth, 39783.

161 **Osbourn, Cyrus**, w, m, 77, 1912, (b) Ohio, (d) Infirmary, widowed, Civil War veteran, mitral insuffication/insepticemia Myocarditis, broken compensation.

162 **Owens, Milton**, w, m, 61, 1911, (d) Infirmary, single, retired, arterio sclerosis, contributing feeble- minded, 18291.

163 **Ozmun, Levi**, m, 69, 1889, (d) Infirmary, widower.

164 **Parcell, Alberta**, w, f, o, 1914, (b) Akron (Charles Parcell, Ohio, Ida Rider, Ohio), (d) 67 N. Broadway, (r) 67 N. Broadway, Akron, acute bronchitis, chronic entero-colitis, 63028.

165 **Paul, Jacko**, w, m, o, 1914, (b) Akron (Samuel Paul, Hungary, Silka Dolich, Hungary), (d) 1132 Andrew St., gastroenteritis, one week no doctor in attendance, 47453.

166 **Pereshitis, Abe**, w, m, 52, 1914, (b) Hungary, (d) Infirmary, married, (r) Barberton, laborer, organic disease of the heart, 11692.

167 **Petrovich, Mike**, w, m, 30, 1914, (b) Austria, (d) City Hospital, married (Anna Petrovich), (r) 186 Spring St., Akron, laborer, peritonitis following operation for intestinal obstruction, 25443.

168 **Pewoski, Joe**, w, m, 39, 1915, (b) Austria, (d) Infirmary, married, (r) 1252 Edison Ave., Akron, common laborer, typhoid fever, 30876.

169 **Pfaiffer, Charles**, w, m, 41, 1912, (b) Germany, (d) Infirmary, widowed, painter, carcinoma of stomach, starvation.

170 **Phillips, Frank**, m, 45, 2318.

171 **Pisciotta, Jasper**, w, m, 24, 1914, (b) Italy, (d) 172 W. North St., single, laborer, lobar pneumonia.

172 **Plark**, w, m, o, 1915, (b) Akron, Ohio, (d) 193 S. Forge (in rear), Akron, stillborn.

173 **Plok, Gavreal**, w, m, 26, 1914, (b) Russia, (d) City Hospital, married, laborer, crushed limb of thigh amputation. Accidentally struck by No. 9 and L Cos. Car, 25177[?].

174 **Plowshitz, Christina**, w, f, 24, 1915, (b) Serbia, (d) Infirmary, married, (r) Barberton, match worker, Barberton Match Factory, tubercular meningitis.

175 **Porter, Albert**, w, m, 62, 1915, (b) Ohio, (d) Infirmary, divorced, farm laborer, cancer of the stomach, exhuastion, 18823.

176 **Puriski, Steve**, w, m, 38, 1912, (b) Hungary, (d) Infirmary, single, acute pulmonary tuberculosis.

177 **Ramder, Erich**, w, m, 54, 1912, (b) Switzerland, (d) City Hospital. widower, accidental fall on side walk fracturing base of skull, 68880,

178 **Ranlus, Levi**, m, 53, 1889, (d) Infirmary.

179 **Reese, John**, w, m, 69, 1916, (b) Wales, (d) Infirmary, none, mitral regurgitation, 40171.

180 **Regonini, S.**, w, m, 45, 1915, (d) Plaza Hotel, Akron, Ohio, acute alcoholism.

181 **Renfrot, Jacob**, w, m, 67, 1915, (b) Findland, (d) Infirmary/County Hospital, single, laborer, mitral heart leakage.

182 **Richards, Eliza**, f, 51, 1908, (d) Infirmary, pneumonia.

183 **Richards, James**, w, m, 0, 1913, (b) Akron (M. Richard, Ohio, Canie Richards, W.V.), (d) Children's Hospital, (r) 107 Lincoln St., Akron, enterocolitis, 72143.

184 **Richards, Wilford**, b, m, 28, 1916, (d) Ohio Canal, drowning in canal probably suicide.

185 **Richardson, Pora**, w, f, 67, 1912, (d) Infirmary, none, carcinoma of uterus.

186 **Richardson, Fletcher**, b, m, 38, 1916, (d) Mt. View Ave., single, laborer, gunshot wound through heart. Homicidal.

187 **Riche, Frank**, w, m, 52, 1914, (d) Infirmary, single, pulmonary tuberculosis, 2 months, 57833.

188 **Ridouot, Amos**, b, m, 53, 1916, (b) Pennsylvania, (d) Springfield/East Akron Sanitarium, East Akron, laborer, pulmonary tuberculosis.

189 **Riley, Mike**, w, m, 44, 1916, (b) Union City, PA, (d) Infirmary, single, (r) Cleveland, common laborer, pleura-pneumonia.

190 **Rose, Jr., John**, w, m, 65, 1914, (b) Missouri, (d) 31 N. High St., married, none, cerebral hemorrage, 5673.

191 **Rosman, John**, w, m, 49, 1912, (b) Germany, (d) Infirmary, single, laborer, rheumatic fever.

192 **Ross, Alvin**, c, m, 35, 1913, (b) Ohio, (d) Infirmary, married, laborer, pulmonary tuberculosis, 72231.

*Appendix A*

193 **Rowell, Mary**, w, f, 18, 1889, (d) Infirmary.

194 **Rusiacky, Constantin**, w, m, 19, 1914, (b) Russia (Wasyl Rusiacky and Maria Rusiacky), (d) Franklin Twp., married, (r) Barberton, Laborer, Struck by train with Sergey Timachovitz, 5743.

195 **Ryan, Patrick**, w, m, 67, 1911, (b) Ireland, (d) Infirmary, single, none, pulmonary tuberculosis, 61744.

196 **Satir, Sophia**, w, f, 0, 1914, (b) Ohio (Nick Latie, Poland, May Nitzki, Poland), (d) Children's Hospital, (r) Akron, endterocolitis, 47387.

197 **Scappin, William**, w, m, 71, 1910, (b) Ohio, (d) Infirmary, single, (r) Akron, laborer, erysipelas, 10962.

198 **Schaffer**, w, m, 0, 1912, (b) Ohio (Chauncy Schaffer, Austria, Lizzie Masteon, Austria), (d) City Hospital, premature birth, 62360.

199 **Schaub, William**, w, m, 30, 1916, (d) Barberton B. & O. tracks, fractured skull, strcuk by B&O freight train.

200 **Schear**, w, m, 0, 1913, (b) Ohio, (d) City Hospital, stillborn, 49222.

201 **Schwind**, w, m, 0, 1915, (b) Akron (Henry Schwind, Austria, Mary Schwind, Austria), (d) City Hospital, still born, 11483.

202 **Scladen, Anna**, w, f, 42, 1909, (d) Infirmary, married, (r) Akron, house wife, pulmonary tuberculosis, 58844.

203 **Seaton, Elizabeth Betsey**, w, f, 74, 1875, (b) Vermont

204 **Selep, George**, w, m, 45, 1911, (d) Infirmary, (r) Barberton, pulmonary tuberculosis, 11635.

205 **Selwester, Annie**, w, f, 42, 1915, (d) 292 Furnace St., divorced (J. H. Schear from Texas and Mina Marietta from Ohio), (r) 292 Furnace St., Akron, housewife, lobar pneumonia, 63106.

206 **Sepdilla, John**, w, m, 43, 1913, (b) Hungary, (d) Infirmary, single, laborer, pulmonary tuberculosis, 55203.

207 **Shalgrue, John**, w, m, 20, 1915, (b) Austria, (d) Infirmary, single, (r) Akron, laborer, pulmonary tuberculosis, 63121.

208 **Shamun, Maggie**, w, f, 56, 1912, (b) Pennsylvania, (d) Infirmary, married, none, carcinoma of uterus, contributing exhaustion, 5744.

209 **Shandor, Valichko**, w, m, 55, 1916, (b) Serbia, (d) 79 N. Case Ave., Akron, laborer, Carcinoma of the stomach, contributing factor exhaustion, 21664.

210 **Shaw, Charles**, w, m, 63, 1911, (b) Massachusetts, (d) Infirmary, married, tinsmith, interstitial nephritis, 40445.

211 **Sherlock, Mike**, w, m, 49, 1915, (b) New York (Ohio resident 49 years), (d) Infirmary, single, laborer, pulmonary tuberculosis.

212 **Sherman, Martin** [Marton?], w, m, 55, 1910, (b) Germany, (d) Infirmary, single, laborer, lobar pneumonia, 63518.

213 **Shortis, Charles**, w, m, 49, 1909, (b) Pennsylvania, (d) Infirmary, single, (r) Barberton, laborer, chronic nephritis, chronic valvular disease, 53931.

214 **Sikova, George**, w, m, 50, 1916, (b) Austria, (d) Infirmary, single, laborer, syphilis.

215 **Simpson, Thomas**, w, m, 67, 1918, (b) Ohio (father from Scotland), (d) Norton Ave, Barberton, Ohio, painter & paper laborer, lobar pneumonia.

216 **Sladen, Harry**, w, m, 58, 1913, (d) Federal St., First ward, single, laborer, cerebral hemorhage, alcoholism.

217 **Slannery, Joseph**, w, m, 28, 1913, (b) Pennsylvania, (d) Infirmary, single, dilation of the heart, chronic valvular heart disease, 5822.

218 **Smith, Mary**, w, f, 70, 1915, (b) West Virginia, (d) Infirmary, widow, senile dementia, arterio sclerosis contributing.

219 **Smith, Neil**, w, m, 0, 1912, (b) Akron, (d) Mary Day Nursery, 315 Locust St., (r) 849 Hammel St., Akron, marasmus, gastro enteritis, 51526.

220 **Smith, Frank**, w, m, 20, 1915, (b) Wisconsin, (d) Infirmary, laborer, typhoid.

221 **Smith, John**, b, m, 40, 1913, (d) City Hospital, septicemia following a cut on cheek coupled by a blow in a fight. Homocide, 42956.

222 **Smith, Joseph**, w, m, 60, 1912, (b) Germany, (d) Infirmary, laborer, senile pneumonia, interstitial nephritis.

223 **Smith, George**, m, 1908, (d) Infirmary.

224 **Smith, John**, w, m, 40, 1916, (b) Poland, (d) City Hospital, (r) 203 E. North St., Akron, laborer, lobar pneumonia.

225 **Smythe**, w, m, 0, 1912, (b) Akron (Augustus Smythe, S.D., Ada Josephine Nichols, St. James, Ohio), (d) City Hospital, stillborn, 57087.

226 **Snyder, Albert**, w, m, 50, 1916, (b) South Africa, (d) City Hospital, married, (r) Silver Lake Jet O, Rubber worker, Firestone, gunshot wound in head, homocidal.

227 **Soos, John**, w, m, 40, 1915, (b) Russia, (d) 405 Bartges St., married, (r) 405 Bartes St., Akron, mill laborer, organic heart disease, 5295.

228 **Spangler, Elizabeth**, w, f, 40, 1911, (b) Germany, (d) Infirmary, (r) Akron, none, meningits/nephritis, 56170.

229 **Speering, Edward**, w, m, 65, 1916, (d) Riverside Hotel, Cuyahoga Falls, heart disease.

230 **Spinrely, Henry**, w, m, 1913.

231 **Spridy, Henry**, w, m, 60, 1915, (b) Ohio, (d) Infirmary, single, (r) Canal St., Akron, laborer, apoplexy.

232 **Stasek, Anna**, w, f, 35, 1915, (b) Austria-Hungary, (d) Peoples Hospital, widow, (r) 896 Holloway St., Akron, housewife, suicidal- from wood alcohol poisoning [methanol], 30855.

233 **Stea, George**, w, m, o, 1912, (b) Ohio (Madaline Stea), (d) Children's hospital, non-assimilation of food (39 days).

234 **Steurn, John**, w, m, 56, 1910, (b) US, (d) Infirmary, single, Akron, laborer, pulmonary tuberculosis, 5270.

235 **Stoner, Benjamin**, m, 70, 1900, (d) Infirmary, stroke (cerebral hemorrhage.

236 **Stovyea, Nova**, w, m, 44, 1914, (b) Serbia, (d) Infirmary, single, laborer, cancer of the stomach, exhuastion, 36528.

237 **Stretarich, John**, w, m, 43, 1911, (b) Austria, (d) Infirmary, married, laborer, pulmonary tuberculosis, 67134.

238 **Stronhacker, Hannah**, w, f, 50, 1911, (b) Ohio, (d) Infirmary, single, none, chronic myocarditis, contributing broken compensation.

239 **Strothers**, w, f, o, 1914, (b) Akron (Harry Strother, W.V., Marcella Weey, IN.), (r) 286 S. Main St., stillborn, 41778.

240 **Supple, John**, w, m, 67, 1916, (b) Akron (1st generation, Irish parents), laborer, pyelonephritis.

241 **Swank**, w, m, o, 1914, (b) Akron (Daniel Swank, PA, Ida Hysong, PA), (d) City Hospital, (r) 320 W. Chestnut, Akron , unknown, the undesired baby was found dead by nurse. For [? Illegible], 69022.

242 **Taft, Martin**, m, 42, 1908, (d) Infirmary, jaundice.

243 **Tantia, Edward**, w, m, 32, 1913, (b) New Jersey, (d) Infirmary, single, laborer, assending pyelitis, 18805.

244 **Tate, Henry P.**, w, m, 42, 1913, (b) Pennsylvania, (d) Infirmary, single, painter, pulmonary tuberculosis, 18808.

245 **Thompson, Calvin**, m, 77, 1889, (d) Infirmary, single,

246 **Thompson, Robert**, m, 1902.

247 **Thorp, Christina**, w, f, 57, 1915, (d) Summit Co. hospital, married, domestic, pyelonephritis.

248 **Timachovitz, Sergey**, m, 31, 1914, (b) Russia (Stefan and Ahafia Timachovitz), (d) Franklin Twp., laborer, struck by train with Constantin Rusiacky.

249 **Tomlin, Edward**, m, 33, 1913, (b) New Jersey, (d) Infirmary, single, laborer, 18805.

250 **Tonin, Lazo**, w, m, 54, 1914, (b) Hungary, (d) Infirmary, married, (r) Akron, laborer, emphysema, exhaustion, 18731.

251 **Trego, Samuel L.**, w, m, 21, 1914, (b) Pennsylvania, (d) City Hospital, single, (r) 970 Johnston St., Akron, rubber worker, meningitis (metastatic), emphysema, 57825.

252 **True, Fred**, w, m, 35, 1909, (d) Infirmary, single, Akron, laborer, chronic endocarditis, cirohsis of liver, chronic nephritis, 43579.

253 **Truman, Henry Leroy**, w, m, 0, 1915, (b) Ohio (Henry Lendiman, Pennsylvania, Ana Truman, W.V.), (d) Infirmary, imperfect development of heart causing congestion of lungs.

254 **Tuko, Geo**, w, m, 33, 1914, (b) Akron, (d) Infirmary, married, rubber worker, pulmonary tuberculosis, 31286.

255 **Vargar, Michael**, w, m, 45, 1916, (b) Austria Hungary, (d) Infirmary, married, (r) Barberton, laborer, suicide by hanging,

256 **Victor, Clara**, f, 61, 1889, (d) Infirmary.

257 **Voihovech, George**, w, m, 53, 1911, (b) Hungary, (d) Portage Twp, widower, (r) Akron, laborer, chronic nephritis/endocarditis, 5714.

258 **Wells, Isaac**, w, m, 72, 1913, (b) Mother born in Ohio, (d) Infirmary, single, laborer, artio sclerosis, terminal pneumonia, 5819.

259 **Weyriels, Lewis**, w, m, 63, 1913, (d) Infirmary, single, (r) Infirmary, septic meningitis, 66342.

260 **Wheeler, Vardusler**, m, 1883.

261 **White, William Richard**, w, m, 3, 1916, (b) West Virginia, (d) 652 Belleview Ave., Akron, cholera infection.

262 **White, James J.**, w, m, 37, 1914, (b) West Virginia, (d) Near Black Dog Causeway of B.&O. RR, married (Emma White), was probably struck and killed by B.&O. train. Body completely decomposed, 36524.

263 **White, James C.**, c, m, 45, 1915, (b) Norfolk, VA, (d) near Bettes Corners, Tallmadge Township, single, B.&O. RR laborer, fractured skull accidentally struck by street car, N.O.T. & L. Co., 69569.

264 **Whitnight**, w, m, 0, 1915, (b) Akron (Ray Farber, Ohio, Christa Whitnight, Ohio), (d) 646 Washington St., stillborn child, 18789.

265 **Wigell, William**, w, m, 0, 1914, (b) Akron (Victor Wigell and Sofa Wawia, both from Finland), (d) 703 Edgewood Blvd., Premature birth, 5644.

266 **Wigell, Victor**, w, m, 0, 1914, (b) Akron (Victor Wigell and Sofa Wawia, both from Finland), (d) 703 Edgewood Blvd., Premature birth, 5652.

267 **Wilkinson, James**, w, m, 56, 1916, (b) United States, (d) Infirmary, (r) 503 Grant St., Akron, laborer, lobar pneumonia.

268 **Williams, Joseph**, w, m, 0, 1916, (b) Ohio (parents Italian), (d) Children's Hospital, renal hemorhage.

269 **Williams, Roy**, c, m, 30, 1916, (d) City Hospital, laborer, pulmonary tuberculosis.

270 **Williams, George**, w, m, 86, 1909, (b) Wales, (d) Infirmary, single, laborer, arterio sclerosis.

271 **Wilson, Sarah**, w, f, 0, 1916, (b) Ohio, (d) Wilson residence, Honodle Ave., Honodle Ave., Akron, measles.

272 **Wilson, Albert**, w, m, 45, 1913, (d) City Hospital, typhoid fever.

273 **Winkleman, Daniel**, w, m, 74, 1914, (d) Infirmary, single, harness maker, apoplexy, 31285.

274 **Wyland, Clair E.**, w, m, 0, 1914, (b) Akron (George Wyland, PA., Annie Barntd, PA), (d) 557 S. Main St., (r) 557 S. Main St., Akron, broncho-pneumonia, influenza, 69079.

275 **Ykoblavic, Eva**, w, f, 39, 1913, (b) Austria (parents Hungarian), (d) 999 Haynes St., married, (r) 999 Haynes St., Akron, housewife, uremia following confinement, cold and influenza(?) case, 72166.

276 w, f, o, 1911, (d) Ohio Canal, Akron, drowned, was found floating in canal wrapped in woman's stocking. 1–5 days old, 61670.

277 w, f, o, 1915, (b) Ohio (Pete Bonitz, Hungary, Katy Boskrish, Hungary), (d) City Hospital, (r) 193 Harter Ave., Akron, still born, 5259.

278 w, f, o, 1915, (d) Old Ohio and PA canal, 6th ward by B&O trestle. probably homicidal. Found in old P.&O. Canal near B.&O. trestle, 18797.

279 w, f, o, 1916, (b) Akron, (d) Ladd St., Akron, stillborn.

280 w, f, o, 1916, (d) Keller Brick Yard, Tallmadge Twp, suffocation, probably homicidal.

281 w, m, o, 1912, (b) Ohio, (d) City Hospital, single, (r) Ohio, premature birth, 62360.

282 w, m, o, 1916, (d) 118 Cole Ave., stillborn found in abandoned cistern.

283 w, m, 26, 1915, (d) Kirwin Farm, half mile north of Tallmadge Ave., suicide from gunshot wounds, 19704.

284 w, m, 30, 1912, (d) B.& O. Railroad tracks, 2nd ward, suicide, was lying on B.&O. railroad tracks with neck across track was run over by train, head being severed.

285 w, m, 30, 1912, (d) B.& O. Yard, murdered from knife strike wounds of chest.

286 w, m, 35, 1912, (d) City Hospital, cirohsis of liver, alcoholism, 51520.

287 w, m, 35, 1915, (d) City Hospital, single, laborer, internal hemorhage, probably struck by train.

288 w, m, 35, 1916, (d) Barberton, found dead in car. Steel blooms crushed skull.

289 w, m, 38, 1914, (d) Mountain Heights, suicide from hanging.

290 w, m, 38, 1916, (d) City Hospital, internal hemorhage, arterio sclerosis.

291 w, m, 40, 1916, (d) N.O. RR roundhouse, body cut in two—accidentally struck by M. O. engine.

292 w, m, 45, 1915, (d) City Hospital, crushed chest struck by metro urban car at Chittenden bridge, 46405.

293 w, m, 45, 1916, (d) Minden Brickyard, organic head disease.

294 w, m, 45, 1916, (d) Akron Lumber Company, organic heart disease.

295 w, m, 47, 1914, (d) Railroad yard, fracture of base of skull accidentally struck by N.O.T. & L. limited, 36412.

296 w, m, 50, 1916, (d) Tallmadge Twp, fractured skull, struck by Erie R.R. co. train.

297 w, m, 50, 1916, (d) Portage Twp, suicide by hanging.

298 m, 55, 1912, Found floating in the canal, death believed to be accidental, 30890.

299 w, m, 60, 1912, (d) C. A. and C. yards, ward 5, skull crushed, legs torn off, arms broken as result of being run over by C.A. & L. train, accidental, 68909.

300 w, m, 65, 1912, (d) Railroad Yard, 6th ward, fracture of skull, struck by a B.& O. freight train.

301 w, m, 65, 1913, (d) 303 Cole Ave., organic heart disease, 55092.

302 w, m, 75, 1913, (d) C.A. & C. yards, ward 7, accidentally struck by C. A. & C. train causing fracture of skull, 5795.

303 w, m, 1912, (d) B.& O. Railroad yard, 6th ward, struck by B. & O. train, left leg cut off, boh arms crushed, right leg crushed.

304 w, m, 1916, (d) Cuyahoga Falls, head crushed, struck by B. & O. train.

305 w, m, 20, 1916, (d) Bluff St. Crossing, fractured Skull, struck by Penn. Train.

306 w, m, 40, 1916, (d) Forge St., Akron, struck by B. & O. train, head severed from body.

307 w, m, 50, 1919, (b) Hungary, (d) Old Forge St., Akron, head, body, and legs crushed and mangled, struck by B.& O. passenger train, 72471.

308 w, m, 60, 1914, (d) Cuyahoga Falls Ave, 1st ward, abdomen crushed left arm and leg fractured accidentally struck by an N.O.T. & L., 41804.

# Appendix B
# CADA Script
## "Along the Graveyard Path"
*by the CADA cast and Wendy Duke*

This is version 4.0, completed on March 24, 2020.

*Editors' note:* this script has been modified slightly for inclusion in this volume. The character roles were anonymized, and the script was shortened by eliminating some stage directions, musical chord notations, and duplicated song choruses. Editors' notes and remaining stage directions are in italics.

*Authors' notes:* all sets and locations will be represented by projected photos and images described as 'slides' below. The central location is Schneider Park in Akron, OH.

## ACT ONE

### SCENE 1—*Summit County Infirmary, 1865*

*Slide: Akron Poor House in 1865. Lights dim, and an old-time newsreel is projected on the upstage screen. The newsreel presents the story of Schneider Park. The company enters as actors with props in a wagon, preparing to perform the play, in small groups while singing.*

Song: "The Graveyard is Telling Its Tale"

Disability
Throughout time
Yours and mine.
The stories are in the bones.
Lasting stones
Hey Hey Hey.
The bones are crying.
Hey Hey Hey.
The truth is flying.
No more No more No more.

Chorus:
The graveyard is telling its tale.
No more. No more. No more.
The graveyard is telling its tale.
No More No More No More.
No more. No more. No more.

*(Actors are seated in a semi-circle on stage surrounding the playing area. They will remain in sight throughout the play.)*

**Narrator**: 2017. A class of anthropology students at the University of Akron are investigating Schneider Park. The Schneider Park mystery draws University of Akron students; an archaeological survey of grave sites is underway. We reached out to Professor Matney, and he agreed to meet us at the burial site in Schneider Park. We learned that the bright green rectangles indicate where people were buried. Grass grows more lush on ground that was dug up. The earth surrounding each grave was trampled upon, and the earth pressed down, making it harder for grass to flourish.

## SCENE 2—*Schneider Park*

*Slide: Schneider Park. Kids in Schneider Park from the 1950s find bones sticking out of the ground.*

**Youth 1:** Hey, look at this sticking up out of the ground—looks like a leg bone.

**Youth 2:** What's it doing here?

**Youth 1:** I heard this park used to be a graveyard.

**Youth 2:** Spooky!

**Old Man:** What are you two doing there?

*(The boys run away, and an old man examines the bones.)*

**Youth 2***: Screams.*

**Youth 1**: Let's get out of here!

**Old Man:** If these bones could only talk, what stories would they tell?

*(He carefully digs into the ground with a stick and reburies the bones.)*

*Song: Chorus from "The Graveyard is Telling Its Tale"*

### Scene 3—Skeletal Remains: A scene based upon archeological research

*Slide: Conference on Paleontology and Compassion*

**Dr. Jordan Euell:** Hello. My name is Dr. Jordan Euell. Welcome to our conference on Paleontology and Compassion. Recent scientific research into early human skeletal remains has revealed that prehistoric humans cared for the sick and disabled. Archeologists propose that far from abandoning those who could not hunt or forage, prehistoric humans took care of those who had limited or no mobility. In the *International Journal of Paleopathology*, an article discussed one skeleton called Burial 9 in a site called Man Bac in northern Vietnam. Unlike the other skeletons, Burial 9 was laid out in a fetal position. This man "had most likely been paralyzed from the waist down due to a congenital disease...and would not have been able to use his arms, feed himself or attend to other bodily needs." (Tilley and Oxenham) However, from studying the bones, researchers concluded the man had lived into his twenties. Therefore, even though he could not participate in hunting, fishing, and taking care of pigs, other people obviously provided care for him. We have some exciting new research today to be presented by Dr. Joseph Moran, Dr. Nicolas Santiago, Dr. Wendy Duke, and Dr. Sid Kranz. First, Dr. Moran. *(Editors' Note: information for this exchange is drawn from two websites. First, The Wellness Journey, an online* *journalism, science, and education sources from Minnesota Wellness Publications, Inc. and particularly from the October, 2, 2021 editorial on Margaret Mead (https://wellnessjourneys.org/2022/10/02/margaret-mead/). And second, from the blog People Thinking Action (https://peoplethinkingaction.blogspot.com/2013/01/disability-in-prehistory.html).)*

*Slide: Shanidar 1*

**Dr. Moran:** 45,000 years ago, a Neanderthal, Shanidar 1, lived to the age of fifty in what is now modern-day Iraq, although one of his arms had been amputated, one of his eyes lacked vision, and he had sustained other injuries.

*Slide: Romito 2*

**Dr. Santiago:** 10,000 years ago, Romito 2 lived until he was a teenager. His skeleton shows that he had a form of severe dwarfism that meant his arms were very short. He was, therefore, unable to live by hunting and gathering among his people, who would have had to provide support in order for him to survive.

*Slide: Windover Boy*

**Dr. Kranz:** 7,500 years ago, Windover Boy in Florida lived to the age of fifteen, although he was born with spina bifida, a severe spinal malformation.

*Slide: Arabian Peninsula burial*

**Dr. Duke:** 4,000 years ago, a young woman on the site on the Arabian peninsula lived to 18. She had a neuromuscular disease, possibly polio, with very thin arms and legs that would have made walking and movement extremely difficult. She would have needed "round-the-clock care." We noted that her teeth were rotting and that possibly she had been fed lots of dates, grown by this group of humans, to keep her from crying.

**Dr. Jordan Euell:** In conclusion, we would like to think that modern society does a great job of providing care for our disabled citizens. We take pride in that we no longer leave disabled infants on mountain tops to die, like the ancient Greeks and Romans. This new research shows us that the impulse to aid and assist, to show compassion, is a trait that goes back to prehuman societies, and evidence of it has appeared throughout thousands of years.

*Spoken word chorus: "Just A Home of My Own"*
Well, my name doesn't matter
This is not about me
For my story is like many millions you see
It's a story that needs to be told right away
Cause it's not in the past no, still goes on today
Like a knife it can cut to the heart—to the bone
What I want isn't much just a home of my own.

### Scene 4—Neanderthal Scene, Adults

*Slide: Neanderthal cave in Croatia. Two parents, Beck and Chud, are holding, cooing, etc. their newborn baby, Tud.*

**Beck**: Aw, look at little Tud! He so precious!

**Chud**: Yes, he truly is blessing.

**Beck**: Wait, something wrong with Tud.... Tud feet don't look right.

**Chud**: You right, and his eye not black, it look like clouds.

**Beck**: We need call Shaman, so he be fixed.

*(Shaman enters)*

**Shaman**: What is problem with child?

**Beck**: He deformed in legs and head.

**Shaman**: Let me take him.

*(Shaman utters a small prayer in caveman talk, and hands Tud back.)*

**Chud**: He is not fixed.

**Shaman**: If nothing change, he was not broken at all.

**Beck**: You must be right. Little Tud perfect!

*(Chud exits, and enter a now adult Tud)*

**Narration**: Time passes. Tud is now a grown man.

**Tud:** You want to see me mother?

**Beck:** Yes, you remember when your father die?

**Tud:** Yes, mother, why ask?

**Beck:** Well, there will come time when I die too. I just want you to be prepared.

**Tud:** Ok…?

**Beck:** Now go. I talk with Shaman.

*(Tud exits, Shaman enters)*

**Shaman:** Yes, Beck?

**Beck:** Shaman, I will die soon. Promise to look after Tud when I go.

**Shaman:** Of course, Beck. We will take care of Tud as one of our own. And when he finally passes, we will bury him with his kinfolk.

*Slide: Landscape at Neanderthal cave site*

*(Beck exits. Tud and other cavemen enter. They pantomime hunting, and Tud is struck by accident. They lay him down, and he dies. They have a burial.)*

*Song: "The Long Haul" (verse 1)*
I was beside you in the darkness of the caves
when fires died, protecting and defending with fearsome pride.
Against my fear, I held you near,
It's been a long haul.

Chorus:
The long haul,
I'm with you and beside you
For the long haul.
One goal together
Over the long haul.

### *Scene 5—Ancient Egypt, youth*

*Slide: Ancient Egypt, a typical residence. Scene starts with Kasmut sitting on a bench with her back to the audience. The priest and are standing with backs to audience.*

**Kasmut:** O good dwarf, come, because of the one who sent you...

**Amenemope:** come down placenta, come down placenta, come down!

**Yuf:** The baby is here!!!

*(Baby cries. Everybody turns around, and Yuf is holding a baby.)*

**Yuf:** He's beautiful!

**Kasmut:** Yes... but look his hands and feet... they're smaller than any I've seen. And his neck is short!

**Amenemope:** Man is clay and straw; the God is his builder.

**Yuf:** Yes! God has sent us such a beautiful baby!

**Kasmut:** Very well, may God's will be fulfilled. We shall name him Seneb.

**Narration:** Ten years have passed. We see Seneb playing on a bench with a piece of metal.

*Slide: Ancient Egypt exterior*

*(Scene changes to Seneb sitting on a bench alone twiddling with a price of metal. Three bullies enter and begin to tease Seneb. Bully 3 is clearly the leader.)*

**Bully 1:** Hey, look! It's the dwarf!

**Bully 2:** Look at his short little legs! And that big head!

**Bully 3:** What've you got there, dwarf? A piece of metal? Hah! You will be useless!

**Narrator:** The bullies surround little Seneb and take his piece of metal. They begin to push and tease him.

**Amenemope:** Children! Leave that boy alone! Beware of robbing a wretch or attacking a cripple. Do not laugh at a blind man, nor tease a dwarf, nor cause hardship for the lame. Don't tease a man who is in the hands of the gods. (*Editors' Note: information and inspiration for this content is drawn from Dr. Judith Felson Duchan's online History of Speech-Language Pathology (https://www.acsu.buffalo.edu/~duchan/new_history/ancient_history/egypt.html).*)

*(The bullies exit.)*

**Bullies:** Sid: Sorry. Amanda: Sorry. Samir: Sorry.

**Amenemope:** Do not worry, Seneb. They know not that dwarves are good luck! If they weren't fools, then they would become friends with you.

**Narrator:** Seneb has had a fascination for metal since he was very young. His mother takes him to a goldsmith to see if he could be an apprentice as a goldsmith.

*(Ancient Egypt goldsmith workshop)*

*(Scene changes to the goldsmith sitting on the bench working. He quickly stands as Seneb and Kasmut come on. Amenemope is also there.)*

**Goldsmith:** What can I do for you?

**Kasmut:** My son here is looking for an apprenticeship.

**Goldsmith:** He's too small.

**Seneb:** I may be small, sir, but I'm strong as an ox and precise as a hummingbird.

**Amenemope:** The Wise Man should respect people affected by reversal of fortune." Who knows, if you train him well, he may very well bring you good fortune.

**Goldsmith:** All right. Well, get to work, and we'll see if you're worth anything.

**Narrator:** Years pass, and Seneb now has his own goldsmith business. He has many famous clients. Including the pharaoh himself

*(Scene changes to Seneb doing metalwork at the bench. The pharaoh enters.)*

**Seneb:** My pharaoh!

**Pharaoh:** I would like a death mask prepared for my mother.

**Seneb:** I would be honored, Pharaoh!

**Narration:** After a long life of service to his pharaoh, Seneb reached the end of his life and was honored with a burial in his pharaoh's pyramid.

*Slide: Pyramid. Funeral music is playing*

**Pharaoh:** It is a shame. He was a valuable worker and a good leader.

**Amenemope:** God makes use of everyone. Even this dwarf was made into a great man.

*Song: "The Long Haul" (verse 2)*
Now when they told me
The challenges that blocked you on your way
I knew that I had nothing more to say.
We have so much to do,
But we'll see it through,
Over the long haul.

Chorus from "The Long Haul"

*Scene 6. Ancient Greece, Adults*

*Slide: Ancient Greece home interior*

**Narrator:** In Ancient Greece, the culture was not accepting of disabilities. We learn what many parents must face and decide when a child is born who is not perfect.

**Georgios:** Oh my! The baby looks very strange!

**Calandra:** Honey, I think he may be deformed.

**Georgios:** Disgusting! I don't want him!

**Calandra:** I don't want him either, but I don't know what to do with him.

**Georgios:** I have heard that Aristotle advises to kill the baby.

**Calandra:** But I don't want to be scrutinized for murder or have to live with killing someone!

**Georgios:** I have studied the law. It says that a baby is not classified as a baby until seven days after birth. This way, we can get rid of it and still have a clear conscience.

**Calandra:** I will take him to the woods while you tell the slaves to be quiet about it.

*Song: "The Long Haul" (verse 3)*
I've got the strength of the mountain
I'm as solid as a stone,
I'm as fierce as the tiger,

You're my child, and you're my own.
You've been with me forever,
I would lay down my soul.
Living waters together
As onward we flow
Over the long haul.

Chorus from "The Long Haul"

### Scene 7—Ancient Rome—youth

*Slide: Ancient Roman dwelling, interior*

**Narrator:** The Romans did not especially like disabled bodies, but an element of practicality and making money shaped their decisions. Let's look in on an upper-class Roman family as they are examining their newborn child.

*(Parents Liviana and Horatio have a baby, Julius. Liviana is excited at first, but they quickly realize that their baby is deformed.)*

**Liviana:** Let me see my baby!

*(Servant Helper hands baby to Liviana.)*

**Liviana:** Oh! There is something wrong with him!

**Horatio:** Let me see!

*(Horatio is dismayed by the baby.)*

**Horatio:** The gods have shown displeasure with us! They have sent us a deformed baby! We must get rid of him.

**Liviana:** No! We can raise him! I don't want to get rid of him! I love him!

**Horatio:** He will be of no use to the family.

**Servant:** Lord, I have heard of deformed persons growing up to be entertainers for rich families or even royalty. He might bring much wealth to the family.

**Horatio:** Hmmmmmm.... We can keep him.... But I don't want to be seen with him in public. I can't have my friends thinking that I am bad luck.

**Liviana**: We will name him Julius

**Narration**: Little Julius is allowed to grow up and is sent to a school to learn how to entertain. His father takes him for an audition.

*Slide: Another Roman dwelling, upper class*

*Julius grows up, learning how to entertain. His father presents him to a rich political family so that he may be hired.*

**Rich Father**: What have you brought before me today, Horatio?

**Horatio**: Sixteen years ago, my spouse and I had a baby. Unfortunately he was deformed.

**Rich Father**: A disgrace!

**Horatio**: Yes, but he has grown up and is skilled in entertaining. Maybe you would want to hire him.

**Rich Father**: Let us see him!

*(Julius enters.)*

**Rich Father**: Oh my! He is an ugly fellow, isn't he? Well, Let's see what he can do.

*(Julius does a silly dance and song, then tells a joke.)*

**Julius**: Why did the cookie go to the doctor?

**Rich Father**: Why?

**Julius**: Because he felt a little crummy!

**Rich Father**: Ho Ho Ho Ho Ho Ho! He is funny! I will hire him, and I will pay him well.

**Horatio**: Thank you, my lord!

*Song: "The Long Haul" (verse 4)*
We walk this path now,
The road that leads you forward on your way.
You're moving down your path
And on the way;
I see you grow
And time will show,
It's for the long haul.

Chorus from "The Long Haul"

### Scene 8—Dark Ages, adults

*Slide: The Dark Ages. Slide: Ancient Britain, pagan/pre-Christian, exterior scene—a forest.*

**Narration:** After the fall of Rome, Europe descended into a time of chaos known as The Dark Ages. Let us see how families coped with disabled children during this time.

*(The scene starts with a man and a woman holding a newborn baby.)*

**Joan:** Thomas, something is boggled with this baby. There is something wrong with his eye. It is cloudy. And his foot!

**Thomas:** It is a club foot. How could a child with wrong feet work the fields?

**Joan:** Me thinks not.

**Thomas:** A child that can't work would only pull us back. We must get rid of it.

**Joan:** Yeah, I suppose.

**Thomas:** I shall leave it by the river.

**Narration:** Thomas departs for the river and sets the baby down, leaving it behind. Another group enters. One is limping, one is holding the arm of the other to see, and one has a twitch and speaks slowly.

**Adam:** What's this here babe doing?

*(Baby crying)*

**Geoffrey:** Methinks he was left by his mum and pop.

**Simon:** We should give it shelter for a while. Come, let us go.

*Song: "The Graveyard is Telling Its Tale"*

### Scene 9—Middle Ages, Youth

**Narration:** We are now in Medieval times, on the monastery grounds, where two monks have found an abandoned child.

*(Two monks stand holding a child)*

**Monk Peter:** Poor babe, left in this world by its parents.

**Monk John:** Look, Brother Peter, his foot be Lame, and his one eye looketh to be blynde.

**Monk Peter:** I see, Brother John. Me thinks we shall take him to our almshouse where he shall be taken care of, and when he is grown he may work the garden or sweep the halls.

**Monk John:** But what if he be too blynde and lame to work?

**Monk Peter:** I am sure we shall find a task that suits God's gifts to him.

**Monk John:** There are those among the clergy that say such deformity is a sign of great sin being punished.

**Monk Peter:** Bah, I say. There are also those in the clergy who see the piety in such as the blind, the lame, and the natural fool. I say they are closer to God's pilgrims passing through purgatory.

**Monk John:** And what of the lepers in Norf'k who ransacked the Abbey?

**Monk Peter:** I have it on good authority the Abbot there was a thief and scoundrel, and the Lepers acted in their defense, but enough of this rhetoric! Let us take this child in so that we may ease his suffering with the seven comfortable works and guide his life with the seven spiritual works.

**Monk John:** Aye, brother. And perhaps one day, the child will make pilgrimage to Canterbury, and God will grant him a cure.

**Monk Peter:** Perhaps. Or perhaps he is already as God sees him to be.

*(The two monks exit with the baby)*

*Song: from "The Graveyard Is Telling Its Tale"*
Hey Hey Hey
The bones are crying.
Hey Hey Hey
The truth is flying
No more. No more. No more.
The graveyard is telling its tale.
No more. No more. No more.

*Scene 10—Renaissance: Disability on stage*

*Slide: the Globe Theatre*

**Narrator Nicolas:** At the beginning of the Renaissance, the churches were disbanded along with the hospitals within the monasteries. Disabled people were left to fend for themselves, homeless, or dependent upon their villages to provide care.

**Narrator Ruben:** Some individuals with intellectual disabilities found work at the courts, entertaining royalty with their wit and humor! In Elizabethan England, disabled characters were portrayed on stage. Let us go to the Globe Theatre, where a production of Shakespeare's Richard III is taking place:

*(Actor comes forward on the stage as Richard the III. Groundlings seated at his feet)*

**Richard the III:** But I, that am not shaped for sportive tricks, Nor made to court an amorous looking-glass; I, that am rudely stamp'd, and want love's majesty To strut before a wanton ambling nymph; I, that am curtail'd of this fair proportion, Cheated of feature by dissembling nature, Deformed, unfinish'd, sent before my time. Into this breathing world, scarce half made up, And that so lamely and unfashionable. That dogs bark at me as I halt by them; Why, I, in this weak piping time of peace, Have no delight to pass away the time, Unless to spy my shadow in the sun and descant on mine own deformity: And therefore, since I cannot prove a lover, To entertain these fair well-spoken days, I am determined to prove a villain And hate the idle pleasures of these days.

*(Actor goes off. Groundlings turn to audience and begin discussing)*

**Groundling 1:** What a marvelous performance!

**Groundling 2:** Truly it was. But can you imagine being deformed such as he?

**Groundling 3:** The suffering and unkindness shown even to a king!

**Groundling 4:** What would happen if one such as us had been born thus?

**Groundling 5:** We could just as easily be struck by a horse and cart in the street and not walk again.

**Groundling 6**: we would be reduced to being beggars like those we see in front of Saint Paul's cathedral.

**Groundling 1**: surely there is some hospital that could care for us?

**Groundling 2**: Nay, Henry the 8th closed them when he banished the Catholic Church.

**Groundling 3**: I hear there was a petition to reopen the almshouses back many years ago.

**Groundling 4**: But it was never paid any mind to.

**Groundling 5**: In my village there was a dwarf of such wit he became a fool for the court.

**Groundling 6**: In my village of Norrige, we had a blind baker of considerable success.

**Groundling 1**: And of course there was Jane the Foole, natural fool and jester to Queen Catherine and Mary the First.

**Groundling 2**: Let us depart and consider the plight of the poor, for surely they deserve our care.

*Song: From "The Graveyard is Telling Its Tale"*
Hey Hey Hey
The bones are crying.
Hey Hey Hey
The truth is flying
No more. No more. No more.
The graveyard is telling its tale.
No more. No more. No more.

### *Scene 11—The Enlightenment*

*Slide: The Enlightenment—Bedlam hospital*

**Narrator**: Eventually, cities began to recognize that disabled people should be cared for, and hospitals were built. The most famous in England was called Bethlehem Hospital, which we now call Bedlam. Although built with good intentions, these places soon fell into conditions that could only be described as horrific. Care for disabled people was now considered an individual and civic duty.

Outcomes were dependent upon social class. Higher-born people could be housed in private "mad houses," while poor people were sent to giant newly built hospitals for care.

*Slide: Eighteenth-century upper-class interior*

*(The scene opens with a midwife handing a baby to the new parents.)*

**Charles**: How does the boy, midwife?

**Midwife**: Well, there may have been a complication…

**Elizabeth**: Well, let it out, girl.

**Midwife**: The child has deformed feet and one clouded eye.

**Charles**: What! Well, my word, an official as high as I cannot have a deformed child in his bloodline!

**Elizabeth (Amanda)**: Whatever shall we do?

**Midwife**: If I might be so bold as to make a suggestion?

**Elizabeth**: Please, do tell of what we may do!

**Midwife**: You and your family are rather wealthy, are you not?

**Charles**: Our wealth is exceptional.

**Midwife**: Then why send your child of excellent bloodline to a filthy hospital for the poor like Bedlam, when he could live out his days in the relative comfort of a private madhouse?

**Elizabeth**: A madhouse? Would that be able to meet his needs?

**Midwife**: Why have your son chained to a bed in Bedlam, when he can instead live in a walled-in estate, with gardens, beagles to hunt with, and indoor games?

**Elizabeth**: Well, chained to a bed does sound horrible. But you don't think God might be punishing us in some way?

**Charles**: Don't be silly Elizabeth. We live during the Enlightenment!

*(Actors glance at the audience for a moment.)*

**Midwife**: Your husband is right. Don't let the word *madhouse* scare you. Madness is not seen as demons punishing us now, but as merely the loss of reason.

**Charles**: Why, Elizabeth, don't you remember? I had my uncle put away in one so we could inherit his estate!

**Elizabeth**: And they have been taking good care of him?

**Charles**: That's what they have been telling me! I mean I haven't checked in a good eight years, but what are the chances such an unregulated system might be fraught with abuse?

*(Actors stare at audience for a moment and then return to character)*

**Elizabeth**: Well then, it must be our best option!

**Midwife**: Excellent! I will take the baby and bring you a bill.

*(Midwife takes the baby off. All actors Exit)*

*Song: "The Graveyard is Telling Its Tale"*

**Narrator**: The madhouses would later come under scrutiny for abuses and be subject to licensing. The Enlightenment was a time full of many events and persons of interest related to disability. Enough that perhaps whole plays could be written on this time and its people alone.

*Slide: Image of the signing of the Declaration of Independence*

**Narrator**: But let us go to America to meet a man you tragically may not have heard of in your history class—founding father and signer of the Declaration of Independence Stephen Hopkins, a politician born with cerebral palsy who is quoted as saying.

*(Stephen Hopkins wheels center stage)*

**Stephen Hopkins**: My hand trembles, but my heart does not.

**Narrator**: His signature, along with many others, helped bring this nation into being.

### Scene 12—Industrial Era

*Slide: The Industrial Era (belching factories in the Victorian era). Sound Effects: factory sounds.*

**Narrator**: Across Europe and America, the rise of factories brought about the Industrial Era. Human labor was put in service to the machines and the mines and furnaces that produced them. The numbers of disabled people increased profoundly through injuries on the job.

*(Human Machine is enacted by the company. Speeds up then breaks apart. Actors transform from cogs in the machine to disabled victims of the factories.)*

**Narrator:** Meanwhile, as the disparities grew between the titans of industry and the laborers who lived to increase their wealth (but not their own), societies had to solve the problem of what to do with those who could no longer produce wealth through their labor. A street in the early days of Akron, Ohio. Beggars are panhandling.

**Beggar 1:** Alms for the poor.

**Beggar 2:** Food for my family, please!

**Person 1:** These beggars are so annoying.

**Person 2:** The city must do something about them.

**Narrator:** The poor house movement in the United States was perceived as a practical solution to both house and provide upkeep for indigents and disabled people.

*Slide: Akron Infirmary. Two workers are digging a grave for a shrouded corpse as a list of burial records scrolls down on the screen. The workers leave, and the ghosts of those buried in Schneider Park arise and come together to sing:*

*Song (duet): "I Want to Say"*

**Singer 1:** I want to say
   That through the years,
   I've always known you've cared.
   In spite of all that's passed,
   I've known that you were there.
   It's just the times you see,
   It's beyond you and me.

**Singer 2:** I want to say
   That through the years,
   We've suffered in our ways,

Apart we've known the truth
We've felt the pain.
We've felt the sting of tears,
The burdens of the years.

**Singer 1**: There used to be a time when such as we
Lived our lives in dignity.

**Singer 2**: Within the family
Upon the Earth.

**Singer 1**: A right of simple times,
A right of birth.

**Singer 2**: Hold to that dream,
The time will come,
When we will all be there.
Awakened from our sleep
We all will care.
For those that are like me,
Yes through advocacy,
We shall be free.

*Intermission Slide: Interview with Jeff*

## ACT TWO

*Slide show: images of people with disabilities throughout the twentieth century (Helen Keller, etc.). Company enters and sings:*

Song: *"Do You See Me as an Equal?"*
Do you see me as an equal?
In your eyes do I unfold?
Do you see me for the person that I am?
Do you see me as an equal?
Free of labels, names and signs?
I'm living well and whole
Here in my plan.

Chorus: They say don't judge the books
Just by their covers.

How can we do less
My sisters and brothers?
For we are truly equal
One people, just the same.
Let's serve each other as we are
Living on this plane.
Did you know that human difference
Is the way we're meant to be?
But only when we know that
Are we whole.
For our differences make us stronger,
Each with our abilities.
Together we comprise
One family whole.

Chorus: They say don't judge the books
Just by their covers.
How can we do less
My sisters and brothers?
For we are truly equal
One Spirit, just the same.
Let's know each other as we are,
Protect each other as we are,
Love each other as we are,
Living on this plane.
Then we'll all be whole once again.
Then we'll all be whole, once again.

### Scene 1—The Twentieth Century

*Slide: Disability as Entertainment/Schlitzie poster.*

**All**: Welcome to the twentieth century!

*Slide: Brooklyn 1909 tenement house/Coney Island Side Show. Sounds: Brooklyn: car horns, traffic, people yelling. Scene: the Metz apartment.*

**Narrator**: 1909, the Bronx. In the small tenement home of Mr. and Mrs. Metz, we meet young Simon. Simon was born with a condition known as microcephaly. It is a neurological disorder and is characterized by a smaller-than-average head. In those days, people like Simon were known as *pinheads*.

*(Mr. and Mrs. Metz at the kitchen table, going over bills and looking worried. There is a knock at the door.)*

**Mrs. Metz:** I'll get it.

*(She opens the door and meets Mr. Mills, a man from the circus sideshow.)*

**Mr. Mills:** Good evening, Mrs. Metz?

**Mrs. Metz:** Yes, I am Mrs. Metz.

**Mr. Mills:** I am here to inquire about your son. I have heard he is quite unusual in appearance.

*(We see Simon peeking out behind a cupboard.)*

**Mr. Metz (JT):** Yes, unusual is the word for him. What do you want, if you don't mind me asking?

**Mr. Mills:** People like your son can make lots of money working at the circus sideshow.

*(He gives a contract to Mrs. Metz.)*

**Mr. Metz:** How much money are we talking about?

**Mr. Mills:** $75 a week to start—who knows how much more after he starts working and traveling on the sideshow circuit.

**Mr. Metz:** $75 a week!

**Mrs. Metz:** This contract is for 5 years! I can't imagine not seeing Simon for five years.

**Mr. Mills:** Oh, you can visit him whenever you like. *(To Mr. Metz)* And we will mail you his income every week. Here's his first week in advance. *(Hands Mr. Metz an envelope of cash. Mr. Metz is delighted!)*

*(Mrs. Metz goes over to Simon, who is hiding)*

**Mrs. Metz:** Come on out of there, Simon. Mr. Mills has a job offer for you!

**Mr. Metz:** Son, there's nothing around here for you. You'd best go with this nice gentleman and learn how to make a living at the circus.

**Simon:** Nooooo.

*(He is clutching a plate from the cupboard.)*

**Mrs. Metz:** Come on, Simon, let go of that plate.

**Simon:** Nooooo.

**Mrs. Metz:** Simon, you need to go with Mr. Mills. Here, let me have that plate.

*(She grabs the plate and puts it out of reach.)*

**Mrs. Metz:** I'm going to pack his suitcase.

*(She exits to pack Simon's suitcase.)*

**Mr. Mills:** Come along now, Simon. I promise you will like the circus.

**Simon:** Nooooo!

**Mr. Metz:** We'll have no more of your sass, boy!

*(Mrs. Metz returns with a suitcase and hands it to Mr. Mills)*

**Mrs. Metz:** I packed a bag for you, Simon. Mr. Mills will take good care of you.

*(She begins to cry)*

**Mrs. Metz:** I will come and visit you; I promise.

*(Mr. Mills leads Simon out of the apartment.)*

**Mr. Mills:** You'll like it in the sideshow, Simon. We'll take good care of you. There's elephants in the circus, Simon—do you like elephants?

*(Once they are outside of the apartment, Mr. Mills becomes sterner.)*

**Mr. Mills:** Come on, kid—quit your bawling.

**Spoken Word Chorus:**
>Now when I was a child, now when I was just small, I lived with my family, though not long at all. The doctor said they ought to put me away for the family. He said it'd be better that way.
>
>Like a knife it can cut to the heart—to the bone. What I want isn't much, just a home of my own.

**Narrator:** The giant hospitals grew into asylums or state institutions that housed and kept disabled people out of sight and out of mind.

Attitudes changed from believing people with disabilities could be helped or treated medically to the notion that they were incurables and should be hidden away from society. Insulting words were used to label people with disabilities.

## Scene 2—The Eugenics Movement in Ohio

*Slide: Schneider Park. Scene: Children are playing in Schneider Park. One pushes another one, who falls down and calls him a moron. Others join and call out: imbecile, idiot, moron, retard. They freeze as the Narrator begins:*

**Narrator:** *Idiot, moron, imbecile*—do you know how those words came to be used to describe people with disabilities? We must look back to a movement in the United States that began in the early years of the twentieth century. It was the Eugenics Movement: "Eugenics" was used to encompass the idea of the modification of natural selection through selective breeding for the improvement of humankind, according to Jeremiah A. Baroness. Meet Henry Goddard. In 1908, Goddard brought Alfred Binet's intelligence tests to the United States, which provided the foundation for IQ testing in the US. He helped define the term *moron* as we see as we visit him giving a lecture.

*Slide: Chart with categories as below. (Editors' Note: content and inspiration for content from Goddard is drawn from the podcast Code Switch's episodes on eugenics from February 2014 (https://www.npr.org/sections/codeswitch/2014/02/10/267561895/it-took-a-eugenicist-to-come-up-with-moron?t=1654063005808).)*

**Henry Goddard:** I would like to explain how the IQ test is used to describe various categories of mental ability. We see on the chart cognitive disabilities fall in three broad categories: "idiot," "imbecile," and "feeble-minded" ("feeble-minded" being the least severe). However, the word was imprecise and unscientific, so I created a replacement. Borrowing a Greek root meaning "dull" or "foolish," I coined the term "moron."

**Narrator:** It is worth stating the obvious: today, none of these words are appropriate as medical terms. In Ohio in the early 1900s, Goddard's thesis that defective children should be segregated during their entire reproductive lives was a major influence in the early Eugenics Movement. An attempt was made to open a segregation colony for such children.

*(A doctor's office. A father is there to hear the results of an IQ test given to his son Danny.)*

**Dr. Jones:** We have the results of your son's IQ test. The good news is he is not an idiot or imbecile; he is what we call a moron. However, his cognitive ability will never develop past that of a twelve-year-old. He will not be able to move through society on his own.

**Mr. Smith (Jordan):** What do you mean?

**Dr. Jones:** Your son is not the only example of a person with this kind of affliction. He and other morons should not be allowed to mingle in society. We are in the process of setting up a camp for those who should not be spreading their kind.

**Mr. Smith:** Spreading? What are you talking about?

**Dr. Jones:** To be blunt, your son should never procreate as his children will undoubtedly bear the same condition or worse. Therefore in order to live in our camp, Danny will be sterilized so there is no chance of him reproducing and creating a new generation of morons.

**Mr. Smith:** Will I be able to visit him?

**Dr. Jones:** No, it is in your best interest and the child's best interest to forget and move on.

**Mr. Smith:** This is my son you are talking about. He is sweet and gentle and has not caused any grief in our home or our community.

**Dr. Jones:** Your son is a danger to our progression as a human race.

**Mr. Smith:** He is only six years old. I cannot let him go. He should have a chance at finding his way through life. There are things that he can do to contribute as he grows older. And so what if he eventually grows up and wants to marry. That is his right as a free citizen in this country.

**Dr. Jones:** Well Mr. Smith, there is a law being proposed in the Ohio State Legislature that would mandate separation of defectives from the general population as well as sterilization. Many scientists and psychiatrists have testified. It is understood that "the character of a nation is determined primarily by its racial qualities; that is the hereditary physical, mental, and moral or temperamental traits of its people." In other words, Mr. Smith, "better breeding" will rid America of its flaws. (*Editors' Note: content here is drawn from eugenicist Harry Laughlin's 1920 testimony to the US House Committee on Immigration and Naturalization.*)

**Mr. Smith:** Nobody is going to rid me of my son! This law has not yet been passed and I am going to work with those who are opposed.

**Narrator:** Eugenics advocates kept pushing for new laws to "protect" the gene pool and "improve' the quality of society. Here is advocate Hannah S. Hall addressing a community group in Ohio in the early 1900s:

*Slide: Assembly hall, Ohio, circa early 1900s*

**Hannah S. Hall** (*eugenicist advocate quoting Goddard*): So to conclude my speech about the appropriate use of eugenics to improve the quality of our society, I would like to quote Henry Goddard: "The idiot is not our greatest problem. He is indeed loathsome. Nevertheless, he lives his life and is done. He does not continue the race with a line of children like himself.... It is the moron type that makes for us our great problem."

(*Audience breaks out in disagreement.*)

**Audience Member 1:** That's not right.

**Audience Member 2:** All the morons are ruining our suh-sy-et-ee.

**Audience Member 3:** We must not allow them to have children!

**Audience Member 4:** You are wrong, sir!

**Audience Member 5:** Morons and idiots are the problem!

**Audience Member 6:** We can't pin all our problems on one group of people!

**Audience Member:** When they are draining millions of dollars and consuming our resources, we can.

**Audience Member 8:** With what you are proposing, even more money will be wasted. Eugenics is based on the belief that we are just mindless animals with one goal to reproduce. We are all human beings!

*Slide: Eugenics ads from contemporary magazines*

**Narrator:** This attempt in Ohio was thwarted, as was the 1915 law that would have gone one step further than Goddard to the sterilization of "defectives." However, in some of the States, people were forcibly sterilized through the 1970s.

### Scene 3—People with Disabilities

**Narrator:** As populations in cities and counties expanded, the old poor houses began to close. These locations were prime real estate. In order to solve the problem of what to do with poor house residents, states began to build giant "institutions for the mentally insane." People with Disabilities were pushed further away from their communities.

*Slide: Interior typical American hospital room. In a hospital, Chad and Becky are paying attention to their newborn son, Todd.*

**Chad:** Isn't he just something, honey?

**Becky:** Yes, dear, he is a beauty.

**Chad:** Wait a minute, what's the problem with his feet? And his eyes look funny!

**Becky:** Oh dear! Doctor, what's wrong with my baby?

*(Doctor Joseph enters.)*

**Doctor:** Let me see the baby, Mrs. McRae.

*(Examines baby)*

**Chad:** Well, Doc? What's wrong with my boy?

**Doctor:** It seems that young Todd has clubbed feet and partial blindness and appears to be mentally retarded.

**Becky**: Ohhh no!

**Doctor**: I recommend that he be institutionalized for life.

**Chad**: What does that mean?

**Doctor**: Well, we'll send him away to a place that will take care of his every need for the rest of his life. He won't suffer as much as he would in the real world.

**Becky**: Well. wait a minute-

**Chad**: Hush now, Darling. Will we ever see him again?

**Doctor**: You can, but I recommend that you simply forget about him. It's better this way.

**Chad**: Well, take him away then.

**Becky**: Wait a minute! He's my baby too!

**Doctor**: Don't worry, Mrs. McRae, he'll be alright. I'll prescribe you a pack of Marlboro Reds for your nerves. So long now!

*Song: "For the Crime of Being Different: by Jeff Moyer*
For the crime of being different
For the crime of being slow
For the crime of not quite fitting in
We sentence you to go
Where you will be with others
Who are also of your kind:
Far, far away from city lights,
Out of sight—and out of mind.

The sentence is quite final
There can be no appeal,
You have no right of protest,
No defense nor free man's bail,
Within the institution
And away from prying eyes
Pain and grinding tedium
Will become a way of life.

Through the power of the people,
And in the wisdom of the State,

We sentence you to go away
And live your star-crossed fate.
Perhaps in time these walls will fall
And this prison will be shunned,
Til that time this sentence stands
And the State's will shall be done.

For the crime of being different,
For the crime of being slow,
For the crime of not quite fitting in,
We sentence you to go
Where you will be with others
Who are also of your kind:
Far, far away from city lights,
Out of sight—and out of mind.

**Spoken Word Chorus:**
>So my clothes were all packed and we drove far away To a big, crowded place where five thousand did stay With no family or love, Crowded rooms with locked doors. Fifty beds, fifty chairs, dirty cold cement floors. Like a knife, it can cut to the heart to the bone. What I want isn't much, just a home of my own.

*(Voices from the state institution based on a collection of recordings called "Lest We Forget," compiled by Jeff Moyer.)*

### *Scene 4—State Institutions*

*Slides: images from state institutions*

**Jordan**: I don't really remember much about my brother. Most of my memories are going to the institution to visit. He had some sort of mental retardation. In today's world, he would have been in a Special Ed class and not sent away for life. As a small child, he was just all over the place. He couldn't focus in school; he was getting bad grades; he didn't have many friends. Of course, this is all based on what my parents have told me. Doctors told my parents to institutionalize him when I was four and he was eight.

We were told to forget him, but we visited from time to time. We treated him not as blood but as an errand to run. A visit to your brother shouldn't be a trip to Acme or something. Over time, he mellowed out. It must've been the drugs and meds they kept pumping into him.

The last memory I have of him was when I was fourteen, and he was twenty-two. I went up to say hi, and he barely noticed. He was slurring his words, he moved slowly, and he was just barely him anymore. They had turned a hare into a tortoise. Even less than a tortoise. A sort of unresponsive snail.

The following week, we learned he had killed himself. We don't know how. To add insult to injury, we couldn't attend his funeral. He was buried in an unmarked location. We never even saw his body.

**Fred:** My wife put me in Orient. I had a seizure and allergies. It felt horrible. The place was crowded and smelled like urine. People in there acted crazy. They were screaming and crying. The staff just stood around. We didn't do anything but sit on wooden chairs. The room was cramped and cold. At night we went to bed in beds that were pushed together. I could hear people crying in their sleep. All I could think about was getting out of there. That was when I was twenty-five. I'm eighty-three today.

**John:** Well my mom and dad died when I was ten. I ain't got no family to take care of me. A sheriff came to my door and put me in handcuffs and put me in his car. I was crying, "What did I do?" The sheriff looked at me and said, "Boy, you don't have anyone to take care of you, so I'm taking you to Apple Creek." That sounded like a nice place. I pictured apple trees and creeks flowing in the backyard. We drove for a long time out into the countryside. We passed big farms and fields with trees. We came to a big gate at the end of a long drive. I smelled something bad. I started to worry.

We stopped in front of a big red brick building. The smell was worse, and I could hear people screaming. (Screams) I didn't want to get out of the car, but the sheriff made me get out and marched me up to the door and into a room, where he gave me to a mean-looking woman.

She looked me up and down and said to her assistant, "Take him to Cottage #5."

The man walked me past many buildings. I heard more screams and smelled more bad smells. We arrived at a huge gray building that said "Cottage #5" on the door. I was taken to large room filled with fifty beds all jammed together so you could barely squeeze through to your own bed. I began crying. They made me take off my clothes and put on some old, raggedy gray clothes. They took my old clothes away, and I never saw them again.

Then they pushed me through another door into a room filled with fifty boys. They were screaming and fighting. Some were rocking back and forth. Some were sitting on wooden benches and wooden chairs. Some were crawling on the floor. Some were trying to climb the walls. Some were trying to get through the iron bars on the windows.

Was this a nightmare? No, this was where I was to live for the next 35 years.

**Laura:** When you think of a place called Apple Creek, you think of rolling hills and warm meadows stretching out into the horizon. You can imagine the smell of sweet flowers and apple-flavored pastries baking. You can almost feel the sun on your skin and the light breeze blowing through your hair...

But when I think about it, I remember the sound of rattling metal and far-off screaming. Instead of vast meadows, there are cramped rooms and long cold hallways, and the only thing you can smell is sadness—pastries aren't allowed.

My parents sent my sister away when she was fifteen. I was twelve. They told me she was sick, and I never heard of her again. Sometimes, late at night, I would hear them whispering about the place called Apple Creek, and I could sleep soundly thinking that she was somewhere nice...safe.

I almost thought I was in the wrong place when I was finally old enough to visit her on my own. This brick building was nothing like I had imagined, and it felt like I was carrying a heavy load on my back as I walked in and requested to visit with her. And then they wheeled her out.

I remember my sister as a bubbly, outgoing girl, but this, this was someone else. We sat in silence for a long time, and it was like her eyes were clouded over. I'll never forget the way she looked at me. She didn't even recognize me. I'm not sure I recognized her.

When she finally spoke, it was in a hushed, gentle voice. She was like a ghost. It was almost as if she never existed, and all I was hearing was the far-off echo of whoever she was years ago, and I realized that I was too late. My sister was gone.... So I left. I left, and I never came back. (Breath) Until today.

**Amanda**: I once was a worker in a state institution—a long time ago. I had ninety people to watch over every day. We kept them in a big room. There was a TV, but they couldn't watch it. The TV was facing the workers. So I spent my day watching TV while they cried, screamed, and rolled around on the floor.

### *Scene 5—Adults: Work*

*[Author's note: The following work scene will appear as an online-only extra scene. It was deleted from the live performance.]*

**Spoken Word Chorus:**

Work. Work. Work. Bright boys went to work. Bright boys leave the cottage every day. We walk to Sunny Side. No sunshine there. Just the dummies. The ones who cannot take care of themselves. They are called the Dummies. We Bright Boys take care of the Dummies. We hose them off, we dress them and feed them. We clean up their messes. Then start all over again: Hosing, dressing, feeding, cleaning up slops. It never stops. We don't get paid, but we get out of our cottage, and if we are friendly, we get privileges.

### *Scene 6—State Institutions, Part II*

**Nicholas**: They don't care. They're cruel. They're disrespectful. I was just eating until a food fight broke out. I thought I was in the right. I thought I stayed out of it, but then a nurse came up to me and said, "You are done." They took my food, even as I begged and pleaded, they took it. The hunger pained me as much as the feeling that I was lower did. I felt upset and misused. I felt like the lowest of the low. Here, the pyramid of life has the patients on the bottom struggling to survive, while the people who are supposed to be helping you, the people you are supposed to look up to, taking all you have.

*Slide: Image of an old clock on a wall at a state institution bench.*

**Joseph**: Tick-Tock. I was cold. Tick-Tock. Every second of every day, stuck on this bench. Tick-T—. No, I can't stand the clock overseeing me like it's my prison warden. I could barely remember why I had been on this bench, as it has been so long. Every day the same. Get up, get sent to the bench, wait, then go to sleep. Get up, get sent to the bench, wait, then go to sleep. Get up, get sent to the bench, wait, then go to sleep. It was a cycle. A cycle meant to punish me. Was I being punished because I had no voice? Was I being punished because my mind and my body were separate? Why am I being punished for something I can't control? It's already horrible to feel like your body is your enemy, but to feel like your "guardians" would rather want you dead. It's heartbreaking. I wonder how much longer I'll sit on this bench, a few hours, a few days, a few months, a few years. Maybe, as the clock continues to tick…. *Sound effect—clock ticking into music track.*

### Scene 7—A day in the life at a state institution

*Slide: Image of a ward inside a state institution. Music: "Third Plane." The actors present a four-minute action without words of a day in a typical Ohio institution in the 1950s—60s. Scene ends as music ends.*

**Narrator:** The movement out of the institutions back into the community gained momentum as parents began to question why their children were being locked and hidden away. One of the earliest parent groups, the Cuyahoga County Council for the Retarded Child, was formed in Cleveland, Ohio, in 1933. By 1950, eighty-eight such parent groups were spread across the United States. In the postwar era of economic boom, the differences between everyday life and institutional life were profound. Parents organized because there were very few resources for support in their communities.

*Song: "You Can't Deny Me Now" by Jeff Moyer*
I was born to you a child with needs,

Through no fault of my own,
You saw me as a cripple,
And turned me from your home.
You did not feed nor clothe me
You left me there to die.

You told yourself it was God's will,
But now you can't deny.
You can't deny me now,
No, No!
You can't deny me now.
You can't deny me now,
No, No!
You can't deny me now.

You threw me in that prison
When I was just a child.
With thousands more you caged away,
In dungeons hard and wild.
The dead were laid in numbered rows
No name, no family tie.
But there will be no more of that
You won't, you can't deny.

Chorus:
You can't deny me now,
No, No!
You can't deny me now.
You can't deny me now.

### Scene 8—*Beginnings of the movement out of state institutions*

*Slide: Conference setting, 1950s.*

**Narrator:** Meanwhile, professional organizations began taking note of the parent groups and reaching out to join forces. The American Association on Mental Deficiency sponsored the first national parents conference in 1950. The featured speaker was Minnesota Governor Luther Youngdahl:

**Governor:** "The point is this, ladies and gentlemen, the retarded child is a human being...and for reasons for which neither he nor his family are responsible, he is retarded. He has the same rights that children everywhere have. He has the same right to happiness, the same right to play, the right to companionship, the right to be respected, the right to develop to the fullest extent within his capacities, and the right to love and affection..." In 1964, the per diem rate for a person living in an institution was $5.57, about one-half the amount devoted to tending animals in a zoo. Even that amount was too much for many states. The Deinstitutionalization Movement was as much about saving money as it was about serving the needs of families. Parent groups began pressuring their governments for local services. The earliest group homes often housed eight to twelve adults with disabilities. Let's take a look at one: You.

*Scene 9—Life in an early group home*

*Slide: Exterior, a Street in Akron, 1970s (Ardmore St?). Scene: a group home in the late '70s. Jimmy is arriving to live in a group home for the first time.*

*(Bill enters with Jimmy.)*

**Bill:** Alright everyone, gather around. This is Jimmy. He is going to live here with you. Say hello. Everyone, introduce yourselves.

**Donald:** I am Donald.

**Ronald:** I am Ronald.

**Danny:** Danny.

**Isaac:** Hi, I am Isaac.

**Bear:** Bear.

**Bill:** This cranky looking one is Victor.

**Victor:** Too many people here already.

**Bill:** Zip it Victor.

**Jimmy:** Well, I am excited to meet you all.

**Bill:** Hey, Bear, why don't you take Jimmy's bags? He's staying with Isaac and Victor.

**Bear:** OK, I can take the bags. Hmm, it's not locked. What's inside? looks interesting…

**Victor:** I don't want anyone else in my room.

**Bill:** It's not just your room. OK, Jimmy, let's go over the house rules. No going out after dark,

**Bear:** That's right.

**Bill:** No talking to the homeless guys outside

**Isaac:** Yeah, stay away from them.

**Bill:** No girls over.

**Danny:** This ain't fair.

**Bill:** In fact no guests without talking to me first.

**Donald:** Aw man!

**Bill:** There's more rules, but I have to start making dinner. We can go over them later.

**Isaac:** What's for dinner?

**Bill:** It's meatloaf night.

**Donald:** I hate meatloaf.

**Victor:** We all hate meatloaf

**Isaac:** I want a salad.

**Ronald:** Pancakes!

**Jimmy:** I like Meatloaf.

**Bill:** See, new guy likes meatloaf.

**Danny:** Of course he does.

**Bear:** Yeah, sure.

**Bill:** OK, I am going for a cigarette. Everyone make Jimmy feel at home.

**Victor:** Hey, Danny, let's talk with Jimmy—

**Jimmy:** Ouch, my foot! You rolled right over my foot!

**Victor:** You touch anything in my room, and I will have Danny push you down the stairs.

**Danny:** Yeah, you watch it, mister.

**Jimmy:** I just want us to be friends.

**Donald:** No one wants to be friends with you, meatloaf.

*(Others leave except Isaac and Ronald.)*

**Sean:** I am sorry it's not always this bad. Victor is just mad because his teeth hurt.

**Ronald:** it's better than where I was before. Hey, let's go eat.

**Isaac**—good idea!

*(Ronald and Isaac leave. Jimmy finds his bag in a corner with all his stuff stolen)*

**Jimmy:** Hey, who took my stuff? Someone got into my bags!

*Song: Company sings: "You Can't Deny Me Now" by Jeff Moyer*

### Scene 10—Advocacy in Action: The Curb Cut Effect

*Slide: pictures of curb cuts. Scene: Berkeley, CA 1971. We see an intersection with able-bodied citizens crossing the street back and forth. Two students in wheelchairs are watching from one side. After the citizens have crossed and exited, the two people in wheelchairs comment:*

**Narrator:** "A curb cut is a solid (usually concrete) ramp graded down from the top surface of a sidewalk to the surface of an adjoining street. It is designed primarily for pedestrian usage and commonly found in urban areas where pedestrian activity is expected." (Wikipedia) The first curb cuts were made in Kalamazoo, Michigan, in the 1940s to help disabled vets get to work. However, the movement for curb cuts really took off in the 1970s in Berkeley, California.

**Mark:** I want to cross the street to go to the grocery store, but I am afraid I will fall out of my wheelchair going across the curb.

**Michael:** I need to go to the drug store, but going over two curbs to get there is dangerous.

**Mark:** I'm tired of not being able to go where I want in this town.

**Michael:** I know what you mean! I have an idea. Let's go back to my place.

*(The two wheel to an apartment, where they continue their conversation while company sings:*

Song: "You Can't Deny Me Now"
You can't deny me now,
No, No!
You can't deny me now
You can't deny me now,
No, No!
You can't deny me now.

**Michael:** I'm going to call my buddy, Nico. He can help us.

*(He picks up the phone and calls Nico.)*

**Michael:** Hello Nico—I got a favor to ask you!

**Nicolas:** Sure, Michael, what can I do for you? Want me to pick up your prescription from the drugstore?

**Michael:** No, this time I want you to pick up a bag of cement from the hardware store so you'll never have to get my prescriptions for me again!

**Nicolas:** What???

**Michael:** Just get the cement and meet me at my place after dark, and I'll tell you all about it.

Company sings:
You can't deny me now, no no.
You can't deny me now

*(Nicolas enters Michael's apt with a bag of cement. Michael shows him a big bucket.)*

**Michael:** Let's mix up this cement and go down to the intersection to make some improvements!

*Company sings:*
You can't deny me now,
No, No!
You can't deny me now.
You can't deny me now,
No, No!
You can't deny me now.

*(Michael, Mark, and Nicolas go to the street. Michael and Mark point out where they want the ramp, and Nicolas pours the cement, shaping it into a rough ramp. He does it again on the other side of the street. As the three inspect their improvements, a police officer patrolling the neighborhood sees what they are doing.)*

**Police Officer:** What's going on here?

*(Examines concrete)*

**Police Officer:** This looks like vandalism. Do you know you can be arrested for destroying city property?

**Mark:** We didn't do it.

**Michael:** How could we do that? We're in wheelchairs!

*(Looking around, the Police Officer sees Brian running off into the night)*

**Police Officer:** Hmm, must've been that guy.

*(He runs off chasing Brian.)*

**Mark:** Let's get out of here before he figures it out!

*(They exit.)*

*(The next day, scene at the intersection. We see Michael and Mark crossing the street using the crude concrete ramps. We also see a woman with a baby stroller, a blind person, and a person with a cane making use of the curb cuts. A city engineer and police officer are there observing.)*

**Police Officer:** *So you want me to get someone in here with a jackhammer?*

**City Engineer:** No, wait! I know this ramp is crude but look at all the people making use of it to cross the street. Not just the guys in wheelchairs. People on bikes, people with canes, baby carriages—having these concrete ramps at intersections makes a lot of sense.

**Narrator:** With a lot of pushing from disability rights advocates, in 1972 the City of Berkeley installed its first official "curb cut" on Telegraph Avenue. It would become "the slab of concrete heard 'round the world."

*Song:*
But now we're strong and growing,
On that you can rely,
Set a new place at the table,
Cause I'll be stopping by.
You can't deny me now,
No, No!
You can't deny me now.
You can't deny me now,
No, No!
You can't deny me now.

### Scene 11—The Story of the 504 Protests

*Slide: Protest signs from 504 in San Francisco*

**Narrator:** The Rehabilitation Act of 1973 and the Story of the 504 Protests.

*Company sings: "Hold On" adapted by Jeff Moyer*
Civil Rights were knocking at our door,
But Carter wouldn't stand on 504.
Keep your eye on the prize. Hold on.
Hold on.
You gotta Hold on.
Keep your eye on the prize. Hold on.

**Narrator:** The Rehabilitation Act of 1973 required affirmative action in employment by the federal government and by government contractors and prohibits discrimination on the basis of disability in programs conducted by federal agencies, in programs receiving federal financial assistance, in federal employment, and in the employment practices of federal contractors. It had been passed into law, but President Nixon refused to sign it, saying:

**Nixon**: "It was a money grab to take the hard-earned dollars from working citizens."

**Narrator**: The law had no teeth until regulations were written and passed by the Department of Education, Health and Welfare.

**Jimmy Carter**: If you elect me president, I promise I will sign the 504 regulations into law.

**Narrator**: Once in the White House, pressures from industry began moving Carter away from his promise.

*Scene: Lobbyists surround Carter, demanding he refuse to sign.*

**Lobbyist 1**: This is going to cost us too much money!

**Lobbyist 2**: You can't expect us to hire these people!

**Lobbyist 3**: This is going to eat into our profits!

*Song:*
After four years of delay,
We came to claim the ground we'd gained.
We had our eye on the prize.
Hold on. Hold on. We gotta hold on.
Keep your eye on the prize. Hold on.

**Narrator**: It was becoming clear—action would have to come from the people. In ten cities across the United States, groups of disability activists gathered to organize a nationwide protest. They were determined to make the government establish rules so that the law could be enforced. Of those ten protest actions, only one held firm—and brought about the necessary changes. This is the story of the 504 protest in San Francisco. The organizers in San Francisco held a teach-in the day before the protest. We'd like to introduce you to some of the planning committee members.

*Slide: image of Mary Jane Owen, 1929–1919*

**Narrator**: Mary Jane Owen was descended from a long line of feminists and fought for civil rights with the Congress of Racial Equality. She was involved with the Free Speech Movement while working on her master's in social work at the University of Berkeley in the 60s. When she lost her sight in 1972, she began to put her energies toward fighting for the civil rights of people with disabilities.

*Slide: Judy Heumann, born 1947*

**Narrator:** Judy Heumann is a leader in the international disability rights movement. At the age of 18 months, she contracted polio and has spent her life using a wheelchair. She had to fight for her rights from an early age, having been refused attendance at her local public school because they called her a fire hazard.

*Slide: Kitty Cone, 1944—2015*

**Narrator:** Kitty Cone was the chief organizer of the 504 sit-in in San Francisco. Misdiagnosed as a child with cerebral palsy (she actually had muscular dystrophy), she was subjected to surgeries that ended up worsening her condition. Facing discrimination in school, Kitty had to fight for her rights every step of the way through college. She joined the Independent Living Center in Berkeley, CA working in the community affairs department.

*Slide: Ed Roberts, 1939–1995*

**Narrator:** Ed Roberts has been called the father of the independent living movement. After contracting polio at the age of 14, he became paralyzed from the neck down. Determined to get an education, he gave up thinking of himself as a "helpless cripple" and chose to think of himself as a "star." He was the first student to use a wheelchair at the University of Berkeley, and his leadership and courage brought about dramatic changes to Berkeley and inspired change across the country and the world.

*Slide: Jeff Moyer, 1949-*

**Narrator:** Jeff Moyer was born in Cleveland, Ohio. He is a disability rights activist, musician and writer. Jeff began losing his sight at age five. His younger brother was born with a cognitive disability and was sent away to a state institution at the age of eight. Jeff's family circumstances led to a lifelong commitment to activism. He has kindly lent his songs to our production, and has helped us with our research and understanding of the disability rights movement.

*Scene: We see people creating signs for the protest. People are coming and going. Someone brings in a pile of handbills for distribution. Jeff Moyer is practicing his new lyrics to "Eye on the Prize." Kitty Cone and Mary Jane Owen are conferring with Ed Roberts and Judy Heumann. Jeff Moyer, musician and bard to the disability rights movement is working on some new lyrics to an old protest song.*

**Kitty Cone:** Judy, are the handbills ready?

**Judy Heumann:** Someone went out to pick them up.

**Ed Roberts:** Hey, Mary Jane, I've been working on my speech!

**Judy**: Do we have a bullhorn?

*(Jeff stops playing his guitar)*

**Jeff**: Oh man, we really need a bullhorn. I will go get one!

*(He puts down his guitar and leaves with another organizer.)*

**Mary Jane:** Keep phoning your friends, but remember to tell them to keep this quiet.

**Amanda**: We don't want anyone at HEW to know.

Company sings:
A movement standing strong and tight
With one dream to win our Civil Rights.
Keep your eye on the prize. Hold on.
Hold on. You gotta hold on.
Keep your eye on the prize. Hold on

*Slide: Outside HEW at United Nations Plaza in SF. Scene: Protest outside HEW. Actors wave signs, pass out handbills, give out buttons to audience members while narration takes place.*

**Narrator**: San Francisco, APRIL 5, 1977—Day One of the 504 Protests. Five hundred people gathered in front of the Department of Health, Education and Welfare. There were over eighty people with signs in wheelchairs. All kinds of people who were Blind, deaf, with cognitive disabilities, friends and families. Local politician Willie Brown spoke in support, as did Reverend Cecil Williams of Glide Memorial Church, as well as leaders from the civil rights movement.

After Mary Jane Owen addressed the crowd, Ed Roberts gave the final speech of the day. He had taught himself to speak away from his iron lung by using frog breathing to pull air into his lungs.

### Scene 12—Ed Roberts Speech at the 504 Protest

**Ed Roberts:** All Right!

It was just, what, three and a half weeks ago that we got here together to begin talking about something that we knew that we could do. we've learned how to be strong, and we've demonstrated that to the people of this country. Winston Churchill once said, "Never have so few, done so much, for so many." And this example, this example of people loving each other, committed to something that is right, is one that I know I will always remember. I thank you. I join you. I celebrate with you. I rededicate myself to work with you, to ensure the future. (*Editors' Note: adapted from Roberts' Sit-In Victory Rally speech of April 1977.*)

(*Applause and cheers!*)

**Judy Heumann:** Let's go in—we're not going to leave until 504 is signed!

**Kitty Cone:** We entered HEW and headed to the fourth floor, where we stayed for twenty-eight days

*Song:*
Well, for 28 days unafraid
Many people with disabilities stayed.
They had their eye on the prize. They held on.
Hold on. You gotta hold on.
Keep your eye on the prize. Hold on.

**Ed Roberts:** This was to be the longest sit-in protest in American history.

**Mary Jane:** During those four weeks we were supported by the Black Panthers, Salvation Army, Safeway, and Machinists unions and many other local and national groups.

**Judy:** Mayor Moscone helped us obtain air mattresses and portable showers.

**Protester 1:** Federal authorities turned off the power at night and all the phones.

**Kitty**: We communicated with the outside world through sign language.

*(Protestor 1 stands at window and signs to the crowd below)*

**Judy**: Interpreters stood at windows, signing to others outside the building. We were determined not to give in!

**Ed**: Joseph Califano Jr. signed the regulations on the twenty-sixth day.

**Mary Jane**: We stayed for two more days until our congressional reps returned from Washington DC.

**Protester 2**: And then we all marched—

**Protester 3**: and wheeled out—

**All**: together!

*Song: "We won't stop until the battle's won"*
We won't stop until the battle's won
And enforcement of the law's begun
Keep your eye on the prize, Hold on.
Hold on, hold on,
Keep your eye on the prize, hold on.
Many years have rolled past that door
But we still must fight for 504.
Keep your eye on the prize. Hold on.
Hold on. You gotta hold on.
Keep your eye on the prize. Hold on.

### Scene 13—*Signing of the Americans With Disabilities Act*

*Slide: GHW Bush and people on stage with him. On stage: a tableau of the image on screen. George Bush signs the bill while other people with disabilities grouped around him.*

**Narrator 1**: With the 504 regulations signed and in place, the disability community soon realized that they had only won the first battle. Many more were to take place. When President Reagan called for deregulation of all rules restricting businesses, one of the chosen targets was 504. The disability rights movement quickly mobilized. Thousands of letters arrived on capitol hill. 504 had effectively granted disabled citizens with minority status. They found allies in other minority movements seeking civil rights.

**Narrator 2:** The 1980s were filled with battles with the courts and seeking corrective legislation that would improve disability rights in education, transportation, employment and housing. Citizens with disabilities gained new negotiating skills and confidence with each victory, while educating the courts and legislatures on the actual challenges facing disabled people.

**Narrator 3:** The Americans With Disabilities act was a culmination of all these battles. It went through several versions on its journey to passage. The ADA was to extend basic civil rights protection granted to minorities and women. Before the ADA, no federal law prohibited private sector discrimination against people with disabilities. On July 26, 1990, America became the first country to adopt a comprehensive civil rights declaration for people with disabilities.

*(Montage: Signing of the ADA with the president on the South Lawn of the White House.)*

*Everyone sings "The ADA Anthem" by Jeff Moyer*

*Song: "The ADA Anthem" by Jeff Moyer*
In the Disability Rights Movement
Are the streams of constant change.
For the worse and for the better
In flux it had remained.
But to move it with decision
Toward human dignity,
We gathered as one,
There was work to be done
For we held only part of the key.

Chorus:
We stand as one to see it through.
Civil rights, overdue.
But to shape new legislation,
Based on laws as then in place,

Bringing power to the people
Whose lives these things embrace.
A coalition cross this land -
The system surely moved.
We gather today,
Now with ADA,
The balance has improved.
We stand as one
to see it through.
civil rights, overdue.

### *Scene 14—Supported Living in Akron 2020*

**Narrator:** The Americans With Disabilities Act has had a profound effect upon the lives of countless people with disabilities. Let's take a look at the differences in housing options from the 1970s to today.

*Slide: A contemporary apartment setting. Scene: Around the kitchen table, three group home residents discuss changes that have recently taken place.*

**Johnny**: I love our new house provider!

**Lisa**: Yes!

**Johnny**: The old provider, Shady Hands, had a van that never worked

**Lisa**: I like our new house manager Clyde!

**Johnny**: He is so kind and supportive!

**Georgy**: He takes us grocery shopping with him so we can pick out healthy food!

**Lisa**: Happy Home Inc's van is very clean and never breaks down!

**Johnny**: Now I'm never late for work!

*(Enter Clyde.)*

**Clyde**: Hey everyone! How are you all doing?

*(Adlib: Georgy—great! Lisa—wonderful! Johnny—super!)*

**Clyde**: Well I just want to say I am so happy that you all voted to have Happy Home Inc be your new house provider! It's only been a couple of weeks, but I am learning every day how to help and support you all.

**Lisa**: You are doing a great job!

**Georgy**: You cook really good!

**Johnny**: And the new van is awesome!

**Clyde**: Well, thank you very much!

**Nick**: Hey guys, I have some news to share.

**Georgy**: What's going on, Nick?

**Nick**: Well, I'm getting married!

**Everyone**: Congratulations! Fantastic, etc.

**Nick**: But I'm sorry I have to tell you, my fiancée and I need to find our own place, so I have to give you my thirty-day notice.

**Nick**: Yes, I have an interview coming up for a part time job.

**Johnny**: That is understandable! A group home isn't exactly a honeymoon cottage!

**Georgy**: We will miss you, Nick!

**Johnny**: You know where you are going to live yet, Nick?

**Nick**: Well my future in-laws have offered us a place. That way we can save money.

**Georgy**: I'm going to miss you buddy. You are the best friend I ever had.

**Nick**: I'll miss you too—you guys are my friends!

**Lisa**: Are we invited to the wedding?

**Nick**: Of course you are invited!

*(Everyone runs to Nick and congratulates him!)*

**Narrator**: Two weeks later.

**Clyde**: Hey, we need to get ready to interview some folks who are interested in moving in to our house. I was wondering, do you need to go over the list of questions you guys put together yesterday?

**Georgy**: No, we're good!

*(Others agree. Clyde brings in Arthur who says hello and they all introduce themselves. Clyde reads from the application).*

**Clyde:** This is Arthur. He's been living at home with his family, but now that he's finished with high school and job training, He'd like to live more independently.

*(The house mates continue asking questions to the applicant.)*

**Lisa**: What kind of job are you looking for?

**Johnny**: What are your hobbies? Do you like group activities like parties, or going bowling or dancing?

**Georgie**: If you came to our game night, what games would you like to play?

**Johnny**: What kind of music do you like? If it is loud, would you be willing to wear headphones?

**Lisa**: How late do you stay up?

**Georgie**: What kinds of food do you like?

**Lisa**: Are you willing to help with chores? We have a job wheel so we can take turns.

**Georgie**: Is there anything you would like to ask us?

**Arthur:** When will I know if I can move here?

**Clyde**: Well we have some more interviews to go through before we can make a decision. We promise we will get back to you one way or another.

**Chris**: Very nice meeting you!

*(They shake hands and he leaves. The housemates converge to look over applications—scene freezes as narration picks up.)*

**Narrator:** The history of the disability rights movement is on-going. We wish we had the time to cover every single act of courage and resistance by both individuals and groups who have transformed their communities. While much progress has been made, there are still battles to be fought and won.

*(Cast comes together to sing final verse of ADA Anthem.)*

*Song:*
And for those labeled, "disabled,"
The change will be perceived -
A freer step across this land
On the road to liberty.
So we'll celebrate this action,
The law that's ours today.
Though the victory's won
Still there's much to be done
As we work for The ADA.
A-D-A,
we stand as one to see it through.
A-D-A,
civil rights, overdue.
Civil rights so very long overdue.

*End*

*Note: these monologues were originally written to end the show, however due to time constraints they will appear online only.*

*Final Scene: The actors present monologues on who they are and how life is going for them.*

- **Samir's Monologue**: Hello, My name is Samir Hammoud. my favorite character is Piglet! I can do the voice of Piglet for you: "Oh dear, what's going to happen right now?" I learned to do film acting for this play. I love acting and singing! My goals in life are to be an actor, voice actor, writer, producer, and director! Look out world, I'm on my way!

- **Sean's Monologue**: I was a C-section born premature. The nurse said I wouldn't survive but here I am. I was always in special ed. I would have to take my tests in a separate room so the other kids wouldn't hear me whisper my answers to the aid. Life is better for me now than when I was a kid, because of technology.

**Brian's Monologue**: My Name is Brian Cogar. In the asylum scene, the play has very powerful emotions. As an actor I had to think about how those people would feel, just like Jeff Moyer felt with his brother living in an institution. If I lived, then I would be scared because I wouldn't know what might happen to me. Society has improved a lot since then and every one of us with disabilities has something to say.

**Joyce's Monologue**: My name is Joyce Wade. I realized I was different from everyone when I was eighteen. I am the type of person who never cared what everyone else thought and I have always been able to talk for myself. I was raised not to say I can't do anything. This play has taught me how people used to get beat up for having disabilities and a lot of people died in the institutions, I would like people with disabilities to get more education in the future.

**Daniel's Monologue**: Hi I am Daniel. I went to Nordonia High School. I liked High School. I like doing theatre and my favorite superhero is Batman.

**Jake's Monologue**: Hi I am Jake Dietz. I love doing animation on my iPad. I like showing people my animations.

*(Video projection: show one of Jake's animations on the screen.)*

I take a lot of inspiration from Attack on Titan and Steven Universe and Scooby Doo! Someday I would like to work with motion capture for movies and video games and do animations for Disney.

**Amanda's Monologue**: Hello, my name is Amanda Bugenske. I have a cognitive disability. My mom said that yes, I was bullied all throughout school, and I want to help stop bullying. While doing this play, I learned about the burials in Schneider park without coffins or headstones. I wish we could do something to honor those buried there. My wish for disabled people in the future is to have everyone with a disability to be treated equal.

**JT's Monologue**: Hello everyone, I am JT Styles and this is my story. I was born with cerebral palsy. In school I had a teacher who told me I wouldn't amount to anything. I would stay at home with my parents and play video games. I didn't think a teacher would say something like that. I hope that the future has more jobs for people with disabilities. I want people with disabilities in the media and the government. I want to hear what politicians are going to do for us. We need to be heard!

**Scott's Monologue:** I am Scott Hudson. I was born with a cleft lip and diagnosed with a cognitive disorder. At school they didn't know what to do with me. I just wanted to be normal, but what's normal? I didn't know what I wanted to do with my life, now I know I want to act! We are a family at Theatre on the Spectrum and we love each other.

**Dre'ia's monologue**: Hi I am Dre'Ia I live with my mom. I was in Special Ed it was ok. I also liked science class. I have always wanted to go to Paris and see the Eiffel tower and all the different shops they have. I hear it's beautiful there. I want people with disabilities dreams to come true. My dream is I would like to be on TV.

**Laura's monologue**: My name is Laura Valendza. I have a learning disability and deal daily with depression and anxiety. I also have fibromyalgia, rheumatoid arthritis, and am a cancer survivor. My life has not been without its struggles, but I have found joy and success through the arts. I attribute my success in life to everything I learned in the theatre. This project has reinforced to me the power of theatre. I believe that theatre has the power to change the world.

**Erica's monologue:** Hello, My name is Erica Crank. The monologues from this show have brought back some of the sadness from my own life. Memories of my past like being bullied in school. Theatre on the spectrum has shown me how to articulate my words and movements. I am becoming smarter every day and making more friends and enjoying playing my ukulele. I don't care what anybody says because it's who I am and I have pride in myself. I make my own decisions as a woman. I don't put up with any drama

**Jude's Monologue**: I began volunteering with youth classes at CADA two years ago. When you don't know how to communicate with someone, it's easy to put them in a box where you think they aren't the same. As we worked, I began to learn how to communicate with each individual. Everyone has their own way of connecting. If only everyone could reach this understanding—we would end intolerance and discrimination.

**Sid's Monologue**: My name is Sid Kranz, I am twenty years old. I have Autism and it makes me different. My brain processes differently. I am very creative and usually have the most energy and enthusiasm of anyone in the room!! Working on "Along the Graveyard Path" has helped me learn how to work with others. I am grateful that I didn't live back then. I am lucky that I have a home with a loving family and a community that supports me.

**Brooklyn's Monologue:** Hello, my name is Brooklyn Brake. Growing up, I found I had a passion for helping people with all types of disabilities. doing this project has helped me grow as a person, I have learned so many things, such as how people with disabilities including children were taken to a state institution and just thrown away. Learning about the past really got to me because I believe everyone should be treated as equals. just because they might be different doesn't mean that they don't have feelings and they don't get sad and hurt, they have hearts too.

**Joseph's monologue:** Hello, my name is Joseph Moran and I was born profoundly deaf in both ears in the summer of 2002. I was also diagnosed with Asperger's Syndrome around the age of ten shortly before Asperger Syndrome was dropped from the books like a brick. Due to these two very different disabilities, I have gotten to meet and interact with people with various disabilities which has taught me an important lesson on just how different yet similar we all are. Some of us were born without the ability to walk. Some of us gradually lost muscle functions as time walked by. Some of us were born with brains that didn't fit the common mold. Despite all those differences though; despite our different experiences and trials; we all share the ability to grow, to do wonderful things just like anyone else. That what's I have gotten from this play, from the history of disabilities, that in the end of the day, all of us, abled-bodied, deaf, blind, autistic, mentally delayed, are capable of great things and are capable of making right of our past's woes. I want to thank everyone who has dedicated their time to this production, and to the great people of not just Akron, but the world, that gradually point the history of disability to a path worth living. Thank you.

**Ruben's monologue:** As a child my parents were parents took care of a young man named Terry he had Down syndrome he was an artist and if the stories are true he even saved my life more than once. I would hear my parents whisper about a place called Apple Creek. When I was around thirty a giant cell tumor ate my tibia. I lost the ability to use my left leg and I walked everywhere with a cane, and then I walked with two canes and finally crutches after my surgery. You can't carry anything when you walk with crutches or canes. So now I don't take my legs for granted. I have a titanium knee. Don't take your body for granted. Don't take your freedom for granted.

**Jordan's monologue:** Hello! I'm Jordan Euell, and I've been working with CADA since I was in High School! Since I've worked with CADA, I have seen many a student grow in the classes of CADA. The space to be free without cruel judgement and isolation. It wasn't until spending my time here that I understood how much one can blossom when given the right guidance and patience. But it wasn't till working on this play how long it took for us to come to this lesson and how far we have to go. As someone on the spectrum, I often try to hide my true self in favor of trying to fit in, in not being an outcast, in just being "normal." But it's not a conversation being normal and weird, we all are on our own paths and need to find what works for us. And that is a process that everyone should have and not trying to conform to an unrealistic standard that we're killing ourselves to match. I longer see myself as an imperfect, a work in progress or an outcast. I'm right where I need to be, a feeling that everybody should have an opportunity to feel.

# Works Cited

25 U.S.C. §§3001-3013 (2006)

43 C. F. R. Part 10

A. W. Bowen & Company. 1898. *A Portrait and Biographical Record of Portage and Summit Counties, Ohio.* A.W. Bowen & Company.

Adams, M. 1978. *Ohio Historic Inventory, SUM-322-11.* Ohio Historic Preservation Office.

*Akron Beacon Journal.* 1849. "Will Be Prepared to Receive Poor on Monday." August 30, page 3, column 5.

———. 1886. February 20, page 1 supplement, column 8.

———. 1886a. "Queries About Public Officers, for the Editor of the Beacon." March 20, page 2, column 2.

———. 1903. "Wants More Room." November 19, page 7, column 7.

———. 1913. "Unclaimed." November 14.

———. 1916. "Sold to P. H. Schneider." August 10, page 11, column 2.

———. 1917. "In the Common Pleas Court of Summit County, Ohio—Cause No. 24891." July 20, page 1, column 5.

———. 1935. "Notice of Appointment." October 25, page 21, column 1.

———. 2017a. "Schneider Park Mystery Draws University of Akron Students; Archaeological Survey of Grave Sites Underway."

———. 2017b. "UA Students Summarize Findings: For Every Visible Grave, Two Lurk Below at Schneider Park," July 8, 2017.

*Akron City Times.* 1887. "Infirmary Investigation." *Akron City Times,* February 9, page 2, column 2–4.

*Akron Daily Democrat.* 1901. "Not a Prayer, Or A Flower At The Burial In The Potter's Field." August 5, page 3, column 1.

———. 1902. "Unclaimed." January 23, page 8, column 5.

*Akron Evening Times.* 1919. "'Johnnie' Pepples, Who Entered Infirmary in Apple Blossom Time 44 Years Ago, Moves Into New Home With Companions." May 9, 1919.

Akron Map and Atlas Company. 1891. *Illustrated Summit County, Ohio, representing her manufacturing interests, commercial houses, public institutions, farms, homes and people, with history, statistics, and general information. Maps of the United States, Ohio, Summit County Townships, Towns, Villages and City of Akron.* Akron Map and Atlas Company.

*Albrecht v. Treon*, 118 Ohio St.3d 348 (2008).

American Society of Planning Officials Information Report No. 16. 1950. "Cemeteries in the City Plan." In *Cemetery Law: The Common Law of Burying Grounds in the United States*, edited by T. Marsh & D. Gibson, 199–205. God's Acre Publishing.

Anderson, B. 1983. *Imagined Communities: Reflections on the Origin and Spread of Nationalism.* Verso.

Anderson, H. D. & P. E. Davidson. 1937. "County Poor Farm Inmates Compared with Their Brothers and the Working Population of the Same Community." *Social Force* 16, no. 2, 231–237.

*Annotation: Use of Cemetery Grounds for Purposes Other Than Interment.* 1941. 130 A.L.R. 130.

Araki, T, M. Nishino, W. Gao, J. Dupuis, G. Washko, G. Hunninghake, T. Murakami, G. O'Connor, H. Hatabu. 2015. "Anterior Mediastinal Masses in the Framingham Heart Study: Prevalence and CT Image Characteristics." *European Journal of Radiology Open* 2 (January): 26–31.

Arnett, P. 2018. "Schneider Park Demographic Analysis." Honors Thesis. University of Akron, Department of Anthropology.

Atalay, S. 2012. *Community-Based Archaeology: Research with, by, and for Indigenous and Local Communities.* University of California Press.

*Beatty, et al. v. Kurtz, et al.*, 27 U.S. 566 (1829).

*Belmont Report: Ethical Principles and Guidelines for the Protection of Human Subjects of Research.* 1978. National Commission for the Protection of Human Subjects of Biomedical and Behavioral Research.

Balk D., T. Pullum, A. Storeygard, F. Greenwell, and M. Neuman. 2004. "A Spatial Analysis of Childhood Mortality in West Africa." *Population, Space and Place* 10, no.3: 175–216.

Bernstein, D. E. & T. C. Leonard. 2009. "Excluding Unfit Workers: Social Control Versus Social Justice in the Age of Economic Reform." *Law and Contemporary Problems* 72: 177–204.

Bierce, L. V. 1854 "Historical Reminiscences of Summit County" Akron, OH: T. & H.G. Canfield, Publishers.

Bindman, A. B., K. Grumbach, D. Osmond, M. Komaromy, K. Vranizan, N. Lurie, J. Billings and A. Stewart. 1995. "Preventable Hospitalizations and Access to Health Care." *JAMA* 274, no. 4: 305–311.

Bixby, W. S. 1921. "Out of Work in Akron." *Families in Society: the Journal of Contemporary Social Services* 2, no. 4, 88–93.

Black, E. 2012. *War Against the Weak: Eugenics and America's Campaign to Create A Master Race*. Dialog Press.

Blackford, M. G. & K. A. Kerr. 1996. *B. F. Goodrich: Tradition and Transformation, 1870–1995*. Ohio State University Press.

Blake, H. T. 1898. *Chronicles of New Haven Green from 1638 to 1862: A Series of Papers Read Before the New Haven Colony Historical Society*. Tuttle, Morehouse & Taylor Press.

Blakemore, E. 2018. "Poorhouses Were Designed to Punish People for Their Poverty." *History Stories*. Accessed January 29, 2019. https://www.history.com/news/in-the-19th-century-the-last-place-you-wanted-to-go-was-the-poorhouse.

Boas, F. 1912. *Changes in Bodily Form of Descendants of Immigrants*. New York: Columbia University Press.

Bohmelt T., V. Bove and E. Nussio. 2020. "Can Terrorism Abroad Influence Migration Attitudes at Home?." *American Journal of Political Science* 64, no. 4: 437–451.

*Brick Presbyterian Church v. Mayor of New York*, 5 Cow. 538 (N.Y. Sup. Ct. 1826).

*Brocket v. Ohio & Pa. R.R. Co.*, 14 Pa. 241 (1850).

Brockmeier, J. 2002. "Remembering and Forgetting: Narrative as Cultural Memory." *Culture & Psychology* 8, no. 1, 15–43.

Brophy, A. L. 2006. "Grave Matters: The Ancient Rights of the Graveyard." *BYU Law Review* (2006), 1469.

Brown M. C. and B. D. Warner. 1992. "Immigrants, urban politics and policing in 1900." *Am. Soc. Rev.* 57, 293–305.

Brown, M. F. 2003. *Who Owns Native Culture?* Harvard University Press.

Bryen, D. N. 2016. "Ethical Issues in Conducting Research Involving Persons with Disability: A View from the Past and Some New Challenges." *Humanities and Social Sciences* 4, no. 2: 53.

Buikstra, J. E. 1997. "Paleodemography: Context and Promise." In *Integrating Archaeological Demography: Multidisciplinary Approaches to Prehistoric*

*Population*, edited by R. R. Paine. Center for Archaeological Investigations, Occasional Paper 24 (367–380). SIU.

Burch Directory Company. 1898. *Akron City Directory.* The Commercial Printing Company: Akron.

———. 1899. *Akron City Directory.* The Commercial Printing Company: Akron.

———. 1902. *Akron City Directory.* The Commercial Printing Company: Akron.

———. 1906. *Akron City Directory.* The Commercial Printing Company: Akron.

———. 1907. *Akron City Directory.* The Commercial Printing Company: Akron.

———. 1911. *Akron City Directory.* The Commercial Printing Company: Akron.

———. 1913. *Akron City Directory.* The Commercial Printing Company: Akron.

———. 1917. *Akron City Directory.* The Commercial Printing Company: Akron.

Burge, L. P. 2014. Akron Soap Company, Akron, Summit County, Ohio. National Register of Historic Places #14000811.

Burnett, A. 1824. "Small Pox and Vaccination." *The Medical Advisor* 38, 134–136.

Campbell-Tiech, A. 2002. "A Corpse in Law." *British Journal of Haematology* 117, 809–811.

Carlson, E. A. 2001. *Unfit: A History of a Bad Idea.* Cold Spring Harbor Laboratory Press.

*Carney v. Knollwood Cemetery Assn.*, 33 Ohio App.3d 31, 514 N.E.2d 430 (1986)

*Carter v. City of Zanesville*, 1898. 59 Ohio St. 170

Castleman, A. 2011. "Graves Dating to 1800s Found in Southern Indiana City Park." *Post Tribune.* December 12, 2011. https://www.wthr.com/article/graves-dating-to-1800s-found-in-souther-indiana-city-park.

Center for Applied Drama and Autism. 2021. *Along the Graveyard Path.* Video series. https://www.youtube.com/@CenterforAppliedDramaAndAutism/videos.

Centers for Disease Control and Prevention. 2018. "Deaths and Mortality." Accessed April 11, 2018. https://www.cdc.gov/nchs/fastats/deaths.htm.

Chamberlain, A. 2006. *Demography in Archaeology.* Cambridge University Press.

Chang, G. H. and S. F. Fishkin, eds. 2019. *The Chinese and the Iron Road: Building the Transcontinental Railroad.* Stanford University Press.

*City of Newark v. Crane.* 1915. 92 Ohio St. 537.

Clark, A. 1990. *Seeing Beneath the Soil: Prospecting Methods in Archaeology.* Routledge.

*Cleveland Plain Dealer*. 1892. "News of the State. A Vigorous Protest from a Western Reserve Dairyman." *Cleveland Plain Dealer*, May 8, page 2, column 1.

———. 1902. "Foreigners to be Deported." *Cleveland Plain Dealer*, June 6, page 8, column 1.

———. 1903. "More Room For Insane Patients." *Cleveland Plain Dealer*, November 17, page 3, column 4.

———. 1906. "Counties Must Not Help." *Cleveland Plain Dealer*, January 14, page 7, column 5.

———. 1909. "Citizens Object to Hospital." *Cleveland Plain Dealer*, July 29, page 9, column 7.

Colopy, M. 1991. *Living History, Dying Art: the History of Glendale Cemetery*. Publisher not identified.

Conn, J. 2017. 2021. "RIP, Unknown Skeletal Remains." *Belt Magazine*, July 24. Accessed January 3. https://beltmag.com/rip-unknown-skeletal-remains/.

Cottrell, D. M. 1989. "The County Poor Farm System in Texas." *The Southwestern Historical Quarterly* 9, no. 2: 169–190.

Cunningham, R. B. 2010. *Archaeology, Relics, and the Law*. 2nd ed. Carolina Academic Press.

Cuno, J. 2010. *Who Owns Antiquity?: Museums and the Battle Over Our Ancient Heritage*. Princeton University Press.

Cusick, S. 2008. "Giving The Abenaki Dead Their Due: A Proposal to Protect Native American Burial Sites in Vermont." *Vermont Law Review* 28: 467.

Dearinger, R. 2016. *The Filth of Progress: Immigrants, Americans, and the Building of Canals and Railroads in the West*. University of California Press.

Deetz, J. 2010. *In Small Things Forgotten: An Archaeology of Early American Life*. Anchor.

Department of Charities and Corrections. 1913. Indiana Department of Charities and Corrections. *The Indiana Bulletin*: 375–468.

Diamond, J. 1991. "The Curse and Blessing of the Ghetto." *Discover*, March, 60–65.

Dinn, R. 1990. "Baptism, Spiritual Kinship, and Popular Religion in Late Medieval Bury St Edmonds. *Bulletin of the John Rylands Library* 72, no. 3: 93–106.

Discamps, E. and S. Costamagno. 2015. "Improving Mortality Profile Analysis in Zooarchaeology: A Revised Zoning for Ternary Diagrams." *Journal of Archaeological Science* 58: 62–75.

*Dobson vs. North Tynesdale Health Authority*, EWCA Civ 1321, 4 All ER 474 (1996).

*Doodeward v. Spence* [1908] HCA 45, 6 CLR 406.
Doyle, W. B. 1908. *Centennial History of Summit County, Ohio and Representative Citizens*. Biographical Publishing Company.
*Drake v. Rogers*. 1861. 13 Ohio St. 21.
Dubelko, J. 2014. *City Hospital*. Cleveland Historical. Accessed July 19, 2018. https://clevelandhistorical.org/items/show/667.
eBay. "Human Remains and Body Parts Policy." https://www.ebay.com/help/policies/prohibited-restricted-items/human-body-parts-policy?id=4325&st=3&pos=1&query= Human body parts policy&intent=human remains&lucenceai=lucenceai&docId=HELP1169.
Ensor, T., S. Cooper, L. Davidson, A. Fitzmaurice, and W. J. Graham. 2010. "The Impact Of Economic Recession on Maternal and Infant Mortality: Lessons from History." *BMC Public Health* 10: 727.
Evans, W. L. 1993. "Who Owns the Contents of Ohio's Ancient Graves?" *Capital University Law Review* 22 (Summer 1993): 11.
*Everman v. Davis*, 54 Ohio App.3d 119, 561 N.E.2d 547 (1989).
*Federman v. Christ Hosp.*, 2013-Ohio-5507 (1st Dist.).
Ferguson, T. J., S. B. Koyiyumptewa, & M. P. Hopkins. 2015. Co-Creation of Knowledge by the Hopi Tribe and Archaeologists. *Advances in Archaeological Practice* 3, no. 3: 249–262.
Fishback, P. V. and S. E. Kantor. 1998. "The Adoption of Workers' Compensation in the United States 1900–1930." *Journal of Law and Economics* 41, no. 2: 305–341.
Flewellen, A. O., A. Odewale, J. Dunnavant, A. Jones, & W. White. 2022. "Creating Community and Engaging Community: The Foundations of the Estate Little Princess Archaeology Project in St. Croix, United States Virgin Islands." *International Journal of Historical Archaeology* 26, no. 1: 147–176.
Frank, J. B. 1976. "Body Snatching: A Grave Medical Problem." *The Yale Journal of Biology and Medicine* 49: 399–410.
Gadson A, E. Akpovi and P. K. Mehta. 2017. "Exploring The Social Determinants of Racial/Ethnic Disparities in Prenatal Care Utilization and Maternal Outcome." *Seminars in Perinatology* 41, no. 5: 308–317.
G. M. Hopkins Company. 1915. *Plat Book of the City of Akron Ohio and Vicinity*.
———. 1921. *Plat Book of the City of Akron Ohio and Vicinity*.
Gaffney, C. and J. Gater. 2003. *Revealing the Buried Past: Geophysics for Archaeologists*. Tempus Publishing Ltd.
Gambini, B. 2017. "UB to Reinter, Memorialize Remains Uncovered from Former County Poorhouse Cemetery." *UBNow*. October 9. Accessed July

25, 2018, https://www.buffalo.edu/ubnow/stories/2017/10/reinterment-service.html.

Garand J. C., P. Xu and B. C. Davis 2015. "Immigration Attitudes and Support for the Welfare State in the American Mass Public." *American Journal of Political Science* 61, no. 1: 146–162.

Gardner, T. 2015. "Grave New World." In *Cemetery Law: The Common Law of Burying Grounds In The United States* edited by T. D. Marsh and D. Gibson, 199–205. God's Acre Publishing.

Garman, J. C. & P. A. Russo. 1999. "A Disregard of Every Sentiment of Humanity: The Town Farm and Class Realignment in Nineteenth-Century Rural New England." *Historical Archaeology* 33, no. 1: 118–135.

Geddes, J. 1823. *Canal Report, Made by James Geddes, Esq. the Engineer Employed by the State of Ohio.* Printed at the Office of the *Columbus Gazette* by P. H. Olmsted.

Gerstenblith, P. 1995. "Identity and Cultural Property: The Protection of Cultural Property in the United States." *BYU Law Review* 75: 559.

*Gilbert v. Buzzard and Boyer [1821]* 161 E.R. 1342

Gippin, J. 2020. *The Forgotten Dead.* Film. https://www.youtube.com/watch?v=54JoDLvIDiM.

Goddard, H. H. & N. J. Vineland. 1911. "Heredity of Feeble-Mindedness." *Journal of Heredity*, 6, no. 1: 103–116. https://doi.org/10.1093/jhered/os-6.1.103.

Goldman, A. S. & F. C. Schmalstieg. 2007. "Abraham Lincoln's Gettysburg Illness." *Journal of Medical Biography* 15, no. 2: 104–110.

Gomes, A. 2011. "Lawsuit Again Stops Kawaiaha'o Work." *Insurance News Net*, November 25, 2011. https://insurancenewsnet.com/oarticle/Lawsuit-again-stops-Kawaiahao-work-%5bThe-Honolulu-Star-Advertiser%5d-a-303423.

Goodman, A. H. and G. J. Armelagos. 1989. "Infant and Childhood Morbitity and Mortality Risks in Archaeological Populations." *World Archaeology* 21, no. 2: 225–243.

Gordie, L. 1922. *Akron Negro Year Book.*

Gotschi, T., J. Heinrich, J. Sunyer and N. Kunzli. 2008. "Long-Term Effects of Ambient Air Pollution on Lung Function: A Review." *Epidemiology* 19, no. 5: 690–701.

Grauer, A. L. 2018. "A Century of Paleopathology." *American Journal of Physical Anthropology.* 165: 904–914.

Grauer, A. L. 2019. "Paleopathology: From Bones to Social Behavior. In *Biological Anthropology of the Human Skeleton*, edited by M. A. Katzenburg and A. L. Grauer, 3rd ed., 447–465. Wiley.

Grauer A. L. and E. M McNamara. 1995. "A Piece of Chicago's Past: Exploring Childhood Mortality in the Dunning Poorhouse Cemetery." In *Bodies of Evidence*, edited by A. L. Grauer, 91–103. Wiley.

Grauer A. L., E. M. McNamara and D. V. Houdek. 1998. "A History of Their Own: Patterns of Death in a Nineteenth-Century Poorhouse." In *Sex and Gender in Paleopathological Perspective*, edited by A. L Grauer and P. Stuart-Macadam, 149–164. Cambridge University Press.

Gray, J. 2000. *Two Faces of Liberalism*. New York Press.

Gray, O. W. 1873. Rail road map of Ohio [Map]. Prepared by O. W. Gray, Philadelphia.

Gravlee, C. C., H. R. Bernard, and W. R. Leonard. 2003. "Heredity, Environment, and Cranial Form: a Re-Analysis of Boas's Immigrant Data." *American Anthropologist* 105, no. 1: 125–138.

Gregorio D. I., S. J. Walsh and D. Paturzo. 1997. "The Effects of Occupation-Based Social Position on Mortality in a Large American Cohort." *American Journal of Public Health* 87: 1472–1475.

Grima, R. 2017. "Presenting Archaeological sites to the Public" In *Key Concepts in Public Archaeology*, edited by G. Moshenska, 73–92. University College London Press.

Grismer, K.H. 1952. *Akron and Summit County*. Higginson.

G. W. & C. B. Colton & Company. 1871. *Map of the Marietta and Pittsburgh Railroad and Its Connections*. [Map] G. W. & C. B. & Co.: New York.

*Hadsell v. Hadsell*, 7 Ohio C.C. 196, 1893 WL 942 (Allen Cir. Ct. 1893)

Hagelberg, K. 2010. *Wicked Akron: Tales of Rumrunners, Mobsters and Other Rubber City Rogues*. Arcadia Publishing.

Hahn, R. A., S. F. Wetterhall, G. A. Gay, S. D. Harshbarger, C. A. Burnett, R. G. Parrish and R. J. Orend. 2002. "The Recording of Demographic Information on Death Certificates: A National Survey of Funeral Directors." *Public Health Reports* 117: 37–43.

Hall, E. 2018. "'When One Shingle Sends up Smoke': The Summit Beacon Advises Akron About the Epidemic Cholera, 1849." *Nineteenth-Century Ohio Literature*. Accessed July 24, 2018. http://ideaexchange.uakron.edu/cgi/viewcontent.cgi?article=1001&context=nineteenthcenturyohioliterature.

*Harris v. Borough of Fair Haven*. 1998. 317 N. J. Super. 226.

*Harris v. Borough of Fair Haven*. 1998. 721 A.2d 758 (N. J. Super. Ch.).

Harris, R. E. 2019. *Epidemiology of Chronic Disease: Global Perspectives*. Jones and Bartlett Learning.

Hart, C. L., G. D. Smith and D. Blane. 1998. "Inequalities in Mortality by Social Class Measured at 3 Stages of the Lifecourse." *American Journal of Public Health* 88: 471–474.

Hatfield, F. *Abandoned Burial Grounds & Their Legal Implication*. https://ohiotownships.org/sites/default/files/Abandoned Cemeteries—What is a township to do.pdf.

*Hayhurst v. Hayhurst*, 4 Ohio L. Abs. 375, 1926 WL 2487 (Hamilton C. P. 1926)

*Haynes' Case* [1614] 77 ER 1389, 12 Co. Rep. 112.

Henri, S. "The Crypt of the New Haven Green." Connecticut Weekender, February 1, 2017. https://ctweekender.com/2017/02/new-haven-green-crypt/.

Hinshaw, J. 1825. Map of the Town Plat of Akron in Portage County, Ohio Laid out on the Canal at the Portage Summit. Online Map Room, *Summit Memory*. https://www.summitmemory.org/digital/collection/new-maproom/id/833/rec/1.

Historic Scotland. 2006. *The Treatment of Human Remains in Archaeology*. Historic Scotland.

Ho, T. L.-M. 2015. "Forgetting the Past: Nineteen Thoughts on Kazuo Ishiguro's The Buried Giant and Chan Koonchung's The Fat Years." *World Literature Today*. September 16, 2015.

Hofmann, D. A., M. J. Burke and D. Zohar. 2017. "100 years of occupations safety research: from basic protections and work analysis to multilevel view of workplace safety and risk." *Journal of. Applied Psychology* 102, no. 3: 375–388.

Holinger, P. C. and E. H. Klemen. 1982. "Violent Deaths in the United States, 1900–1975: Relationships between Suicide, Homicide and Accidental Deaths." *Social Science & Medicine*. 16: 1929–1938.

Horlick, D. 2015. "Grave Recycling." In *Cemetery Law: The Common Law of Burying Grounds in the United States*, edited by T. Marsh and D. Gibson, 111–114. God's Acre Publishing.

Hosoi, K. & F. C. Stewart. 2013. "Differential Diagnosis of Mediastinal 'Tumors.'" *Archives of Internal Medicine* 47, no. 2: 230–258.

Hubert, J. & C. Fforde. 2002. "The Reburial Issue In the Twenty-First Century." *Heritage, Museums, and Galleries* 2002: 116–32.

Hunt, D. R. 2017. *The Robert J. Terry Anatomical Collection*: Accessions 100714(1927); 279804 (1967). September 1, 2017. http://anthropology.si.edu/cm/terry.htm.

*In re Disinterment of Frobose*, 163 Ohio App.3d 739 (6th Dist. 2005).

*In re Disinterment of Glass*, 182 N.E.3d 22, 2021-Ohio-4645 (2d Dist. 2021).
*In re Disinterment of Glass*, 2022-Ohio-28 (2d Dist. 2022).
*In re Disinterment of Swing*, 26 N.E.3d 827, 2014-Ohio-5454 (6th Dist. 2014).
*In re Estate of Eisaman*, 110 N.E.3d 96, 2018-Ohio-1112 (3d Dist. 2018).
Ishiguro, K. 2015. *The Buried Giant*. Vintage Press.
Jackson, P. E. 1950. *The Law of Cadavers and of Burial and Burial Places*. 2d ed. Prentice Hall.
Jameson, J. H. 2004. "Public Archaeology in the United States." In *Public Archaeology*, edited by N. Merriman, 21–58. Routledge.
Jelin, E. 1994. "The Politics of Memory: The Human Rights Movements and the Construction of Democracy in Argentina." *Latin American Perspectives* 21, no. 2: 38–58.
Johnson, J. K., Ed. 2006. *Remote Sensing in Archaeology: An Explicitly North American Perspective*. University of Alabama Press.
Johnson, S. A. 2006. *Industrial Voyagers: A Case Study of Appalachian Migration to Akron, Ohio 1900–1940*. PhD dissertation. The Ohio University.
Jones, J. 2016. "History of Ogden's Pest Houses." The Dead History. Accessed July 19, 2018.
Joyner, C. 2010. "Family Cemeteries Conflict with Land Development." *U.S.A. Today*, October. 5, 2010. http://usatoday30.usatoday.com/news/nation/2010-10-05-family-burial-plots_N.htm.
Kaler, S. G. 2008. "Diseases of Poverty with High Mortality in Infants and Children—Malaria, Measles, Lower Respiratory Infections, and Diarrheal Illnesses." Annals of the New York Academy of Sciences 1136: 28–31.
Karinshak, Z. S. 1997. "Relics of The Past—To Whom Do They Belong—The Effect of an Archaeological Excavation on Property Rights." *Emory Law Journal* 46: 867.
Kelly, E. 2012. "Homes May Be Built on Wood County Cemetery." *WTOL*, Mar. 9, 2012, https://www.wtol.com/article/news/homes-may-be-built-on-wood-county-cemetery/512-e255d6f3-5c83-456a-81d6-bb4cd99f7dea.
Kimmerle, E. 2022. *We Carry Their Bones: The Search for Justice at the Dozier School for Boys*. William Morrow.
Knapp, P. C. 2009. *The Architecture of Education: Public Schools in Akron, 1890–1920*. Master's Thesis. Program in History. Youngstown State University.
Knepper, G. 1990. *Summit's Glory: Sketches of Buchtel College and the University of Akron*. The University of Akron Press.

Krauskopf, B. J. 1958. "The Law of Dead Bodies: Impeding Medical Progress." *Ohio Law State Law Journal* 19, no. 3: 455–476.

Kvamme, K. L. 2006. "Magnetometry: Nature's Gift to Archaeology." In *Remote Sensing in Archaeology: An Explicitly North American Perspective*, edited by Jesse K. Johnson, 205–234. University of Alabama Press.

Lakoff, G. & M. Johnson. 2003. *Metaphors We Live By*. The University of Chicago Press.

Lamott, A. 1995. *Bird by Bird*. Knopf Doubleday Publishing Group.

Lane, S. A. 1892. *Fifty Years and Over of Akron and Summit County*. Beacon Job Department.

Larsen, C. S. 2002. "Bioarchaeology: the Lives and Lifestyles of Past People." *Journal of Archaeological Research* 10, no. 2: 119–166.

Laqueur, T. W. 2015. *The Work of the Dead: A Cultural History of Mortal Remains*. Princeton University Press.

Lawrence, J. 2000. "The Indian Health Service and the Sterilization of Native American Women." *American Indian Quarterly* 24, no. 3: 400–419.

Lerman, P. 1985. "Deinstitutionalization and Welfare Policies." *Annals of the American Academy of Political and Social Science* 479: 132–155.

Lombardo, P. 2011. *A Century of Eugenics in America: From the Indiana Experiment to the Human Genome Era*. Indiana University Press.

Loudon, I. 1991. "On Maternal and Infant Mortality 1900–1960." *Social History of Medicine* 4, no. 1: 29–73.

*Louisville & N. R. Co. v. Wilson*, 123 Ga. 62, 51 S.E. 24 (1905)

Lovett, L. 2007. "'Fitter Families for Future Firesides': Florence Sherborn and Popular Eugenics." *The Public Historian* 29, no. 3: 69–85.

Lown, M. 2006. *Munroe Falls Historical Society Newsletter* 82.

Madoff, R. D. 2010. *Immortality and the Law: The Rising Power of the American Dead*. Yale University Press.

Manderson, L., J. Aagaard-Hansen, P. Allotey, M. Gyapong and .J Sommerfeld. 2009. "Social Research on Neglected Diseases of Poverty: Continuing and Emerging Themes." *PLoS Neglected Tropical Diseases* 3, no. 2: e332.

Maples, J. L. 1974. "The Akron, Ohio Ku Klux Klan 1921–1928." Master's thesis. The University of Akron.

Marsh, Tonya D. 2015. "The Grave is Full of Instruction." In *Cemetery Law: The Common Law of Burying Grounds in the United States*, edited by Tonya D. Marsh and Douglas Gibson, 2–8. God's Acre Publishing.

———. 2105. "Key Principles of U.S. Cemetery Law." In *Cemetery Law: The Common Law of Burying Grounds in the United States*, edited by T. Marsh and D. Gibson, 11–14. God's Acre Publishing.

———. 2012. "The Sale of Human Remains." In *Cemetery Law: The Common Law of Burying Grounds in the United States*, edited by T. Marsh and D. Gibson, 192–194. God's Acre Publishing.

———. 2015. "The Legal Status of Human Remains." In *Cemetery Law: The Common Law of Burying Grounds in the United States*, edited by T. Marsh and D. Gibson, 182–183. God's Acre Publishing.

———. 2015. "The Common Law of Disinterment." 2015. In *Cemetery Law: The Common Law of Burying Grounds in the United States*, edited by T. Marsh and D. Gibson, 362–365. God's Acre Publishing.

Mastromarino, M. A. 2002. "Fair Visions: Elkanah Watson (1758–1842) and the Modern American Agricultural Fair." PhD dissertation. Department of Arts & Sciences, College of William & Mary.

Matthews & Taintor. 1856. Summit County Map. Matthews and Taintor.

McCarrier, K. P., F. J. Zimmerman, J. D. Ralston and D. P. Martin. 2011. "Associations Between Minimum Wage Policy and Access to Health Care: Evidence from the Behavioral Risk Factor Surveillance System, 1996–2007," *American Journal of Public Health* 101: 359–367.

McClain, S. R. 1975. "The Contributions of Blacks in Akron 1825–1975." PhD dissertation. Department of History, University of Akron.

McClellan, B. 2014. "Tracking a journey from Poor House to Potters Field to Final Resting Place." *St. Louis Post-Dispatch*. April 25, 2014. http://www.stltoday.com/news/local/columns/bill-mcclellan/mcclellan-tracking-a-journey-from-poor-house-to-potters-field/article_e5cc4d25-2783-5067-a223-d7dc75954150.html

McGimsey III, C., R. 1972. *Public Archaeology*. Studies in Archaeology Series. Seminar Press.

McHenry, E. 2002. *Forgotten Readers: Recovering the Lost History of African American Literary Societies.* Duke University Press.

Mennel, R. M. and S. Spackman. 1980. "Origins of Welfare in the States: Albert G. Byers and the Ohio Board of State Charities." *Ohio History Journal* 92: 72–95.

*Methodist Prot. Church of Cincinnati v. Laws*, 4 Ohio C. D. 562 (1893).

Mirowsky, J. and C. E. Ross. 2000. "Socioeconomic Status and Subjective Life Expectancy." *Social Psychology Quarterly* 63, no. 2: 133–151.

Mora, A. P., M. T. Mora and A. Davila. 2007. "The English-Language Proficiency of Recent Immigrants in the U.S. during the Early 1900's." *Eastern Economic Journal* 33, no. 1; 65–80.

*MSNBC.* 2014. "Arizona Republican Suggests Sterilizing Poor Women." https://www.msnbc.com/rachel-maddow-show/arizona-republican-suggests-sterilizing-poor-women-msna412631.

Murphy, E. M. 2008. *Deviant Burial in the Archaeological Record.* Vol. 2. Oxbow Books.

Murray, E. A. and A. J. Perzigian. 1995. "A Glimpse of Early Nineteenth Century Cincinnati as Viewed from Potter's Field: an Exercise in Problem Solving." In *Bodies of Evidence*, edited by A. L. Grauer, 173–184. Wiley.

Nash, P., Z. Hussain, M. Parkes, K. Mannings, R. Bhatt, N. Kalish, P. Sohal, S. Sighu, C. Carson, and K. Hart. 2015. *Multifaith Care for Sick and Dying Children and Their Families: A Multi-disciplinary Guide.* Jessica Kingsley Publishers.

*Nat'l Archives & Records Admin. v. Favich,* 541 U.S. 157, 168 (2004)

*Native American Graves Protection and Repatriation Act (NAGPRA),* Pub. L. 101–601, 25 U.S.C. §3001 et seq.

Nelson, D. 1988. *American Rubber Workers & Organized Labor, 1900–1941.* Princeton University Press.

*New York Times.* 1889. "False Death Certificates." May 31, page 1, column 4.

Novak, N. L., N. Lira, K. E. O'Connor, S. D. Harlow, S. L. R. Kardia, & A. M. Stern. 2018. "Disproportionate Sterilization of Latinos Under California's Eugenic Sterilization Program, 1920–1945." *American Journal of Public Health* 108(, no. 5: 611–613. doi: 10.2105/AJPH.2018.304369.

Ohio Attorney General Opinion 1953-2978.

Ohio Attorney General Opinion 2003-034.

*Ohio Cemetery Law Task Force Report and Recommendation* (Sept. 29, 2014).

Ohio Rev. Code §517.21

Ohio Rev. Code §517.23

Ohio Rev. Code §517.24

Ohio Rev. Code §1715.02

Ohio Rev. Code §1721.15

Ohio Rev. Code §1721.21

Ohio Rev. Code §2108.70

Olexa, M. T., N. T. Hodge, and T. L. Owens. 2006. "No Grave Like Home: Protecting the Deceased and their Final Resting Places from Destruction Without Going Six Feet Under." *Drake Journal of Agricultural Law* 11: 51.

Olexa, M., N. T. Hodge, T. Owens, and C. Hampton. 2012. "A Grave Situation: Protecting the Deceased and Their Final Resting Places from Destruction." *Florida Bar Journal* 86, no. 2: 35.

Olin, O. 1917. *Akron and Environs—Historical: Biographical, Genealogical.* The Lewis Publishing Co.

Ohio Board of Education, Akron. 1884. *Annual Report of the Board of Education.* Werner Printing Company.

Ohio Board of State Charities. 1868. **Annual Report of the Board of State Charities to the Governor of the State of Ohio for the year 1867.** L. D. Myers & Bro., Columbus. State Printers.

———. 1870. **Annual Report of the Board of State Charities to the Governor of the State of Ohio for the Year 1869.** L.D. Myers & Bro., Columbus. State Printers.

———. 1887. *Twelfth Annual Report of the Ohio Board of State Charities.* G. J. Brand and Company, State Printers.

———. 1896. *The Ohio Bulletin of Charities and Corrections* 2, no. 1. The Laning Printing Company.

———. 1910. *The Ohio Bulletin of Charities and Corrections* 16, no. 1. Office of the Ohio Board of State Charities, Columbus.

———. 1916. *The Ohio Bulletin of Charities and Corrections.* 22, no. 2. Office of the Ohio Board of State Charities, Columbus.

Ohio Commissioner of Railroads and Telegraphs. 1906. *Annual Report of the Commissioner of Railroads and Telegraphs, to the Governor of the State of Ohio, for the Year 1905,* Vol. 38. The Springfield Publishing Company.

Ohio State Board of Health 1886. *First Annual Report of the State Board of Health.* Myers Brothers State Printers.

Orwell, George. 1949. *Nineteen Eighty-four.* Secker & Warburg.

*Oxford Reference.* 2021. "Unbaptized Babies." Accessed March 24, 2021, https://www.oxfordreference.com/view/10.1093/oi/authority.20110803110604183. Oxford Reference.

Palmer, Robert. 2012. "Cemetery Evidence Could Stall Walmart." *Times Daily.* April. 2, 2012. www.timesdaily.com/archieves/cemetery-evidence-could-stall-walmart/ article_e7bb306d-e9e7-517d-a8f0-a4e18e9de8da.html.

*Pansing v. Village of Miamisburg,* 21 Ohio C.D. 130, 31 Ohio C.C. 130, 11 Ohio C.C. (n.s.) 511 (1907).

*Past Pursuits: A Newsletter of the Special Collections Division of the Akron-Summit County Public Library.* 2006, Spring: 5.

Paul, J. 1968. "The Return of Punitive Sterilization Proposals: Current Attacks on Illegitimacy and the AFDC Program." *Law & Society Review* 3, no. 1: 77–106.

Paulson, G. 2012. *Closing the Asylums: Causes and Consequences of the Deinstitutionalization Movement.* McFarland Press.

Pearson, M. P. 1999. *The Archaeology of Death and Burial.* Sutton Publishing.
Perrin, W. 1881. *History of Summit County, Ohio.* Baskin and Battey Publishers.
Pew Research. 2015. "America's News Anchors Are Less Recognizable Now, But Network News Is Still Alive." http://www.pewresearch.org/fact-tank/2015/02/12/americas-news-anchors-are-less-recognizable-now-but-network-news-is-still-alive/.
Pillay-van Wyk, V. and D. Bradshaw. 2017. "Mortality and Socioeconomic Status: the Vicious Cycle between Poverty and Ill Health." *The Lancet* 5, no. 9: E851–852.
Preston, S. H. 1975. "The Changing Relation between Mortality and Level of Economic Development." *Popular Studies* 29, no. 2: 231–248.
Price, M. 2009. "Poor Lost Souls of Akron." *Akron Beacon Journal.* May 18, 2009.
Pugel, C. 2019. *The Forgotten Dead Documentary: Behind the Scenes.* Film. https://youtu.be/WXgaYBybp3o.
Pyburn K. A. 2011. "Engaged Archaeology: Whose Community? Which Public?" In: *New Perspectives in Global Public Archaeology,* edited by K. Okamura K. & A. Matsuda, 29–41. Springer.
Rasmussen, M., M. Sikora, A. Albrechtsen, T. S. Korneliussen, J. V. Mareno-Mayar, G. D. Poznik, C. P. E. Zollikofer, M. S. P. de León, M. E. Allentoft, I. Moltke, H. Jónsson, C. Valdiosera, R. Mahli, L. Orlando, C. Bustamante, T. W. Stafford, Jr., D. Meltzer, R. Nielsen & E. Willersley. 2015. "The Ancestry and Affiliations of Kennewick Man." *Nature* 523, no 7561: 455.
Rectigraph Abstract & Title Company. 1910. *Atlas and Industrial Geography of Summit County.* The Rectigraph Abstract & Title Company.
*Regina v. Kelly & Lindsay,* [1999] 3 All E. R. 741
*Renihan v. Wright,* 25 N.E. 822 (Ind. 1890)
Ritchie A. & J. Steiger. 1974. *Soil Survey of Summit County, Ohio.* Ohio Department of Natural Resources.
R. L. Polk and Company. 1889. *Grand Rapids City Directory.* R. L. Polk and Company.
R. L. Polk and Company. 1914. *Polk's Medical Register and Directory of North America.* R. L. Polk and Company.
Roberts, C. A., D. Lucy and K. Manchester. 1994. "Inflammatory Lesions of Ribs: an Analysis of the Terry Collection." *American Journal of Physical Anthropology* 95: 169–182.
Roberts, C. A., A. Boylston, L. Buckley, A. C. Chamberlain and E. M. Murphy. 1998. "Rib Lesions and Ruberculosis: the Paleopathological Evidence." *Tubercle and Lung Disease* 79: 55–60.

Rodgers, D. T. 1982. "In Search of Progressivism." *Reviews in American History* 10(4), 113–132.

*Schaeffer v. Unknown Heirs.* 1961. 86 Ohio L. Abs. 425, 16 Ohio Op.2d 301, 175 N.E.2d 776 (8th Dist.).

Schaper, D. 2005. "O'Hare Growth May Mean Moving a Cemetery." *NPR.* Nov. 19, 2005. https://www.npr.org/templets/story/story.php?storyId=5020426.

*Schoonmaker v. Reformed Protestant Dutch Church of Kingston.* 1850. 3 Code Rep. 232, 5 How. Pr. 265, 271 (N.Y. Sup. Ct.).

———. *Schoonmaker v. Reformed Protestant Dutch Church of Kingston*, 1850. 5 How. Pr. 265, 271 (N.Y. Sup. Ct.).

Seidemann, R. 2013. "How Do We Deal with All of The Bodies—A Review of Recent Cemetery and Human Remains Legal Issues." *The University of Baltimore Journal of Land and Development* 3. 1.

Seidemann, R. and R. Moss. 2009. "Federal Legal Protection for Cemeteries." In *Cemetery Law: The Common Law of Burying Grounds in the United States*, edited by T. Marsh and D Gibson, 1387–391. God's Acre Publishing.

Selden, S. 2005. "Transforming Better Babies into Fitter Families: Archival Resources and the History of the American Eugenics Movement, 1908–1930." *Proceedings of the American Philosophical Society.* 149, no. 2:199–225.

Sessions, M. 1918. "The Feeble-minded in a Rural County in Ohio." Printed by the Ohio State Reformatory (unironically).

Sexton, J. 2001. "Not A Park or Mere Pleasure Ground: A Case Study of The New Haven Green." *Town Greens.* Accessed April 16, 2018. www.towngreens.com/DOCUMENTS/tg_newhaven_case.pdf.

Shackel, P. A. 2004. "Working with Communities: Heritage Development and Applied Archaeology." In *Places in Mind: Public Archaeology as Applied Anthropology,* edited by Shackel, P. A. and E. J. Chambers. Routledge.

Shaffer, C. A. 2003. "The Standing of the Dead: Solving the Problem of Abandoned Graveyards." *Capital University Law Review* 32: 479.

Shanks, M. & C. Tilley. 1992. *Re-Constructing Archaeology: Theory and Practice.* 2nd ed. Routledge.

Siener, W. H. 2008. "Through the Back Door: Evading the Chinese Exclusion Act along the Niagara Frontier, 1900–1924." *Journal of American Ethnic History* 27, no. 4: 34–70.

Smith, D. W. and B. S. Bradshaw. 2006. "Variation in Life Expectancy during the Twentieth Century in the United States." *Demography* 43, no. 4: 647–657.

Smith, G. S. & J. E. Ehrenhard [Eds.] 1991. *Protecting the Past.* CRC Press.

Snivel, R. M. 1935. City Gets $800,000 Legacy. *Detroit Free Press,* December 28, page 9.

Sorlie P. D., E. Backlund and J. B. Keller. 1995. "US Mortality by Economic, Demographic and Social Characteristics: The National Longitudinal Mortality Study." *American Journal of Public Health* 85: 949–956.

*Spanich v. Reichelderfer*. 1993. 90 Ohio App.3d 148, 628 N.E.2d 102.

Special Collections Division. 2006. The Old Summit County Infirmary. *Akron-Summit County Public Library*, 5(1), 1, 3.

Stark, L. 2011. *Behind Closed Doors: IRBs and the Making of Ethical Research*. University of Chicago Press.

*Stark County Democrat*. 1878. "The Valley Railroad." October 17, page 5, column 3.

*State v. Glass*, 56 Ohio Op.2d 391, 273 N.E.2d 893 (4th Dist. 1971)

Statista Research Department. "Distribution of Snapchat Users in the United States as of February 2016, by Age." Feb 17, 2016. https://www.statista.com/statistics/326452/snapchat-age-group-usa/.

Stewards of Historical Preservation. 2017. "Schneider Park Cemetery." July 21. https://historicakron.wordpress.com/2017/07/21/schneider-park-cemetery/ (site discontinued).

Sulik, S. T. 2020. "Waving the Red, Black, and Green: The Local and Global Vision of the Universal Negro Improvement Association in Akron and Barberton, Ohio." PhD Dissertation. Philosophy in History. University of Texas, Arlington.

Sutter, R. C. 1995. "Dental Pathologies among Inmates of the Monroe County Poorhouse." In *Bodies of Evidence*, edited by A. L. Grauer, 185–196. Wiley.

Tackabury, Mead & Moffett. 1874. *Combination Atlas Map of Summit County, Ohio, Compiled, Drawn and Published from Personal Examinations and Surveys*. [Map] Tackabury, Mead, and Moffet.

Taylor, J. S. 2003. "The Story Catches You and You Fall down: Tragedy, Ethnography, and 'Cultural Competence.'" *Medical Anthropology Quarterly N.S.* 17, no. 2: 159–181.

*The Cleveland, Columbus and Cincinnati RR. Co. v. Keary*. 1854. 3 Ohio St. 201.

*The Baltimore Sun*. 1946. "City to Move 170 Bodies: Will Pay to Transfer Those Buried on Airport Site." September 27, page 19.

Tilley, L. & M. F. Oxenham. "Survival against the odds: Modeling the social implications of care provision to seriously disabled individuals." *International Journal of Paleopathology* 1, no. 1 (2011): 35–42.

Trexler, P. 2014. "History Comes Alive in Akron at Glendale Cemetery's 175th anniversary celebration." May 30. *Akron Beacon Journal*.

Tsosie, Rebecca. 2012. "NAGPRA and the Problem of Culturally Unidentifiable Remains: The Argument for a Human Rights Framework." *Arizona State Law Journal* 44: 809.

Tucker, R. L. 1999. "Information Superhighway Robbery: The Tortious Misuse of Links, Frames, Metatags, and Domain Names." *Virginia Journal of Law & Technology.* 4, no 1.

United States. Bureau of the Census. 1922. Fourteenth Census of the United States, 1920 (Vol. 5). US Government Printing Office.

United States Congress. 1920. Biological aspects of immigration: Hearing before the committee on immigration and naturalization. (April 16–17). US Government Printing Office.

*United States Federal Census.* 1870. p. 71, family 510, NARA microfilm publication M593 (Washington D.C.: National Archives and Records Administration, n.d.); FHL microfilm 552,180.

———. 1910. Akron Ward 1, Summit, Ohio, United States; citing enumeration district (ED) ED 121, sheet 4B, family 105, NARA microfilm publication T624 (Washington DC: National Archives and Records Administration, 1982), roll 1233; FHL microfilm 1,375,246.

———. 1912. *Thirteenth Census of the United States: 1910: Vol. I, Population.* US Government
Printing Office.

———. 1930. *Ward 8, Akron, Summit, Ohio. Enumeration District 66.* T626 (Washington DC: National Archives and Records Administration, 2002). Image 23 of 92.

———. 1940. *Ward 8, Akron City, Akron City, Summit, Ohio, United States*; citing enumeration district (ED) 89-208, sheet 3B, line 60, family 64, Sixteenth Census of the United States, 1940, NARA digital publication T627. Records of the Bureau of the Census, 1790–2007, RG 29. Washington, D.C.: National Archives and Records Administration, 2012, roll 3180.

University of Buffalo. 2017. "Erie County Poorhouse Cemetery." *University of Buffalo News Center,* October 11, 2017. Accessed July 25, 2018. httxp://www.buffalo.edu/news/key-issues/erie-county-poorhouse-cemetery.html.

Urbanus, J. 2018. "Letter from Brooklyn: New York City's Dirtiest Beach." *Archaeology* 71, no. 5: 56–63.

Van Dyke, R. M. 2019. "Archaeology and Social Memory." *Annual Review of Anthropology* 48, 207–225.

Vander, M. 2015. *The Law-Making Process.* Bloomsbury Publishing.

Verea, M. 2018. "Anti-immigrant and Anti-Mexican Attitudes and Policies during the First 18 Months of the Trump Administration." *Norteamerica, Revista Academica Del CISAN-UNAM* 13, no. 2. https://doi.org/10.22201/cisan.24487228e.2018.2.335.

W. H. Parish Publishing Company. 1898. County Building. [Photograph]. W. H. Parish Publishing Company.

Wagner, D. 2005. *The Poorhouse: America's Forgotten Institution.* Rowman and Littlefield Publishers: Lanham.

Washington, H. A. 2007. *The Dark History of Medical Experimentation on Black Americans from Colonial Times to the Present.* Doubleday.

Weinick, R. M., S. C. Byron and A. S Bierman. 2005. "Who Can't Pay for Health Care?: *Journal of General Internal Medicine* 20, no. 6, 504–509.

Weiss, E. 2001. "Kennewick Man's Behavior: A CT-Scan Analysis. "*American Journal of Physical Anthropology Supplement* 32, 163.

Whitehead, C. 2019. *The Nickel Boys: A Novel.* Doubleday.

Whitman, L., L. Metzger, A. Donkin & M. Davis. 2008. *Report on the Historic Research and Archaeological Investigation of Munroe Falls Metro Park, and Old Summit County Home Property and Cemetery in Summit County, Ohio.* Community Archaeology Program, Department of Classical Studies, Anthropology, and Archaeology, University of Akron.

*Whitney v. Cervantes.* 2014. 328 P.3d 957, 960 (Wash. App.)

Wickes, S. 1884. "Interment in England." In *Cemetery Law: The Common Law of Burying Grounds in the United States*, edited by T. Marsh and D. Gibson, 111–114. God's Acre Publishing, 2009.

Wilson, K. M. 2016. "Building Memory: Museums, Trauma, and the Aesthetics of Confrontation in Argentina." *Latin American Perspectives* 43, no. 5: 112–130.

Winchell, F., J. C. Rose and R. W. Moir. 1995. "Health and Hard times: a Case Study from the Middle to Late Nineteenth Century in Eastern Texas." In *Bodies of Evidence, edited by* A. L. Grauer, 161–172. Wiley.

Winkleby, M. A., Jatulis, D. E., Frank, E., & Fortmann, S. P. 1992. "Socioeconomic Status and Health: How Education, Income, and Occupation Contribute To Risk Factors for Cardiovascular Disease." *American Journal of Public Health* 82, no. 6: 816–820.

Winter, M. 2012. "Storm Unearths Very Old Skeletons in New Haven Park." *USA Today.* Oct. 31, 2012.

Witten, A. J. 2006. *Handbook of Geophysics and Archaeology.* Equinox Publishing.

World Health Organization. 2013. "Health Risks Associated with Stagnant Water. Recommendations for Occupational Health and Safety Following Disasters." World Health Organization. Accessed December 1, 2018. http://www.wpro.who.int/philippines/typhoon_haiyan/media/health_risks_associated_with_stagnant_water.pdf.

Yang, Y. and K. C. Land. 2013. *Age-Period-Cohort Analysis: New Models, Methods, and Empirical Applications*. Taylor and Francis.

Zander, M. 2004. *The Law-Making Process*. Cambridge University Press.